The Parley Vous
A Novel by Don Campbell

978-0-578-01678-8

This is a novel about a restaurant named the Parley Vous where there is no "No Smoking" section. Four men meet there each morning to discuss women, sex, piercing, Elvis, Viagra and hundreds of other topics, including why corn is often found in elephant dung. Take a rollicking ride through small town America with your hostess, a beautiful widow named "Dolly," and meet a cast of characters that include the poet laureate of Indiana, the piss sisters, Dennis, the homosexual dentist, baptizing Burt and a lawyer who defends his wife in a trial where she is charged with murdering her lover.

"Raunchy, funny, sexy, a great read. Don is an astute observer of the human condition and his dialogue is remarkable. He has made his fictional Hoosiers come alive." Indiana State Congressman F. Dale Grubb

This is a work of fiction. Although some of the historical characters are real, the rest are not. Since many friends and members of the family will read this book, I should point out that none of the content is based on anything that really happened. In other words, I made all this shit up.

Debbie Hummel-Marconi created a very clever painting entitled "The Restaurant" and used it to design the cover of this book. Debbie can be reached at P.O. Box 989 in Bonita Springs, FL 34133. Telephone her at (239) 992-6989 or
Visit her on the web at www.hummel-marconi.com

This book is dedicated to my amazing wife, lover and friend.

CHAPTER ONE:
THE RESTAURANT

She had stopped smoking years ago, but the restaurant had not. She would open the doors each morning at 5:00 and within minutes the men would begin to assemble. They were farmers mostly, but a few hourly workers from the meat processing plant together with a funeral director, a doctor, a lawyer, and a deputy sheriff were almost always in attendance. It was the kind of place that featured country fried steak, fish on Friday, and chicken on Sunday and chili and breakfast all day every day.

There are still places in Southern Indiana that remain loyal to tobacco. After all, Indiana is fifth in the nation in smoking, (Kentucky is number 1) and fourth if you count only pregnant women. Defensive proclamations such as "My daddy smoked for fifty years and it never hurt him" and "Cigarettes smoked in moderation may even be good for you", together with the ever popular "Tobacco's been awfully good to Southern Indiana", were often heard in the restaurant. Carcinoma was thought to be an automobile dealership in California located somewhere in the wine country. And so it was that at 5:04 or so every morning matches were struck and lighters were lit and the smoke that never really went away rose from stagnation with an indolent ferocity. Coughing was common, of course, and it was tolerated, accepted, even ignored. There is a gag reflex that occurs, however, when caffeine and nicotine collide and its sound is instantly recognizable and uniquely disgusting. It is also contagious. A stranger entering unaware would think that a dozen men had all decided at once to put fingers down their throats. Vomit was rarely produced but when it was, the olfactory nerves became involved and the contagion arose and intensified until the restaurant sounded like a tubercular ward located on a garbage scow.

Presiding over all this frivolity was Clarice. She was 24 years old and had lived in Paris Crossing all but two years of her life. Her mother had converted a grocery store and named it the Parley Vous in honor of its location. Clarice painted it red several years ago but the sun bleached it pink as a September petunia.

"Goddamn place looks like a beauty parlor for geriatric whores," Doc Cross said. "It's bad enough eating in a place with a pansy name. The color makes me want to get my nails painted and my tits enlarged".

"Your tits are bigger than mine already." Clarice said. She was only half joking. Tall and slender with long legs and a clear, clean complexion, she was just attractive enough to intimidate the local men.

She was always friendly and never morose but just as her non-smoking ways was different, so was her unwillingness to socialize. While she would banter with the men she had not had a date in months after breaking off her relationship with a dentist in Louisville just when everyone thought she had finally met her match. Some thought her aloof and pretentious but men who cannot bed the object of their desires often denigrate women.

"She must be queer." smiled Red the cop.

"Why Red, did Clarice turn you down again?" Doc smiled in return. "You're probably right. A woman would have to be a lesbian to turn down a fat, ugly, married, racist..."

Red Cox's real name was Red Cox. His father, Fred Cox, was a loyal Indiana

University fan who already had two sons named after him, Fred Cox, Jr. and Fred Cox II. Both had moved to Hanover and mercifully ended the Fred Cox tradition. Old Fred chose Red because it sounded like Fred and his favorite I. U. cheer was "Go big red." Fred could envision himself yelling his cheer while his son played basketball at Assembly Hall. In fact he wrote the famous coach telling him of Fred's hopes and dreams for Red's future. The coach even replied telling Fred to look the coach up when Red graduated from high school because "I know that all of us here at Indiana University want to have Red Cox."

Every child with a bad name or a physical imperfection begins life with one or maybe two strikes against him. Lives are shaped, formed, even predetermined by buck teeth, pimples and names like Red Cox or Sandy Beach. Red had too much respect for his father to ever change his name and so he decided to live with it. This gave him imperviousness to insult and the ability to laugh at himself. He loved his job, his wife and his child and he worshiped Doc, who in turn always insulted Red with venom diluted with affection. No one could deny that Red was good at his job. Even though the famous coach never came calling, at eighteen Red saved the Harris baby from drowning in Tom Miller's pool and an appointment to the Jennings County Sheriff's department soon followed. The Indiana Merit Board system ensured Red of retirement as a lawman and he wanted nothing more out of life, except maybe three hours naked with Clarice.

CHAPTER TWO:
RED COX

Red was fat, although he thought of himself as burly and big boned. To a certain extent, both were true. At six three, Red could carry a lot of weight, still he was a lot heavier than when he left the Corps 10 years ago.

Red was not ugly. He was blessed with an abundance of brown wavy hair, good teeth and a friendly face. Most women thought him handsome, including his wife, Debbie. She had met Red while waitressing at a trendy, overpriced restaurant in Louisville. Debbie was little but like many small people, she was aggressive, defensive, and overconfident. Red ordered a cheeseburger and a beer.

"Not very creative are you, cowboy." Debbie said.

"I'm not going to order anything I can't pronounce." Red replied. "This menu must have been written by people unfamiliar with the English language."

"It is pretty pathetic, isn't it?" Debbie said. "I think the owner believes he can get away with charging more by using foreign phrases to disguise the food."

"I'm not good at foreign phrases," Red said. "Except for maybe 'bonito como un cuadro', I learned that from a Mexican I served with in the Marines. It means 'pretty as a picture' and that sure describes you. What time do you get off?"

Hours later at her apartment, it seemed they had talked continuously from the moment Red got into Debbie's car. Engrossed in what he was saying, he followed her into the bathroom and was startled when she began to pee. He was strangely pleased and aroused when he heard how strongly her urine struck the water.

"I think we should make love," she said, "but not tonight I'm having my period."

"I don't mind." Red said.

"Men always say that as if they are the only ones capable of being repelled by the mess." Debbie replied. "Besides, it's not your sheets, or your bed. I'm not working Thursday and I should be done by then. Will you still be interested enough to see me Wednesday night?"

He was consumed by her promise to "make love," not go to bed, not fuck, but make love. Four days later on Wednesday evening Red knocked on Debbie's door. She greeted him wearing only a bra and panties as he had almost known she would. Four hours later she wore nothing as they ate spaghetti from a can and talked about marriage. They were wed a month later in the Coffee Creek Christian Church just west of Paris Crossing and they moved into Red's house on Montgomery Street.

For the first few months of their marriage Red thought he had died and gone to heaven. Debbie never turned down an invitation to make love, except during her "blood days" when she became moody and depressed. After her period she seemed almost insatiable for the first few days, often awaking Red by taking him in her mouth while she satisfied herself. When finished she would spoon into Red's back and give him her moist fingers to suckle.

Debbie and Paris Crossing, however, were not a good fit. She was a city girl and while Red took her to North Vernon or Madison or Columbus on most weekends it was Louisville she wanted and Red avoided. Somehow he thought if Debbie returned she might not come back. The county car was all they "owned" and so in order to kill time while Red was gone, Debbie walked. At first her sojourns were only for a few blocks. Then Debbie walked a mile and finding that no tough task, she began to walk several miles a day. Although she would not admit it Debbie walked in search of Red.

Sometimes she'd find him; and while he'd always acknowledge her presence by waiving to her from the car, he'd never stop. On one occasion during Debbie's hiking days she spotted Red lecturing a motorist he'd stopped on State Road 3 near Commiskey. Smiling at herself, she walked up behind Red and started playing with his ass. Angered and mortified, Red accused Debbie of stalking him. Visibly shaken, Debbie turned and began to run toward home. Red quickly disposed of the grinning motorist and pulled alongside Debbie.

"Honey, I'm sorry," Red said.

"Fuck you," Debbie predictably replied.

Red sped away, but drove to his house fifteen minutes later. He did not go inside but stood in the open doorway. The clever repartee began anew stopping only when the front door was slammed in Red's mournful face.

Debbie announced three days later that she was forgiving Red only because she missed his company in bed. Or as she put it:

"You are still in the doghouse, but I'm freeing your dick." Normalcy returned, if there was such a thing in the ever more complex marriage of Red and Debbie Cox.

There could be no doubt that they loved one another but what Red was beginning to suspect was that Debbie did not crave sex so much as intimacy and his almost constant presence and attention were required. He had even stopped going to the restaurant every day for lunch because Debbie would always be there and would always be needy. Red knew he would never leave Debbie but he fantasized about Clarice and about how a more independent woman might need less

maintenance.   His occasional flirtations,
however, meant nothing as Clarice well knew.
He was Debbie's husband and he took his role
seriously,   often   musing   to   himself   that
Debbie was every man's dream and he should be
happy he had her.

Indiana has long been known as the most
southern,   northern   state   and   it   logically
follows that southern Indiana seems more like
Kentucky or even Tennessee.   There are bigots
that   live   there   just   as   there   are   bigots
everywhere else.   It is the openness of the
racism that sets the region apart.   Below the
city limit sign of an Ohio River town was the
warning,   "Nigger don't let the sun set on
you here."   The sign was not removed until
the sixties: the nineteen sixties.   Red was
an   exception.   His   simple   John   Wayne
patriotism caused him to believe that it was
country and not color that mattered.   He had
served with blacks in the corps and found
them not much different from whites.   He
could not even muster up hate for Arabs even
though he had spent time in the hell hole
that was Saudi during Desert Storm. Mostly,
he pitied them.   Imagine not being able to
see an uncovered woman's ass in the daylight
without feeling guilty.   How can life be
worth living without looking at breasts or
pussies, Red mused.   Their religion says that
they can't do that until after they're dead.
What kind of religion is that?   Do their
embalmers give them perpetual hard-ons?   I
mean what do they think they can do with a
dead dick?

Our interstate highway system not only
speeds us to our destinations, it also gives
us   protection.   White   people   can   drive
through Watts, Cabrini Green and East Saint
Louis   without   ever   really   being   there.

Blacks can do the same with places like Meridian, Montgomery and Selma. Many would argue that isolation only intensifies prejudice and their position is difficult to dispute. Unfortunately, these days we seem more to want to avoid trouble than to confront problems so we grow farther apart, and so it was that Red got painted with the racial smear by a black Kentucky state congressman named Benjamin Simpson.

Ben Simpson was on a roll. Flushed with success at how well his Urban League speech had been received in Indianapolis, Ben was happily driving his B.M.W. convertible south on Interstate 65. At 28 Ben was already being touted as the next United States senator from his district. He was not a physically imposing person. In fact, Ben was a little guy but he was well liked and he had a booming voice that seemed to make him much taller than the five foot seven inches he claimed. He was a very black man who had a fascination with his color. Ben had majored in history at Georgetown and had authored a book that sold quite a few copies. The book titled
The Blacker You Are, The Harder It Is sounded autobiographical. It was not. Ben Simpson's intelligence and affability combined to make his blackness irrelevant.
The Indianapolis audience had been entertained by the retelling of Hitler's rise to power. "It was not until the Nazis stopped wearing brown and started wearing black did they become the embodiment of evil." Ben had said, repeatedly replaying his speech in his mind with greater and greater satisfaction until the low fuel light went off. Ben impulsively turned off the interstate at the next exit, which he noted was numbered 41. "Damn it all to hell," he exclaimed when nothing remotely resembling a

gas station appeared at the exit. He turned left onto 250 thinking at first that it ran parallel to the interstate. As the road took a more easterly turn, the congressman began to panic, and then he saw the sign: "Paris Crossing, 10 miles" it said. It was a comforting sign, large and green. Briefly it crossed his mind how colors can relieve tension and he wondered how much study had been put into green. "See I told you we're not lost" and blue "Thank God a place to pee." Plenty of money had been spent figuring that out, Ben thought, his political mind ready to take issue with future projects that revealed obvious answers such as "Farts smell bad, study reveals" or "Population increases when more children are born." Ben referred to these headlines as "No shit" statements because whenever anyone heard or read them, their immediate, sarcastic reaction was "No Shit." Although Ben had never heard of Paris Crossing he knew that the Beemer had another ten in her, and he was sure that even though the gas was probably going to cost him, it was bound to be there. "Maybe even more than one station," Ben said aloud thinking again of the size of the sign and its official, soothing greenness.

Gradually the terrain changed. The road narrowed and began to dip. The crops lining it took on a different character. Instead of corn and soybeans, patches of tobacco plants began to appear and somehow their presence seemed menacing and dangerous. "Tobacco and cotton," Ben surprised himself by saying, "Slave crops." Even though he had said it he was still unsure of its meaning. Probably something he had heard growing up and yet had he? Ben's father was a lawyer and his mother was a college professor. The congressman was raised in an affluent Louisville suburb and his parents disdained what they called "country darkie" talk. Howling Wolf and Lighting Hawkins were not musical favorites of his parents. Instead, Ben grew up to the music of Sinatra, Count Basie and Barry Manilow. He never failed to be nauseated whenever he heard "Mandy." A pickup truck passed going the opposite direction and its driver openly gawked at the BMW and its lone, black occupant. "God damned redneck" Ben thought. Another truck passed and the incredulity of the first driver was replaced by a look of contempt and disgust. "Pissed because my car cost three times more than your F-150?" Ben thought, his pride now tinged with fear. "What in the hell have I gotten myself into?" he said aloud. The road narrowed even more, and the dips became hills punctuated by curves that appeared for no apparent reason, as if the highway engineer had been on LSD. "LSD; Lake Shore Drive" Ben thought. "Wish to hell I was there. Wish to hell I was anywhere other than here. Where the shit is that goddamn town?"

Although he didn't see another vehicle, Ben sensed one behind him. Suddenly he thought of that terrifying TV movie where the driver of a car (Dennis Weaver, was it Dennis Weaver?) is pursued by a gigantic truck. (You never saw the truck driver just the goddamn truck) Reactively Ben began to increase his speed. "If this were a movie there would be shrill, minor cords screaming." thought Ben remembering Psycho and Jaws.

As you enter Paris Crossing from the west, the forty-five mile an hour speed sign is followed immediately by a thirty-five mile an hour sign. It is not a speed trap but a necessity mandated by a sharp turn in the road. Ben's mind was more on his real or imagined pursuer than it was on his imminent peril. Horrified as he entered the curve, now too late aware of impending disaster, Ben tried to brake. The little car shuttered and spun. A man appeared in the middle of the highway crossing the street. Ben did not know if it was his scream or the noise from his tortured brakes he was hearing. The car, as if sensing an encounter with flesh and blood, stopped inches from the knees of Red Cox.

Those two allies fear and instinct, fueled by adrenaline more powerful than explosives, overruled rational behavior. Red knowing nothing other than what his instinct told him, reached for his gun. Ben, seeing death in a brown uniform, employed his most effective weapon, "Stop right there you black, hillbilly, racist son of a bitch" he thundered. Later the participants would agree that the silence that followed was profound. "It was as if God had pushed the mute button," Ben remembered. Although the absolute stillness lasted but a moment, it seemed to take the deputy and the congressman several ticks of the clock to decipher what had been said. Then Red began to laugh. It was laughter that was not preceded by a giggle or a grin. The laughter that rocked Red's body exploded from his mouth, his eyes and his gut. Red was so convulsed that he could not speak. He began to hop in a circular motion, finally collapsing just off the blacktop, still braying with delight.

"That's not what I meant to say" said Ben trying to salvage some dignity and suppress the laughter that was definitely becoming a problem.

"No shit" sputtered the now hysterical Red.

"The Nazis started out wearing brown uniforms just like yours and then they changed to black," pontificated the congressman.

"First you try to kill me, then you slander me and now you're giving me a history lesson. Are there credits available for this, professor?" Red sputtered still gasping for breath.

"I think this is an appropriate time for me to tell you to go fuck yourself," said Ben, no longer able to disguise his relief at not being followed or killed and now laughing aloud. "Is there a gas station in this backward piece of shit place?"

"No" said Red, "but I've got a five gallon can in the police car which is damned near full and it's yours if you buy me a cup of coffee. As a matter of fact, I just might be able to get Clarice to fry you some chicken. Isn't that what you people eat?"

"You prick" said Ben. "You sound just like that golfer. Say, doesn't he live around here?"

"You must be thinking about Tiger Woods. I think he lives in Florida. Say ain't you a cute little fellow." said Red, helping Ben out of his car.

"Holy Christ" Ben said. "A redneck faggot; talk about a classic oxymoron." Clarice poured the coffee and the two men lingered, unwilling to let the moment end.

CHAPTER THREE:
PARIS CROSSING

Paris Crossing is located in Jennings County which is named after Indiana's first Governor. It is also the only county in the United States which is named Jennings. Turn on the computer, enter Jennings County, hit search and you will find Jennings County without ever having to mention that it's in the State of Indiana.

There was a Paris before there was a Paris Crossing. Now a ruin, Paris was once a thriving community located southeast and less than a mile from what was to become Paris Crossing. Southern Hoosiers are a peaceful lot, so instead of wrestling the land from the Indians around 1800, they actually paid good money for it. The going rate was $1.25 an acre. The beads and blankets commonly exchanged for Indian dirt was thought to be a fair way of doing business by our ancestors. No wonder the Indians became pissed off.

Some of the original settlers came from Paris, Kentucky and the town was probably named Paris, Indiana because of their influence. Marie Barbe Francois Lakenel might tell you otherwise. She came from France, the real, by God, France in the early 1800's and her presence may have given the town its name. Clarice's mother claimed to be a descendant of the aforementioned Marie Barbe, but Clarice had claims of her own, one of which was that her mother desperately wanted to have a famous ancestor.

Other settlers came from Virginia, New York, and Wales. Some had fought in the Revolutionary War. The original dwellings were log cabins. When newer style homes were built they were often constructed around the log cabins so that families would have someplace to live while the new home was being built. The idea was to tear the cabin down once the new dwelling was completed. That often never occurred. Nearly all of the homes that once proudly stood in Paris have crumpled and died like the town itself, but less than 30 years ago there was one home still standing that had a log cabin within its walls.

When the Ohio and Mississippi branch line of the railroad from Jeffersonville to North Vernon was built in 1854 it bypassed Paris and it was bye, bye, Paris. Paris Crossing was a village before the railroad came to town, but it gradually began to overshadow Old Paris with the advent of rail traffic and the coming of the Civil War. At one time 14 passenger trains a day came through and seven of them stopped at Paris Crossing. Businesses that had abandoned Paris moved to Paris Crossing and new businesses soon followed. The salesmen who traveled by rail had to have places to stay and boarding houses sprang up to accommodate them. Taverns were built and churches were formed. Most southern Indiana towns have an equal number of taverns and churches. "When there is more of one than the other you have disharmony" Pres Hart the lawyer said one morning at the restaurant. "People either pray too much or drink too much. The ying and the yang get all fucked up."

There was nothing civil about the Civil War. From all accounts, it was carnage, pure and simple, and it was personal. Men looked men in the eye while they killed or were slain. The Enola Gay dropped a bomb that killed more than 40,000 Japanese, yet the men who did the killing never had to see the agony, smell the blood, or hear the screams of the dying. No wonder it is so easy to wage war when a missile can be launched from your chair. Forty eight men fought for the union from Paris and Paris Crossing.

There had to be southern loyalists. Many of the original settlers from Kentucky and Virginia were still alive when the war began and continued to rage until its bloody end in 1865. General John Hunt Morgan CSA, known as "The Great Raider" took a cavalry force into Paris in 1863 and destroyed a bridle and saddle shop. No Confederate troops had gotten so far north. During the same campaign, Morgan with 2,500 men actually captured the nearby towns of Lexington and Versailles. Morgan was one cool dude with a full mustache and a Van Dyke beard. He wore a hat with a raffish brim, and he buttoned only the first four bottom buttons of his uniform top leaving his full chest and the top of his small belly exposed. You can say all you want about the Confederates, but their officers sure knew how to dress. There is nothing more romantic than a losing cause. In addition to *Gone With The Wind* there must be thousands of novels about the glorious South. Poems were written, too. This one from *The Kentucky Belle* best describes how many in southern Indiana romanticized General Morgan: "I went to warn the neighbors. He isn't a mile behind. He sweeps up all the horses, every horse that he can find. Morgan, Morgan the raider and Morgan's terrible men."

"Just about every classmate of mine knew that rhyme when we were growing up here in the seventies," said Pres Hart. "My grandfather said that his dad bragged about the fact that Morgan stole his horses. 'Morgan stole only the best', great granddaddy would say. Of course, that was utter nonsense. Morgan stole any horse that would give his raggedy ass troops a ride, and he would leave his exhausted nags as if he was making a fair trade."

CHAPTER FOUR:
THE RESTAURANT

The Parley Vous looked out on the highway and for its customers it had only one door which did double duty as the entrance and the exit. The restaurant itself was narrow and fairly deep. Houses that had the same appearance were called "shotgun homes" because anyone standing twenty feet away from the front door with a double barreled sawed off version could spray everyone in the place with buckshot. There was a back entrance that was used only by Clarice. Her apartment was located at the top of the stairs that were to the left of the rear entrance.

Only one sign adorned the front door - "Cash Only" it said. From time to time, Clarice would get calls from credit card companies wanting her "to bring the Parley Vous into the twenty-first century" as a salesman from Master Card once put it. Clarice believed that credit card companies were a front for the Internal Revenue Service. This notion came from her mother who told Clarice, "Every time someone puts a cup of coffee on his credit card, it goes into your file." Unlike most of her mother's paranoid pronouncements, this one had a ring of truth to it and Clarice embraced it wholeheartedly. She could visualize a room filled with bespectacled suits gleefully preparing indictments. She also could see that the men had erections tenting their tailored trousers. This too came from her mother who had said, "If you think someone's trying to screw you, check out his crotch and remember that some men get hard when they think about hurting you."

Clarice's mother was named Dolly. Her maiden name was Le Beau, and that is what she went by after Clarice's father died. Dolly's married name was Morris. Thorny Morris had been Clarice's father. Dolly made a lot of money during her lifetime, mostly by not reporting much of her income. "If you don't cheat, you don't eat," Dolly was fond of saying.

Dolly had also designed the restaurant, but she had given no thought to the ventilation system. As you walked through the front door, you noticed at once the overhead fans. The smoke stirred and moved quickly, but it had no place to go. There were no windows. Dobbins's garage shared her building on the right and the real estate office occupied the remainder of the shared building to her left. One day, several years ago when Clarice was an insecure 17 year old, Dolly came up with the notion that she could vent the building upstairs through the apartment. Dolly had a local handyman build a hollow 'fireman's pole,' the bottom of which was placed in a hole which had been drilled in the ceiling of the restaurant. It then went into the apartment, exiting through the roof above. Clarice was both mortified and enraged. She had come home from school to find a pole in the middle of her bedroom closet, with most of her clothes folded neatly on her bed. Dolly had not bothered to consult Clarice or even warn her in advance.

"It's not enough that we don't live in a house like normal people. It's not enough that we don't have a yard. It's not bad enough that I never had a swing or a sandbox," Clarice yelled at Dolly, "because now I come home to find that I don't have a closet. What's next? Have you rented my room? If so, I want to meet the cretin who would want a room that has no closet." Clarice paused for effect, "Oh, now I've got it, you've sold my bed. Admit it mother. Admit that you don't give a shit about me or my feelings and you never have."

"Clarice," Dolly began, "I probably should have given you some warning, but I called Bud Miller two months ago about ventilating the restaurant and he just showed up this morning with that hollow pole and before you know it he was drilling a hole. I couldn't just tell him to stop while I ran to school to get your permission. I probably wouldn't have seen the son-of-a-bitch for another two months."

"But why my closet?" Clarice implored. "Why did you have to put that enormous fucking thing in my closet?"

"It was the most out-of-the-way place in the apartment." Dolly explained. "Would you rather have it in the middle of the living room? And it's not that big. It's only about a foot around. If you get rid of all those old clothes I put on your bed you'll still have lots of room for the rest of your clothes and the new clothes you're going to buy when I give you two hundred dollars and let you take the car to Louisville this weekend, and by the way you know I don't like to hear you use that kind of language. It sounds so coarse."

"You think you can buy my forgiveness for two hundred dollars?" Clarice said incredulously.

"Alright, three hundred." Dolly replied.

"Four hundred" said Clarice, "and if you ever do anything like that again, I promise to redefine the meaning of coarse. I will spew filth. I will make Rosanne blush, and I want twenty dollars for gas. Deal?"

"Deal" said Dolly.

The pole worked for awhile. One could stand outside the restaurant and watch the cigarette smoke pour from its top.

"Looks like the College of Cardinals has elected a new Pope," Doc said from outside the Parley Vous a few days after the pole was installed.

The smoke, of course, had a yellowish tinge that became more apparent as the weeks passed and the nicotine accumulated inside the pole. Then the pole began to leak. The droplets were small at first and they were quickly dispersed as they hit the fan blades and went flung throughout the restaurant. Anyone stuck by a wayward droplet thought little of it dismissing the moisture as spittle from the person seated opposite them. With time, however, the size of the drops increased and they began to smell. Because of their color they were readily apparent when they ended up in coffee or mashed potatoes. Dolly tried denial at first, but when that ploy failed and the men began to abandon her establishment, Dolly feverishly began to attempt to repair the problem. Nothing seemed to work, however, and the final straw occurred when what appeared to be nicotine stained part of a pigeon feather was flung by a fan into Todd Marks split pea soup. The very same day the hole in the roof was covered and when Clarice came home from school she burst into the restaurant shouting: "Mother come quick, someone stole the pole. "

"Sarcasm does not become you Clarice, " Dolly said and in good weather or bad, the doors both in front and in back stayed open at least a crack. Everyone thought that helped but smokers are experts at self deception. It took a stranger to accurately describe the restaurant's continued foul odor. As he opened the door he was overheard to malaprop, "If you could see cancer, this is what it would smell like. "

If you stood inside the restaurant with your back to the front door, you would be facing south and you would see a line of three tables in the middle with aisles on each side. On the east wall were four booths running north to south. The west wall had but three booths and a large round table that was in an alcove at the south end of the wall. This was where Pres Hart, Bill Walsh, Doc Cross and Red Cox usually gathered.

A counter separated Clarice from her customers. A swinging door on the west side of the counter was what she used to serve the men and it also gave her some degree of separation from the men. Customers were free to observe and converse over the counter, but Clarice would politely "cut you a new asshole" if you tried to enter her kitchen. You were likely to be served cold eggs for at least a few weeks while Clarice silently judged the sincerity of your latest apology.

In fact, Clarice did not like having anyone in her kitchen. She had no employees after her mother's admonition to not leave a paper trail.

"You hire someone, you have to get a federal identification number, pay on their social security, withhold their taxes and pay worker's compensation insurance," Dolly had said. "You're just telling the IRS, 'Here I am. Where's my audit?'"

There were several local women who baked cakes, pies, cookies and doughnuts that they sold to the Parley Vous and Debbie Cox could usually be counted on to show up about 11:00 a.m. Debbie seemed delighted to wait tables. Clarice knew it was so Debbie could be with Red without annoying him. Red had once again begun to eat lunch at the restaurant since Debbie was "working" there. Clarice gave Debbie free coffee and half the tips for helping out.

The walls were paneled from the linoleum floor to about six feet from the ceiling. The six foot area was covered with photos. Some of them were of Dolly and Clarice as both of them aged. Most, however, were of

the men.   There were sixteen pictures of
camouflaged men standing by, over, or holding
aloft, deer carcasses, antlers, or heads.
Somehow, in most of the pictures, the deer
appeared to be more intelligent than the men.
There were three pictures of hunters with
dead turkeys.   The unfortunate birds lost
their nobility in death.   The men in the
photographs holding the turkeys looked
embarrassed. While dead deer retain a regal
appearance, the turkeys looked obscene. A
dead turkey's neck can no longer support its
head and the hunters in the photographs
appeared to be displaying a grotesque
feathered mass with a flaccid penis. Red's
picture was there twice, once as a Marine
graduate and the other with Ben Simpson.
Both Red and Ben were grinning foolishly when
Clarice took their picture.
     The letter from the famous coach had
once been on the wall, but someone had stolen
it.   There were other pictures of men holding
things; a watermelon, a fish, a gun and a
black Labrador puppy. There were no pictures
of women other than Dolly and Clarice.

CHAPTER FIVE:
THE ROUND TABLE

Simon and Garfunkel, melanoma, corn borer disease, football, Captain Marvel, Jimmy Durante, Hawkeye Pierce, colonoscopies, women, hunting, the weather, round barns, funerals, the lottery, Vietnam, Buddy Holly, baseball, David Letterman, the cost of healthcare, pollution, automobile racing, computers, beagles, cloth diapers, Dolly Parton's breasts, heaven, golf, Yogi Berra, embalming fluid, the Pope, diesel engines, Ivory soap, Matt Dillon, WD 40, balls, the Beatles, Ben Gay, The California Coastal Highway, Italian food, Marlon Brando, Volvos, the butterfly migration and Vicks Vaporub were just a few of the topics that were discussed during January, 2000. The men got along with one another well enough to look forward to meeting each morning. For that very reason the sharp edges of divisive topics were avoided and national policies were shunned. The subjects of their conversations were designed to soften the impact of their oncoming day and their mortality.

Today's topic evolved into what had become a familiar theme; "We were so poor that..." Bill Walsh was the first to bring it up. Typically, poverty was preceded by a discussion about the lavish riches possessed by the youth of Paris Crossing. Cell phones were today's catalyst. "We never even had a phone until I was in the third grade," said Bill, who at fifty was the oldest now seated at the table. "Even then we were on a party line with four other people, so there was no privacy because all of the other people on your line could listen in on everything that was said."

"We must have come full circle then," said Red, "Cell phones send and receive radio waves that are easily intercepted; anyone with the right equipment can hear everything that is said during a cell phone conversation."

"No one wants to keep their conversations to themselves anyway," said Pres Hart. "Go to any supermarket and you can hear people speaking loudly about personal matters that no one gives a shit about. It's as if they want strangers to know about their daughter's yeast infection."

"And how would you like to have your money invested in telephone booths?" asked Doc. "There are no more booths, just cubicles for the upper half of your body and with the use of cell phones no one even uses these anymore. We have destroyed Superman by depriving him of a place to change clothes."

"Has it become a rite of passage?" Bill Walsh queried. "Do all kids get cell phones on their sixth birthday, cars when they are sixteen, a college education provided by their parents, and condoms and birth control pills so they can fuck themselves silly without worrying about the consequences? How can we expect them to ever mature? What's the divorce rate these days, Pres?"

"I don't know what's happening overall," said the lawyer, "but my divorce clients seem to get younger and their reasons for wanting out seem to get more and more trivial. Does 'not wanting to watch television with me' warrant a cancellation of vows sworn to not more than two or three years ago in the presence of God and the entire Methodist choir? I've stopped giving wedding gifts because I'm tired of having people quarrel over them. Even worse is having the former bride tell me that a present I selected for the happy couple is not worth fighting about."

"Maybe if you're poor when you're young you stand a better chance of becoming a well-adjusted adult," reasoned Bill Walsh.

"There are some folks on the south side of Chicago who would disagree with that," Doc said.

"Of course you're right," said Bill, "but if you could place these kids in the same environment we were in when we were growing up, with the same level of poverty, maybe their futures would be brighter."

"Kids today will sue their parents if they're not provided with the 'necessary luxuries,'" Pres said. "Did you know that the children of divorced parents are better off from a higher education standpoint than the children of parents who stay married? If your parents are divorced and you want to go to college, a Judge will order your parents to pay for most of your education. If your folks stay married, it's up to them to decide how much money, if any, they contribute towards your higher education. What kind of message does that send? Makes a kid who wants a college education think about putting lipstick on his father's fly and rubbers in his mom's purse."

"The only luxury we had was a two-holer outhouse," said Bill Walsh. "We didn't have indoor plumbing, so we had to do our business in the privy that sat out back. Froze my nuts off in the winter. At least I had it better than my little sister. I'd just pee in the yard when my folks weren't looking, but Emmy, being a girl, had to use the outhouse. Most people in our neighborhood only had one-holers, but in my family, at least, peeing and shitting were social occasions. Emmy hardly ever peed by herself. Seemed like mom would always go with her, and Dad would sometimes go with me. Hell, the folks would go out together with flashlights after dark and sit and shit and read."

"Did you and Emmy ever shit together?" asked Pres.

"Goddamn it Pres, you're going to have to stop representing perverts, because quite frankly, you're starting to sound like one. No Emmy and I were never in the outhouse at the same time," replied Bill. "She never spent any more time in there than she had to anyway because she was so afraid of spiders. They were relentless. Shit attracts flies..."

"I never heard of such a thing," Red interrupted.

"And flies are just about a spider's favorite meal," Bill continued, ignoring Red. "So the shithouse spiders would weave their webs someplace between your ass and the mounds of brown below and no matter how hard you tried to drown them with piss or bomb them with shit, the spiders would return, determined to catch the flies, or as Emmy thought, to bite her on the ass."

"I'd like to bite Emmy on the ass," said Pres. "And while we're on the subject, did I ever sing you the song I wrote about figure skating? It goes, "I'd pay to see Katrina Witt shit. I'd give a lot---just to see her twat..."

"You have inspired me to recite my favorite poem," said Doc, *The Passing Of The Backhouse* by James Whitcomb Riley."

"Oh, for Christ's sake," said Pres, "we should have seen this coming."

Though he was often interrupted by hoots, moans, cat-calls and even an arm-fart, Doc was undeterred and once started, never stopped reciting the verses that were credited to his grandfather's drinking buddy and dearest friend.

"When memory keeps me company and
moves to smiles or tear,
A weather-beaten object looms through
the mist of years.
Behind the house and barn it stood, a
half a mile or more
And hurrying feet a path had made
Straight to its swinging door.
Its architecture was a type of simple

classic art,
But in the tragedy of life it played a
leading part,
And oft the passing traveler drove
slow and heaved a sigh,
To see the modest hired girl slip out
with glances shy.
We had our posey gardens that the
women loved so well,
I loved it too, but better still I loved
the stronger smell
That filled the evening breezes so full
of homey cheer.
And told the night-o'ertaken tramp
That human life was near.
On lazy August afternoons, it made a
little bower
Delightful, where my grandsire sat
And whiled away an hour.
For there the summer mornings its
very cares entwine,
And berry bushes reddened in the
streaming soil behind.

All day fat spiders spun their webs to
catch the buzzing flies
That flitted to and from the house
Where Ma was baking pies.
And once a swarm of hornets bold,
had built a palace there.
And stung my unsuspecting Aunt,
I must not tell you where.
Then father took a flaming pole, that
was a happy day.
He nearly burned the building up, but
the hornets left to stay.

When summer bloom began to fade
And winter to carouse,
We'd bank the little building with a
heap of hemlock boughs.

But when the crust was on the snow
And the sullen skies were gray

In sooth the building was no place
Where one would wish to stay.
We did our duties promptly, there one
purpose swayed the mind.
We tarried not, nor lingered long on
what we left behind.
The torture of that icy seat would
make a Spartan sob,
For needs must scrape the goose flesh
with a lacerating cob,
That from a frost encrusted nail, was
suspended by a string,
For father was a frugal man and
wasted not a thing.
When Grandpa had to "go out back"
And make his morning call,
We'd bundle up the dear old man with
A muffler and a shawl.
I knew the hole on which he sat,
'twas padded all around,
and once I dared to sit there, 'twas
all too wide I found.
My loins were all too little and I
Jack-knifed there to stay,
They had to come and get me out or
I'd have passed away.
Then father said ambition was a thing
that boys should shun,
And I just used the children's hole 'till
childhood days were done.

And still I marvel at the craft that
cut those holes so true.
The baby hole, and the slender hole
that fitted Sister Sue;
That dear old country landmark, I've
tramped around a bit
And in the lap of luxury my lot has
been to sit.
But ere I die I'll eat the fruit of trees
I robbed of yore.
Then seek the shanty where my name
is carved upon the door.
I ween the old familiar smell will

sooth my jaded soul.
I'm now a man, but none the less, I'll
try the children's hole."

CHAPTER SIX:
DOLLY

The "Hanging Rock Hill" has always been dangerous. It appears out of nowhere in flatland Indiana and to the unwary, the descent into Madison looks as if it had been carved out of the side of a Colorado mountain. It began as an Indian trail and was traveled heavily by the time Indiana was admitted to statehood. People coming and going from the Ohio River demanded a road they could more easily travel by horseback and by carriage, and gravel was laid down shortly after the Civil War.

Just west of the hill are the tracks of what once was called the Madison and Indianapolis Railroad. Completed in 1850, its construction was hailed as an engineering marvel. Locals referred to it simply as "the cut." It was the steepest railroad grade in the United States, and a special engine had to be built in England to ascend it. Horses on the hill would panic, rear and try to throw their riders upon seeing the monstrous engine belching smoke and fire. Those who lived nearby knew to keep their horses off the road from nine until ten in the morning when the leviathan made its descent and from four until five thirty in the afternoon when the mighty engine slowly and painfully rose from the depths of the old river town.

Hanging Rock Hill is also quite beautiful. In the spring and fall the foliage is nearly as spectacular as the view from the top. The hanging rock itself is a massive piece of limestone that juts out on the east side of the road, creating a rather large parking area below it. Tourists climbing the hill would often pull over on the right, off the highway and under the overhang to make way for faster traffic and to marvel at the rock. When the streams above the rock overflow, the water pours from its top creating a waterfall that is the subject of postcards. Children and lovers enjoy playing in the water and hiding in the cave created by the overhang of the rock.

The hill was paved in the early twenties to accommodate motor traffic but not much could be done to change its characteristics. It remains a hazard, its grade is nearly as steep as the nearby railroad but while the train is afforded a straight climb and descent, motorists on the road must negotiate curves that whip and twist. People that travel the hill often think nothing of speeding down it. They know how to handle the hill's treachery. Strangers to the hill frustrate the locals, slowing the traffic down to a crawl. Windows are rolled down and the fearful tourist from Wisconsin or Georgia must listen to shouts of "Move it, chickenshit," as if the hill itself was not terrifying enough. Occasionally, frustration would give birth to stupidity and a local motorist would try to pass a flatlander on a curve. Although there were mitigating circumstances that is pretty much what happened on August 8, 1978.

It had rained earlier in the day and Todd French was running late. His grocery truck had made its deliveries to Austin, Dupont, New Washington and Vernon but the biggest part of the load was still on board and he had to be unloaded in Madison before 5:00 p.m. That was when the crew at the Kroger went home and after that time, Todd would have to unload the truck himself. Among the remaining groceries on the truck were 10 cases of Alpo each weighing 60 pounds and Todd knew that his 56-year-old back would betray him and maybe cause him to lose more work. His boss had already frowned on the number of sick days Todd had burned. "You have been off 12 days and it's still July," the asshole had said two weeks ago, as if Todd had been faking the migraine headaches that had lately taken charge of his life. One was lurking now as Todd saw the Illinois car in front of him as he began his descent to the south down the Hanging Rock Hill into Madison.

Predictably, the car bearing the Illinois plate, a late model Buick, began to slow down. Todd's truck was an old, double axle, International with a stick shift that loudly complained when Todd began to try to find a gear low enough to accommodate the speed of the Buick in front of him. The cargo portion of Todd's truck was a wide metal box. It was twenty feet long and a foot taller than the cab of the truck. Its sides were a foot wider than the cab on both sides. All in all, it was an unwieldy little beast but it was infinitely preferable to a semi. The big trucks avoided Hanging Rock Hill.

Ahead of the Buick and the old truck just off the left side of the road was the Hanging Rock. The streams above the rock had swollen and burst and the water was falling from the rock with unusual force pouring out into the road. The spray created by the collision of the water with the limestone below the falls was enticed by the emerging sun to create colors of red, yellow, pink and green. A Japanese couple driving up the hill from the south, viewed the rainbows with delight and drove their rented Volkswagen behind the stream into the parking area. The waterfall hid them out of the sight of traffic coming down the hill; indeed it would have been difficult for any southbound driver to see anyone coming up the hill.

Flashbulbs went off behind Todd's eyes. The cable encircling his head tightened and waves of nausea similar to those caused by knees to the nuts, all struck at once. "I've got to pull over," Todd said aloud.

To his right was nothing but stern guardrails to prevent his descent into the abyss created by glaciers and the river millions of years ago. There was nothing but granite to his left, and the Buick had slowed to a crawl in front of him; then the Buick stopped. Todd cursed, but he understood the reason for the Illinois driver's hesitation. The Hanging Rock and its spectacular waterfall was only about fifty yards away and the Buick driver was both overwhelmed by the sight and terrified to proceed into an area that would rob him of sight. To Todd, however, the parking area created by the overhang of the hanging rock looked to be a safe haven where he could rest long enough to get rid of at least the vicious part of the headache so he could proceed safely down the hill.

Todd pulled out around the Buick. He didn't take the time to laboriously shift into a higher gear to get up to speed. He didn't have to. Todd stood on the clutch, disengaging the gears, and gravity did the rest. The old truck with only a partial load, still weighed more than eight tons; steel being its primary structural component. Only seconds had passed but the truck had already gone 30 yards. Todd knew he was taking a chance by staying on the left side of the road, but nothing was coming through the waterfall, and if he continued at what was now about forty miles an hour Todd thought he could pull into the north cave entrance before a vehicle might emerge from the falls. He was right. He began to brake. An involuntary sigh of relief gave way to a scream of horror when he saw through the mist, what appeared to be a figure pointing a camera at the old truck. Todd turned to the right, but the truck's left bumper struck what Todd now saw was clearly a man. A head-on collision then ensued with a north bound automobile. The car was struck with such force that its motor ended it its back seat together with its driver.

Three people were killed that day. Two of them died instantly: Asio Hiramoto of Osaka, Japan and Thorney Morris of Paris Crossing, Dolly's husband of seven weeks and four days. Todd French would not speak at the scene. His silence continued at the hospital. Doctors believed him to be "dazed and disoriented." He was neither. His grief was so deep and profound that he was no longer living. When he was briefly unattended around 9:30 that evening, he pulled the IV from his arm and staggered out of the hospital. In fact, he was not physically injured in the collision but his migraine had gone into another dimension. His brain now felt as if it was the contested prize of warring hyenas. He could feel their paws squeezing and pulling until the gelatinous tissue in his skull began to tear. Madison is usually quiet on a week-night and someone must have heard the screams of the tortured truck driver as he searched through eyes burning with self-loathing and disgust, for his apartment on Second Street.

Todd's headaches had begun during his wife's third chemotherapy treatment. Both Todd and Linda knew the treatments would not save or even lengthen her life by much, but they could not bear the thought of doing nothing. Four months later when Linda died on July 5, 1975, the headaches had taken up permanent residence in back of Todd's eyes, growling on good days, snarling and showing its teeth on bad ones. Two weeks before her death, Todd had told Linda about the migraines. We all do it. We complain to the blind about our cataracts. We tell amputees about the blisters on our heels or the warts on our hands. Maybe we are trying to relate, or just trying to make conversation. Much of the time, however, we complain in response to complaints.   We tire of hearing about you, and want you to hear about us.

Linda had urged Todd to get another job. "I'm afraid you'll have an accident or hurt yourself, or worse, kill somebody," she said. As he opened the door to his apartment what was left of his mind screamed, "But you didn't and now you did." His tongue probed the hole at the end of the barrel of his twenty-gauge as his toe wrapped around the trigger. He was humming "What a friend we have in Jesus" when the gun went off.

CHAPTER SEVEN:
DOLLY GOES TO INDY

Like many country people, Dolly had a deep distrust of lawyers. After Thorney's death, food and advice arrived in equal quantities. Deviled eggs, fried chicken, potato salad, and "you hire yourself an Indianapolis attorney, girl" were common themes. Although she did not know for certain, Dolly suspected she was pregnant. What she did know beyond a doubt was that she was alone, broke and devastated. Thorney had been her first and only love and while she ate the chicken and thanked the people who crowded her kitchen, she wanted only to be left alone. During the funeral, while Thorney was being buried in a casket Dolly could not afford, her friends came into her house and removed Thorney's clothes. The origin of this tradition is lost in time and it is no longer practiced in most urban areas, but it is alive and well in Southern Indiana. Its purpose is to help the living cope by reducing memories of the dead. The friends and neighbors who perpetuate the ritual all mean well and sincerely believe they are easing the grieving process. Dolly did not understand. For awhile, she thought that maybe Thorney was alive after all and the absence of his clothing proved it. But where was he and why had he left her? She was almost relieved when a friend asked if Dolly wanted Thorney's clothes donated to the church or the Salvation Army.

Everyone seemed to know Pres Hart. Although he had not been in the town very long, his presence was a boost to the prestige of Paris Crossing. He was the only lawyer in town and the first lawyer to practice law there since Harley Trimble died twelve years ago. The sign in his window said "D. Prescott Hart, Lawyer". Dolly had met Pres through the Jennings County biking club. It was a loose, mostly unorganized group that met on Sunday mornings at Hardees to take bicycle rides through the countryside. Both were avid cyclists and they were the only two in the group who smoked, so she and Pres would sneak away from the rest to share a kinship created by their common addiction. Pres did not act like a lawyer. He was not uppity and he never seemed to think he was better or smarter than anyone else. In addition, Pres seemed always to be happy. He would sing or whistle while walking down the street or striding through the courthouse. While Dolly felt him to be a friend, she was reluctant to trust him with what her friends told her was a case meant to be handled by "only the best."

Dolly was just a country girl raised by country parents. Alarmingly beautiful at twenty three years of age, she was shrewd but not city-smart. She could barely spell, and her reading was only at the fifth grade level. Her math skills, however, were way above any member in the senior class when she was in the sixth grade, and she knew men. She was a virgin when she married Thorney, not because she wanted to be, but because her folks had convinced her that men would not marry trashy women. Dolly wanted to be married, and even more than that, Dolly wanted no one to look down upon her.

Nonetheless, she let her sister talk her into making an appointment with an Indianapolis lawyer. His name was Robert Trent. He had handled Dolly's sister's divorce when Marlene was living in Marion County and, "His office is right on the circle," gushed Marlene. "We can see him in the morning and shop all afternoon. Or would you rather see him in the afternoon and shop all morning?" Dolly didn't care. It had been only twelve days since Thorney's death and Dolly's grief still held her heart in its hands. It squeezed hard every few minutes and it was all she could do to breathe.

Indianapolis is a fearful place for country people. Louisville and Cincinnati are big cities, but they are almost southern. It's as if the Ohio River has softened the north side of one and the south side of the other. River towns have a down comforter feel about them. We love to look at water and the tranquil Ohio seems to soothe and reassure.

Indianapolis is north and it has all those highways and all those cars. Dolly thought its people were uncaring and aloof. Worse, she thought Indianapolis people believed that people from southern Indiana were in the same category as Kentuckians. Marlene put on Indianapolis airs, but she didn't fool Dolly who knew that her sister had lived out of town and had seldom ventured as far in town as the circle, which is the heart of the city.

Most of us spend more time selecting cereal than we do choosing a lawyer. Robert Trent specialized in divorce; as a matter of fact that was all he did. He had stolen the Toy's-Are-Us motto and had business cards printed saying "Divorces Are Me." He had done a good job for Marlene in helping her get rid of Hugh. "That cheating, lying, son-of-a-bitch" would always follow Hugh's name whenever it was spoken by Marlene. Marlene's two year old Ed, when asked about his dad, would tell everyone, including his paternal grandma Martha that her son was a "cheating, lying, son-of-a-bitch," much to Marlene's silent delight.

"Honestly, mother Martha I don't know where he ever heard that kind of language. Probably Hugh taught it to him before leaving us penniless," Marlene would protest.

Marlene was all excited when she picked Dolly up for her appointment. Dolly loved Marlene. She was Dolly's older sister and had always been Dolly's best friend. Dolly had observed other sisters competing for their parents' attention and love. In most families, it seemed that one sister would try to make herself smell better by slinging shit at the other. Marlene had her faults. She had fallen hopelessly in love with a no account son-of-a-bitch, and Dolly knew that if Hugh ever came back that Marlene would welcome him with open arms and dropped panties. Dolly would have cut Hugh's dick off and put it down the garbage disposal, but Marlene was loyal, forgiving and incredibly stupid when it came to men, thought Dolly. Marlene was also a terrible driver. Her major fault behind the wheel was that she had no fear. In addition, she would look at her passengers while she talked, and she was always talking. Without thinking, Marlene would hasten left into the passing lane and slow down when the conversation demanded all her attention. Then, urged by the horns from enraged semis, Marlene would retreat to the right, only to repeat the process when a new idea emerged.

Both Dolly and Marlene wore skirts and blouses. Marlene was always well dressed. She was not as attractive as Dolly, but Marlene had a seductiveness about her that made her irresistible to men. Thorney had been an admirer of Marlene's charms and had even taken Marlene to a school dance when Marlene was a sophomore and he was a senior. Dolly was only in junior high at the time, but when Thorney saw her sitting with Marlene, Thorney strangely felt as if he had betrayed Dolly by dating her sister.

When Indianapolis was laid out by the original surveyors, the circle was the very center of the city. In the middle of the circle stands a structure known as the Soldiers and Sailors Monument. It is only fifteen feet shorter than the Statute of Liberty and at its top is Lady Victory. She holds a sword and she is facing south to greet her victorious Union Army as it returns from battle. If you come from southern Indiana, the statute looks menacing. It seems to say, "Keep your hillbilly ass out of here."

There are only two streets in and out of the circle. Meridian Street runs north and south and Market Street runs east and west. Of course, because of the monument, when entering the circle you cannot go straight. Regardless of whether you enter the circle from Market or Meridian you would turn right to get on the circle. Traffic in the circle itself moves one-way counter-clockwise just like it does on the nearby Indianapolis Motor Speedway.

Marlene completed the drive from I-65 to South Meridian Street without doing anyone harms. As she neared the circle, Marlene told Dolly how the traffic moved one-way left. "All you need to know about driving around the circle is to keep turning left just like A.J. Foyt does when he drives around the track". And that was what was going through Marlene's mind as she turned left off of Meridian into the path of a city bus.

Marlene screamed and both women peed. Reflectively, Marlene jerked the steering wheel left and stood on the brake. The car spun and miraculously ended up facing the right direction. Ignoring the horns and shouts of "stupid bitch" that filled the air, Marlene turned right back onto Meridian Street. The car was redolent with the smell of fear and urine. "Just keep going south" said Dolly. "I've wet my pants and one or both of us smells like a hog fart."

"It must be you that stinks, little sister, cause I'm sitting in a pool of eau de cologne", said Marlene, shifting her weight while glancing across at the urine that had started to drip to the floor from Dolly's seat. "Looks like both of us are about a pint of piss low."

"When we get back home, I'll call Trent and explain to him why we couldn't make the appointment," said Marlene.

"You be sure and emphasize that both of us were sensitive to the effect we might have on his other clients," said Dolly. "We wouldn't want them to think that he was consorting with the piss sisters."

"Sweet pee and Urinella. Will you still see him if I make another appointment?" said Marlene. "He has the cutest ass."

"Marlene, I don't need a nice ass right now. I need a good lawyer. I have no money, my man is dead and I think I'm pregnant," said Dolly.

CHAPTER EIGHT:
THE ROUND TABLE

Credence Clearwater Revival, the cost of postage, muzzle loaders, Chinese food, diarrhea, Mike Ditka, bowling, the Russian Revolution, the Sound of Music, beards, women's nipples, Lake Michigan, Wayne Newton, pollution, fortune telling, Bill Gates, Pete Rose, septic tanks, Alabaster Alabama, Little Richard, the size of dicks, sand hill cranes, mustard, powdered milk, Queen Elizabeth, Mario Andretti, mushrooms, hotels, peptic ulcers, People Magazine, Fords, throwed rolls, jumper cables, and speed limits were popular topics in February, 2000.

Clarice poured Doc another cup of coffee. "There you go, darling," she said.
"You call everybody darling. And everybody calls you, darling, too." Pres sang the first few stanzas of the familiar old song to a smattering of applause
"Do you have a song for every occasion?" asked Bill Walsh.
"When did she start with this darling shit?" asked Red. "And why doesn't she call me darling."
"You're not old enough," said Bill. "It started with me about 15 years ago when I was alone in a motel restaurant in Kentucky. I ordered a meat loaf or fried chicken or one of those meals you think can't nobody fuck up and the waitress said "thank you, hon". She wasn't exactly gorgeous but even a homely woman can make you feel good when you're alone and I came right back at her with a remark that still makes me cringe. I said, "I'll be up and waiting for you in room 402."
"You are one silver-tongued son-of-a-bitch" said Red.

"That's what I was hoping to prove to her," replied Bill. "She never came back to my table. The guy who showed me where to sit brought my food and the bill at the same time. It wasn't until I checked out the next morning and the sweet young thing behind the counter said, 'did you have a nice stay with us sweetheart,' did it dawn on me that the women weren't flirting. Goddamn them, they were saying sweet things because they thought of me as old. Like their grandpa, for Christ's sake."

"It's traumatic when it happens the first time," said Doc. "You've got this picture of yourself in your mind and you've edited out all the lines in your face, and the hair growing out of your nose and your ears."

"You no longer have a belly, your hair is thicker and darker," added Pres.

"And you know when that cute, little bank teller says, 'Good morning, honey' that if you weren't in a public place she'd be on her knees unzipping your pants," said Doc. "Then you overhear her call that ugly old bastard who was in line behind you 'sweetheart' and your dick and your ego shrink as small as that parsley on your plate."

"Do you know the difference between parsley and pussy?" asked Red. "Very few people eat parsley."

"Nothing could be finer than my lips on your vagina in the morning."

"Nothing could be sweeter than her mouth upon my peter at the dawning," sang Pres.

"Didn't oral sex become common after World War Two?" asked Red.

"That's what most people think," answered Doc. "The rich were saving it for themselves and when the poor went to Europe they learned what they were missing and brought it back to America. The preachers, who were poor themselves, condemned it from the pulpit without really saying what it was. Wasn't it a crime in Indiana, Pres?"

"Yes," said Pres. "It was called 'The abominable and detestable crime against nature.' It was a felony and it included oral and anal sex between consenting adults. You could go to jail for twenty years for licking your wife and she could be sentenced to do the same time for giving you a blow job."

"Well, not everybody" said Bill. "When I was a kid I worked in a shoe factory with a lot of World War II vets and I remember one guy who smacked his Parisian girlfriend when she started to go down on him. He equated all oral sex with homosexuality, 'I ain't no goddamn queer,' he told her."

"I had a professor in med school tell us that cunnilingus would lengthen our lives," said Doc. "Doctor Barton his name was, and as far as I know his theory was never published, but everyone embraced it because it prescribed the kind of medicine that everyone wanted to take, sort of like beer will lengthen your penis. In any event, he believed that since women outlived men by about seven or so years it had to be because of their hormones and the only way men could ingest them and derive the same benefits was to drink from the source."

"Give her a licking and your heart will keep on ticking," sang Pres just as Clarice appeared with coffee.

"What were you singing this time?" asked Clarice. "I never get to hear you sing."

"Nothing much," said Pres. "You've heard my nonsense before."

"Pres Hart, I've never heard you sing a complete song," said Clarice. "All I get are little snatches." Red laughed aloud. The other three tried not to look at Red or one another but Doc began to sputter and Pres and Bill immediately followed.

Clarice appeared bewildered and then she realized that she had used one of the 457,000 words men use to describe female genitalia. Furious, she turned to go to the kitchen. She was almost there when she spun and walked back to the round table.

"I want to ask a question," she said. "Do men ever mature? Look at you, especially the three of you," said Clarice, pointing to Doc, Pres and Bill. "I know what a little boy you are," she said to Red who blushed, thinking that Debbie had been telling Clarice about Red's recent behavior in bed.

"But you three are older than dirt. You are all college educated and two of you have your doctorates," Clarice said indicating Pres and Doc. "When you get to be eighty will you start to snicker when some woman refers to her cat as pussy?" Red laughed again. Ignoring him, Clarice angrily forged ahead.

"Answer me," Clarice insisted. "Do men ever grow up? Doesn't anyone have anything to say for themselves?"

After a few moments of silence, Doc raised his hand.

"Yes?" asked Clarice.

"He started it," said Doc pointing at Pres.

"Did not," said Pres.

"Did to," said Doc.

"Did not," said Pres.

"A pox on your entire gender," said Clarice as she headed for the kitchen. This time she did not turn around.

CHAPTER NINE:
PRES HART

Dolly and Pres rode their bikes for the same reason. You could forget about mental stress for a time and let your muscles worry about how to make the next climb. Then, when the summit was reached, you could dismiss your trouble entirely while the child in you emerged to feel the wind that sang of pleasant danger; to exhilarate in the 25 mile an hour descent on wheels too narrow to deal with a walnut on the road.

Reality always re-introduced itself at the bottom of each hill and while it was usually pleasant for the ever-optimistic Pres, it remained a hell for Dolly, only a few weeks removed from the death of her young husband. Dolly had not been looking for Pres that Wednesday morning, yet she knew that Pres liked to ride early on weekdays and she was hopeful that the rider about a quarter of a mile in front of her was the lawyer.

Dolly was a strong rider and she needed the solitude that comes with biking through the countryside. In the weeks after Thorney's death, she had ridden every day. As soon as she returned from the Indianapolis trip with her sister, Dolly had leaped upon her bike and rode a furious twenty miles to Vernon. Her route northbound was upon the well-traveled Route 3 and she had ignored the drivers who passed her, often coming within inches of her bike and body. She hadn't bothered to shower and had changed only her skirt for jeans. Once in Vernon, her fury spent, she made her way home by taking county roads, now hoping to get back to Paris Crossing without being seen or smelled.

It did not take Dolly long to catch Pres and she smiled when she heard him singing a balderized version of "Blueberry Hill." At that moment, her brain briefly registered a thought unique to those who have lost loved ones. "You did not think of him," Dolly said to herself. "A moment passed without pain." The thought brought both relief and guilt but the lawyer spoke before Dolly could digest this new sensation.

"Has anyone ever sung Hello Dolly to you?" asked Pres gently.

"Not lately," said Dolly.

"Well don't worry," said Pres. "I do a bad Carol Channing and my Louis Armstrong sounds like Pinky Lee."

"I think you have a nice voice," said Dolly.

"Thank you kind lady," said Pres and they rode for a few moments in silence.

"How are you doing, Dolly?" asked Pres.

"Not very well," answered Dolly. "Do you have a cigarette?"

"Sure," said Pres. "That maple on the right up ahead looks in need of human companionship."

The two rode to the tree and dismounted. Pres handed Dolly a cigarette and pointing at her battered Huffy said, "When are you going to get a new bike, girl?"

Tears welled in Dolly's eyes.

"God Dolly, I'm sorry. What a stupid thing to say. You probably don't have a dollar to spare. Forgive me, please", said Pres.

"Are you embarrassed, Pres?" blubbered Dolly.

"Yes, I am," answered Pres guardedly.

"Well, you're not one half as embarrassed as I am," Dolly cried. "I went to see another lawyer."

It took several minutes for Dolly to make her confession. She didn't leave out any details.

"Both of you wet your pants?" asked Pres.

"Yes," Dolly replied.

"At the same time?" asked Pres.

"I guess" said Dolly. "God-damn-it Pres I'm trying to apologize."

"Apology accepted," said Pres. "But I'm still wondering if it's genetic. Most people placed in a dangerous situation have a fight or flee reaction. In you and your sister's case it was fight or pee, or maybe it was flee and pee, or pee and flee."

"Shut up, Pres" said Dolly trying not to smile. "Will you take my case?"

Before Pres' reply, Dolly again briefly forgot, and this time her brain had time to comprehend that she would heal. She might never quite be the same, but she would heal.

Pres Hart was born and raised in Sellersburg, located only 20 miles or so north of Louisville. Both of his parents taught music. Pres' mother was the only female band teacher in southern Indiana. Pres' father taught voice. "There was always music in my parents' house," Pres would often say. Most of it came from vinyl. Like new books and good wine, vinyl had a smell to it that was almost sensual. The big seventy-eights spun out joy from five in the evening when his parents returned from work, until they went to bed at ten. The record player was Pres' alarm in the mornings and it sang all weekend long. His parents preferred popular music and for the first 10 years or so of Pres' life, the music of the thirties, forties and fifties was ever present. Subconsciously, or perhaps through osmosis, Pres' brain absorbed the words and music until he knew all of his parents' songs by heart. Later he bought a record player of his own and played vinyl that contained the songs of his generation. He remembered those too, all of them. He knew the words and music to traveling songs like the Happy Wanderer, I'll Walk Alone; You'll Never Walk

Alone, Walking After Midnight and Traveling Man.

He remembered songs about Proud Mary, Maria, They Call the Wind Maria, Marie, Mary, Carol, Donna, Dawn, Jean, Gigi, Gloria, Sweet Adeline, Misty, Lily Marline, Oh Susanna, Susan, If You Knew Susie Like I Know Susie, Wait Till the Sun Shines Nellie, Banging Away on Lulu, Lupe, Be Boppa Lula, Lela, Long Tall Sally, Stella By Starlight, Sylvia's Mother, Sioux City Sue, My Cherona, Lady in Red, Amy, Ricky, and Peg of my Heart. He knew Breathless, The Rocking Pneumonia and The Boogie Woogie Blues, Fever, Old Black Joe, Sam's Song, Brennen on the Moor, Johnny Be Good, Henry the Eighth, The Ode to Billy Joe, Frankie and Johnny, Tom Dooley, The Piano Man, Why Can't a Woman Be Like a Man, YMCA, You are My Sunshine, Be Prepared (that's the boy scout's marching song), The Hallelujah Chorus, Hallelujah I Just Love Her So, Baby Baby Don't Get Hooked on me, Baby Face, Dang Me, The Battle of New Orleans, Galveston, A Rainy Night in Georgia, Stars Fell on Alabama, Back Home Again in Indiana, The Tennessee Waltz, Georgia, The Carolina fight song, Long Distance Information, I Left My Heart in San Francisco, The Atchison, Topeka and the Sante Fe, The Chattanooga Choo-Choo, Folsom Prison Blues, Jackson, I've Got a Gal in Kalamazoo, Kokomo, Shenandoah, My Old Kentucky Home, Those Old Cotton Fields Back Home, Way Down Upon the Suwanee River, Suwanee, It's a Long Way to Tipperary, The White Cliffs of Dover, From the Halls of Montezuma, Going Back to Houston, Gary, Indiana, Every Thing's up to Date in Kansas City, Oklahoma, North to Alaska, Take the Last Train to Clarksville, There's No Place Like Home (click them ruby red slippers, bitch), Home, Home on the Range, This Old House, Frosty the Snowman, Bury Me Not on the Lone Prairie, Mule Train, My Baby Likes the Western Movies, The Theme from High Noon,

Davy Crockett, You've got to Walk that Lonesome Valley, The theme from Picnic, Go Bum Again, and ten thousand more.

A staunch heterosexual, he knew but did not sing, I Enjoy Being a Girl, I Feel Pretty, My Sweet Little Alice Blue Gown, and I Want to Be Bobby's Girl.

Pres wrote his first song when he was nine. He sang it in the Methodist Church on Easter Sunday to the delight of his parents. It had no title. The words were:

"When Jesus was a tiny baby,
His father said to him,
Oh, my son, you must die a death of agony,
To save this world from sin,
Oh, isn't it a shame,
Oh, isn't it a shame,
For the way we live our lives today,
Looks like Jesus died in vain. "

"Oh, the years flew by,
Like leaves in a hurricane,
Then an army of Pilate's men,
Pounded nails in the tree,
That stood on Calvary,
And we all were born again. "

"Oh, isn't it a shame,
Oh, isn't it a shame,
We must start today,
We must hope and pray,
That he did not die in vain. "

As his sophomore year at DePauw University neared its end, Pres discovered two things. He was not cut out to be a music major. His voice was only adequate and his ability to play an instrument had not progressed beyond rudimentary guitar 101. His second discovery took him entirely by surprise. Her name was Marie and she was in love with him.

Sad people are often attracted to happy people. The morose view the cheerful like a jumper views a parachute. The opposite can also occur. The urge to support, help and heal is overpowering in some people, and when the strong find the weak, the attraction can be irresistible. Pres never had not thought seriously about love until Marie unexpectedly blurted on just their second date, "I love you and I want to marry you even though I know you could never love me."

"Of course I could love you," Pres replied, embarrassed by the declaration. "I mean anyone could love you Marie. You're pretty and you're smart, a lot smarter than me. Didn't you ace that religion test?" Pres continued to ramble on but Marie wasn't listening. All she had heard was that Pres could love her.

For the remaining three weeks of the semester, Marie seemed to always be where Pres was. At first Pres was flattered by the attention and welcomed the envious looks of his male classmates when Marie greeted him with a kiss. Cloying, however, can be annoying and soon Pres' irritation with Marie began to surface. Sensing the emerging tension, Marie made her move.

"I've got a room reserved at the Best Western," said Marie.

"You do?" said Pres, not quite grasping what Marie had said.

"I think it's time we slept together," Marie said pressing a motel key into Pres' suddenly sweating palm. "I've already checked in. There's an outside entrance, so no one can know that I'm going to have company."

"You've thought of everything," said Pres.

"Yes, I have," said Marie. "I even made a list. Look at number six."

Pres looked at the small piece of paper Marie produced. Number six read: Remember to tell my honey to bring rubbers.

Pres retreated to his room. It took the sun a long time to go down that afternoon. As it got closer to the horizon, the more conflicted and confused Pres became. His dick and his brain were familiar adversaries. He tried to tell himself that he could simply "fuck her and leave her" but Pres could not bring himself to take advantage of Marie even though he knew that she was taking advantage of him. "If I go to her, I will eventually have to marry her and it will probably be sooner rather than later," Pres thought. "If I don't go to her I'll really hurt her and I'll be missing out on a rare piece of ass." Absently, he began to sing "Caught in a Trap", followed by "Prisoner of Love" and when he put his key in the motel door, he had just finished singing "Temptation." As he turned the key, he thought bewilderedly, "How in the hell did I get myself into this?"

Marie had been crying. "I didn't think you'd show up," she said. "Am I so unattractive to you that you can't stand the thought of making love to me?"

"Marie, I think you're gorgeous," Pres said. "I just wanted to be sure I wasn't seen. This could get us expelled from good old strait-laced, church-owned DePauw U." As he spoke, Pres took Marie in his arms and realized she was trembling. "Are you cold?" he asked.

"I'm fine," she said, but her body betrayed her.

"You're terrified, aren't you? Look, Marie, we don't have to do this." said Pres.

"No, I want to." Marie said. "It's just that I want to tell you everything, I've got to tell you everything before we do this.

I need to tell you everything. Do you understand?"

"I guess," Pres said. "Jesus, Marie calm down."

Marie then told Pres about her "uncle" Jimmy (Sonny) Hawkins, her father's first cousin, a high school basketball legend who was revered by Indiana sports fans and in particular, Marie's father. Sonny was Marie's favorite "uncle" and she was not overly concerned at age thirteen to be awakened by the touch of Sonny's big hand rubbing her back. "I just thought I'd give my sweet niece a back rub," Uncle Sonny had said. Marie had not even thought it unwise to remove her panties when asked.

"Please don't tell me how stupid I was," Marie said. "He was the only adult outside of my father who really paid attention to me and I was so starved for affection that I didn't want to lose this wonderful man who everyone looked up to. I thought I was really special. I was being caressed by a hero."

"Oh, God," said Pres. "Oh, God, Oh, God," as he spoke, Pres grabbed and held Marie close.

"At first he just rubbed my behind as if it was the normal extension to a massage. He even warned me not to let anyone else but him touch my "little bottom" as he put it. Soon, it became a routine. Every time I stayed with Uncle Sonny and aunt Elia, I could expect good old Uncle Sonny to pay me a visit. I would even take my panties off before I went to bed, so my favorite uncle's back-rub would not be interrupted," Marie said.

"Where was Elia all this time?" asked Pres.

"I've asked myself that question hundreds of times. I guess she either didn't know or didn't care. Anyway, he soon started fingering me and then when I was sixteen, he began to have intercourse with me."

"You poor baby. My God, Marie," said Pres. "You must have known there was something wrong then."

"Oh, I knew it was wrong, alright," said Marie, "but by then I had fallen in love with him."

Pres was stunned. "You were sixteen years old."

"You were never a sixteen year old, small, homely, girl whose mother hated her. I'm not asking you to understand right now, I just want you to know why I am, who I am, and why I need you so much. Please don't be scared. I know if I have you, I can survive. I'm not sure I can make it without you."

"Is the son-of-a-bitch in jail?" asked Pres.

"No, he's in Oregon," replied Marie. "Portland, I think."

"I don't understand," said Pres.

"I never told anyone. My father worships Sonny. I couldn't hurt my dad. Besides, it was as much my fault as it was Sonny's."

"Marie, you are so wrong," said Pres.

"That is what my counselor says, but you're the ones that are wrong. I laid in bed in my uncle's house with my panties off and I couldn't wait for him to come touch me, to make love to me. How was I not at fault?" asked Marie.

"You were a baby, a child, a victim of the worst species of human who ever lived. Every time that kind molests a child, he ruins a life. When did he finally start leaving you alone?" asked Pres.

"After Elia caught us in bed together," Marie replied.

"What a wonderful experience that must have been," Pres said.

"He sends me money," said Marie. "He was a partner in my father's law firm in

Crawfordsville; then he and Elia got a divorce and he moved away. He must be doing well because he sends me a money order for a hundred dollars every week. "

"Hush money," said Pres and then he said no more because Marie had begun to undress. He watched as she removed everything but her bra and covered herself with the top sheet of the bed, carefully folding down the blanket and bedspread. Pres turned off the overhead light. Marie turned on the light by her side of the bed. "I want to watch you undress," she said. That pretty much did it for Pres. He was already disgusted with himself for becoming aroused during Marie's confession of abuse. The sight of her near nakedness and her spoken desire to see him unclothed caused him to come without being touched.

"Honey, are you alright?" asked the bewildered Marie as Pres hastily retreated in shame to the bathroom.

"Pres, what's wrong? Did I embarrass you? Answer me honey, please, you're scaring me."

The come seemed to be everywhere. "I'm fine. I'm fine," Pres said. "I just need to take a quick shower."

"No you don't," Marie said. "You always smell so sweet and clean," but the shower had already started to run.

"What's the matter with your under shorts?" Marie asked the shower curtain from her seat on the stool. Her fingers gave her the answer as she lifted Pres' briefs from the tiled floor. The curtain parted just as Marie touched the cotton jockeys with her tongue. Her eyes never left his as she took the shorts and rubbed them up and down his hardening cock. As she bent to take him in her mouth, she said, "I told you not to take a bath."

She refused to remove her bra until the lights were out and they were both covered with the sheet and blanket. "I don't have much up there," she said as Pres reached for her breasts. Indeed, she was small, but her nipples were large and responsive. As Pres entered her, both he and Marie thought of Sonny. Pres wondered if Marie had ever lavished the oral attention he had received on her "uncle." Marie's thoughts were "I think maybe I can get over Sonny now."

Pres and Marie were married in Crawfordsville two weeks after both of them had graduated from DePauw. Uncle Sonny did not attend the services, but he sent Marie a money order for a thousand dollars which she received the day before the wedding. Marie's father, Harry Hawkins kept toasting Pres referring to him as the man who had made Marie happy. "Even though he is a goddamn DePauw Danny," Harry said repeatedly. Harry was a graduate of Wabash College, which is located in Crawfordsville. Pres met Marie's mother for the first time at the wedding. Mildred Hawkins lived in Naples, Florida in a condo on the beach which had been community property before her divorce from Harry. Marie had lived there until she was sixteen but Marie had always been "Harry's little girl" and she was glad to return to Crawfordsville to live with daddy.
Marie was happy. "I have everything I ever wanted." She told all who would listen. "I'm back home with my daddy and I've got a man who loves me as much as I love him."
Pres supposed he was happy, too. He was to spend the summer working in Harry's law firm: Hawkins, Hawkins and Hawkins it said on the door. He would take the LSAT and if everything went well, Pres would go to law school and enter Harry's firm as a full partner.

"Can you imagine me having a goddamn DePauw graduate as a partner in my firm?" Harry said to Judge Smyth in Pres' presence. "Pres, you may be the only male DePauw graduate in the whole damned county. Judge Smyth and I always thought DePauw was a girl's school, didn't we Barry?" Harry went on to say, as the two older men laughed. Wabash was an all-male institution and many of the young women from Crawfordsville went to nearby DePauw.

Wabash College, like DePauw, is a proud and prestigious institution. The two schools have a friendly rivalry but it did not take Pres long to tire of Harry's remarks denigrating DePauw, which were beginning to sound personal. There is a fine line between teasing and meanness and Harry crossed it often. Pres' father had always told Pres to watch a man playing poker to get a true picture of his nature. Harry was a good poker player, but he was a verbal thug, ridiculing anyone who called with a lesser hand. At his regular game, which took place at the VFW on Friday afternoons, Harry would often try to raise the limit so as to empty the wallets of the just-paid, minimum wagers on whom he preyed.

Pres also resented Harry for giving Pres advice about how to handle Marie, "You don't want to make her mad," Harry told Pres. "You'll just get her all depressed again. You don't know how much money I had to spend to get her back to normal again. Why she's been seeing a shrink since she was twelve years old. Besides, she's got a terrible temper. Just like that bitch of a mother of hers."

"As a matter of fact," thought Pres the day before taking the LSAT, "I don't like the son-of-a-bitch. If I only had the balls, I'd tell him to take his full partnership and stick it up his ass."

Unfortunately, at that stage of his life, Pres' balls were minuscule. He had let Marie talk him into everything. She had stopped seeing her counselor, they had set up housekeeping in her home town, he had gone to work for her jerk of a father and she was still accepting money from the man who had repeatedly raped her. "What next?" thought Pres. "Oh yeah, I remember, Daddy's gonna pay my way through law school. You weak, pathetic bastard."

The next day Pres thought seriously about filling in the wrong blanks and writing, "How in the fuck should I know" responses to the essay questions. His competitive nature ultimately overpowered his rebelliousness and he knew when he had finished the test that he had done well.

At first Marie wanted Pres to commute to his law school classes in Bloomington while she remained in Crawfordsville in the furnished apartment her father had provided. Pres' balls grew a little when for the first time he could remember, he refused to give in to Marie. She surprised him by quickly changing her mind and agreeing to the move. "I think Daddy's gonna give us his old Lincoln, so we can come back and stay with him on weekends. Would that be okay, darling?" Marie asked.

"Of course," said Pres, surrendering the high ground he had just won, as his balls became microscopic.

Marie's father gave a lot of money to Indiana University and Harry had no trouble finding a duplex that was within easy walking distance of the law school. Another young couple was already in the other half. She was named Enid and she wanted to be a nurse. His name was Bill and while he was ambivalent about his future plans, he thought he would probably wind up being a mortician like his dad.

Law school was challenging but doable for Pres. Marie got a job at a pizza parlor working from noon to eight on Mondays, Tuesdays and Thursdays and Pres got offered a gig at a local tavern to play and sing from five till midnight on Fridays. Pres anticipated a major showdown with Marie. Her weekends back home with Harry in Crawfordsville were precious to her and a pain in the ass to Pres. If he accepted the performing job, he and Marie would not go back to Crawfordsville until early Saturday morning. Marie agreed to a two week trial run and shortly after midnight on the next two Saturday mornings, Marie drove the dark, lonely, eighty mile distance without any help from Pres who played for drinks and tips. The tips were scarce but the drinks were not and Pres curled up in the back until Marie helped him into her father's house.

After the second weekend, Marie suggested (demanded) that Pres either quit his job or she would go to see Harry by herself. She seemed relieved when Pres agreed that she should go home without him. "I need to spend more time here at the library on weekends anyway and we could use my tip money for cigarettes. Every little bit helps," Pres said, thanking God for letting Pres have his weekends away from his obnoxious father-in-law.

By the fourth Friday, it had become apparent that Pres was attracting customers. Law students are easily amused. They ordinarily don't turn into pricks until after they pass the bar exam. Pres had composed several jingles to help him memorize significant cases and on Friday he would intersperse them among his standards. Soon the jingles outnumbered the music and Pres sang them all to the tune of "Good Night Irene". Two follow:

According to Keller v Keller
26 Indiana 349
If you dangle your dickie in public
You'll pay an outrageous fine.

"That's not really what the case says, but it's a hell of a lot more amusing than bailment," shouted Pres to his mostly drunken comrades.

At 482 Ind 14
Is the case of Smart vs. Smart
Which holds that public indecency
Can consist of letting a fart.

It didn't take long for other students to volunteer lyrics of their own, and soon audience participation became part of Pres' act. His boss was so pleased with the increase in alcohol sales that he started giving Pres tips. One Friday in December Pres was handed twenty-five one dollar bills. Feeling flush, Pres bought a carton of cigarettes and a Playboy magazine.

Wednesday mornings were cleaning days for Marie and when she turned the mattress on their bed she discovered the Playboy magazine. Pres came home late that afternoon to find that his remaining seven packs of cigarettes had been cut in half and the cigarette halves were in the trash sodden with left over coffee. Most of the Playboy was in there too but it appeared to have been burned before it was tossed. The Playmate of the week had been saved from the conflagration. She was on the living room rug, a turd obscured her otherwise perfect left breast.

The bedroom door was closed. Pres turned the knob and was surprised to find it unlocked. Marie was sitting up in bed, fully clothed, smoking furiously. "You've never liked them, have you?"

"I don't know what you're talking about," Pres said.

"Don't play innocent with me, you rotten son-of-a-bitch," Marie hissed through clenched teeth.

"Marie, honey please..." Pres implored.

"My tits, my breasts, my boobs, or lack thereof, you unfeeling, uncaring, merciless asshole. It's not my fault" she began to scream. "It's not my fault. It's not my fault." She was yelling now as loudly as she could.

"Marie, please, Bill and Enid will hear," Pres pleaded.

"I don't care if the whole fucking town hears," Marie said, making no attempt to diminish the volume. "As a matter of fact, I want everyone to hear how little Pres Hart cares for his wife's feelings."

Marie then left the bed and jabbed at Pres with her lit cigarette. Pres thrust out his arms to deflect the attack and shoved Marie with such force that she landed back on the bed. Hatred appeared in her eyes. She pulled the car keys out of her purse and headed for the door. As she left she yelled, "You'd better get rid of your whore laying on the rug. I think somebody shit on her."

Marie did not return that night or the next morning. Pres was miserable. Marie was due at work at noon and on impulse Pres called the restaurant. Marie answered the phone. At first Pres said nothing. Marie tired of saying hello to an unresponsive phone.

"Pres, is that you?" she asked.

"Yes," he said. "I didn't know if you would be there or not. Will you be home for supper?"

"Of course I'm here. I've got to work. I don't want my father to have to pay for everything. I don't know if I'll be home tonight or not. Is that bitch gone?"

"Yes," Pres said.   "Honey, I'm sorry.
I didn't mean to hurt you."
    "If the slut is gone then I'll be home.
Just remember, if this is your way of
complaining about my inadequacies, you've
made your hurtful point.   I don't want to see
her or any of her silicone sisters in my
house again.   Understood?" said Marie,
hanging up the phone.   Four months passed
before she removed her bra in his presence
again.   Pres quit his job at the bar and went
to Crawfordsville with Marie every weekend
and every holiday.   He agreed with every word
Marie spoke and his balls vanished.

CHAPTER TEN:
VEEDERSBURG

Harry was not quite true to his word. Although the sign on the door was changed to read Hawkins, Hawkins, Hawkins and Hart, Pres' portion of the firm's income was to start at twenty percent. Harry took forty-five percent, his brother, Mack got thirty-five and Pres got the rest. The other Hawkins was Sonny who was out in Oregon getting his head on straight after his divorce. Pres was told that Sonny was making big bucks working for a firm that specialized in immigration law, but one day he was sure to come home. Pres couldn't' wait.

The Hawkins firm was well known in the area for defending insurance companies. Harry was an accomplished trial lawyer and the plan was for Pres to gradually take over the trial work. There was only one problem; even though he was fresh out of law school and new to the area, it readily became apparent that Pres was going to be good. Harry was quick to take the credit. "He didn't know shit when he first came here," Harry said. "I thought I was going to have to fire his ass and tell Marie to ditch the dummy and marry someone smart, but miracle of miracles he turned out to be teachable. Doesn't it figure that it would take a Wabash graduate to turn an undereducated DePauw retard into a decent lawyer?"

Juries liked Pres and he liked them. His success grew to such a degree that the insurance clients began to ignore Harry and take their cases to Pres. At first Marie basked in Pres' radiance. It was the happiest time of her life. Then she began hearing people talk about how Pres was twice the lawyer Harry had ever been. Although she was proud of her husband, Marie was hurt by the insinuations that her father's skills paled in comparison to those of her talented husband. Pres basked in the attention. He regularly stopped at the Friendly Tavern on his way home. There Pres could drink with fellow lawyers and court personnel. He could sing rock and roll and try out songs that were gestating, most of which, he would not finish. One of these was titled, "Melting quarters down."

Strange things were happening to the price of silver. It was later revealed that a Texas billionaire was trying to corner the market on the precious metal. His actions propelled silver's price to unheard-of levels. Quarter, dimes, halves and dollar coins were pure silver in those days, and for one brief period before the billionaire was foiled and the market collapsed, the face value of the silver coins was exceeded by the value of their silver content. Pres sang his song as he thought Burl Ives might and it went like this.

"Save your silver dollars boys,
Your half dollars too.
Save your quarters, save your
        dimes
They're worth more than that to
        you.
Throw them in that red hot pot,
Stir them all around,
We can make a fortune boys,
By melting quarters down."

Veedersburg, located in Fountain County, was a forlorn little town located halfway between Crawfordsville and the Illinois state line. Pres passed through it often on his way west from Crawfordsville to Covington, the Fountain County seat, to try lawsuits on behalf of one insurance company or another. Founded in 1804 by a man named Peter Veeder, Veedersburg was the home of a foundry that belched foul smoke on every traveler that passed through its sorry environs.

Pres left court early on a sunny Friday afternoon. His career as a trial lawyer had taken off. The three-day trial in Covington had been resolved in his favor. It was his third victory in a row. Most of the time, Pres took the interstate back to Crawfordsville, but today was different. The trial had been a hard one to win and he wanted to take the long way home to savor his victory.

Driving through Veedersburg on U.S. 136, Pres was seized by a muse that grabbed him by his left nut and squeezed. He slowed and drove a few more miles while the words to his song began to take shape. His excitement at his clever creation was causing him to actually tremble. Breathlessly, he pulled over and rushed into a tavern he knew in Hillsboro, the next town east of Veedersburg. The place was called "A Drinking Establishment" and it was owned by a woman named Mildred who lusted after Pres. He had helped Mildred's daughter through a divorce that should have been simple were it not for a custody battle over a nasty monkey named Harlot. Mildred's daughter was awarded the filthy beast and Mildred told Pres that she owed him "a little something extra for his efforts." Up until now, Pres had avoided Mildred but he needed someplace to write down the song that might escape if he tried to hold on to it for many more miles.

Thankfully, Mildred was not at her usual spot behind the bar and Pres was happy to see three insurance adjusters who greeted Pres warmly. Insurance people were always happy to see Pres. Harry had given Pres permission to spend the firm's money on beer for their insurance clients and Pres was eager to oblige.

There was an old acoustical leaning in the corner and Pres began to sing softly while he tuned the guitar and drank his Pabst. The art of memorization frequently distracts from inspiration. Pres never wrote anything down, so the first line had to be repeated until the second line appeared; then the first and second lines were sung until the third line emerged. By the time the entire song was completed, Pres was frequently sick of his first several lines. Exacerbating the difficulty was beer and the need to be social to the people who were responsible for much of the firm's income.

Finally, after three hours and six Blue Ribbons, Pres began to sing aloud to his companions. By this time, early Friday afternoon had turned into happy hour and the tavern was packed. Hillsboro is barely in Fountain County, six miles east of Veedersburg and thirteen miles west of Crawfordsville. The people in the bar that evening were all from nearby and more than a few were from Veedersburg.

His insurance companions cheered when Pres completed his song and the fifty or so others who were in attendance began to good-naturedly complain about not hearing the song. Urged on by Mildred, who had just recently made her appearance, and the insurance adjusters who were still drinking on his money, Pres stood on the bar and began to sing his ode to Veedersburg to the tune of "My Darling Clementine."

"Peter Veeder, Peter Veeder,
Was a hardy pioneer
Fought the injuns
Fought the white man
Ended up six miles from
    here."

"Oh he roamed this
Whole world over
For a town to bear his name

Bring him glory, bring him
          honor
Bring him ever-lasting fame. "

"Near a sulfur-smelling
          eyesore
Where the pigeon droppings
          fall
Stood an old, abandoned shit-
          house
Which he converted
into City Hall. "

"Oh, how fitting
Oh, how proper
How indicative of your worth
Ignoble city, you sure ain't
          pretty
You're the asshole of the
          earth. "

The police surmised that the beer bottle
that struck Pres in the temple was probably
thrown by someone from Veedersburg. This
observation was seconded by Pres when he
learned at the hospital several hours later
that the bottle was nearly full. "Only a
Veedersburgerian would be dumb enough to
throw away a perfectly good beer, " said Pres
before lapsing back into unconsciousness.
     All of the insurance adjusters had
cameras and several different pictures of
Pres appeared in the Crawfordsville paper the
following day. By Sunday, Pres' visage
became known to newspaper readers in
Lafayette, Terre Haute, Indianapolis, Fort
Wayne and even Evansville. The most popular
photo depicted Pres on the floor behind the
bar; his bloodied head nestled in Mildred's
ample bosom. It was also one of Marie's
personal favorites.
     The captions were all variations on the
same theme; "Lawyer Assaulted, alcohol
thought to be a factor, " read the

Crawfordsville Journal Courier. "Prominent Crawfordsville Attorney Injured in Bar Fight," blared the Indianapolis Star. The *Lafayette Journal Review* took a slightly different approach "Injured Lawyer Comforted in Bar by Lady Friend," was the caption that appeared under the picture of Pres and Mildred.

In fact, there was no bar fight. There was no fight at all. When Pres was struck and fell, most of the people fled the tavern. Some ran because they were certain a fight would ensue. Others fled believing that Pres had been killed; and of course the bottle thrower ran for reasons uniquely his own.

Marie was at the hospital when the ambulance arrived. At first, Pres seemed to be coming around, but then he lapsed into a coma. The doctors appeared concerned and Marie was terrified. "When he comes to, I'm going to kill him," Marie told Harry through tears that belied her anger. "Not before me, kiddo," said Harry. "This is a small town and this kind of publicity scares clients, especially insurance people."

Pres remained unresponsive until Saturday evening. By this time, Marie had seen all the pictures in the Crawfordsville paper and she had with her the one showing Mildred smothering Pres with her big breasts. Pres opened his eyes. His head was killing him and he had no idea where he was. Marie threw herself upon him screaming, "Doctor, nurse, I've got my husband back."

His first thoughts were that he had been in a car wreck. Pres remembered vaguely drinking too much and he feared that he had hurt someone by trying to drive home.

"Marie, was anyone else hurt?" he asked.

"Only me," she had replied. "We'll talk about it tomorrow. I've been here for over fifteen hours and I was afraid I'd lost you. You're back now and I'm going home to get some rest. You need some, too. You also need to explain why you seem to need women with cow's udders," she said showing the picture of Pres and Mildred to him.

Marie then kissed Pres on the forehead, spun on her heels and left at the same time as her injured husband's much-relieved doctor entered the room.

In every small town, the same lawyer that is revered by some is despised by others. Try representing the unfaithful wife of the preacher or the Masonic brother who stole from his lodge. It was even worse when lawyers represented insurance companies. Little Sue was pummeled by coals that fell from a truck and everyone in town knew that she deserved to be compensated for the loss of her left leg. If you were Harry, you knew it too, but your insurance clients paid you to defend the drunks the companies hired to drive their trucks and you did your job well. You even bragged in bars and restaurants when you had held the verdict down. Other lawyers may have admired your skills, but you did not boast only to them, and your neighbors were often filled with revulsion when they learned how you had taken money from a one-legged girl.

The Lafayette paper's photograph with its unfortunate "lady friend" caption was published in the Crawfordsville paper on Monday. Pres' marriage could probably have survived had not the photograph with its implication of both drunkenness and infidelity appeared, but someone wanted Harry and his boy wonder to hurt and bleed. Marie was their unknowing, pain-inflicting instrument.

Marie's world was swerving. The foundation of the insecure is built upon the sugar poured by the ones who love them. Every compliment serves to support a wall. Each kiss bolsters a floor. Every hug raises a girder. Every slight, every betrayal, real or imagined, is magnified. Sugar dissolves in an instant and the house that may have taken years to build collapses with the first tear, the first hint that you knew all along that you were not good enough.

"Marie, honey, I barely know the woman," Pres said.

"Why would she say that she was your girlfriend?" Marie asked.

"The paper said lady friend, honey..." Pres began.

"Do you think that's any less humiliating to me? Why would she claim to have any relationship with you at all?" asked Marie.

"When I was representing her daughter, I thought that Mildred might have a crush on me, but Marie, I never did anything to encourage it. I love you and only you. That's the way it is and it will always be that way," said Pres.

Marie stared at him. It was Tuesday afternoon and Pres knew that the doctor would likely release him from the hospital in about an hour. Marie had quieted and Pres thought that he had won her over with his explanation and his protestations of undying love. He was wrong.

"Let me see if I have this right," Marie said. "There must be a dozen bars between here and Covington, but you chose the one owned by a woman you knew was in love with you. Am I right Pres? Do I have my facts straight, mister high and mighty lawyer?"

"She wasn't there when I stopped and I wouldn't have gone in if she had been there." Pres was floundering and he knew it. "Didn't you hear what I said? I love you."

"No you don't. You never have and you never will. No one ever will," replied Marie. She then stood, turned and left.

Instead of going home from the hospital, Pres went to his office. Even though it was after 6:00 in the evening, Harry was there. Harry was almost always there. He had nowhere else to go.

"You sure shit in your nest, boy," Harry said. "If you weren't married to my daughter, I'd fire your ass."

"Thanks for the vote of confidence, Harry" said Pres.

"Mack and I have been talking and we think you should lay low for a while. Maybe you and Marie could take a trip. Go to Hawaii or Peru or some fucking place a million miles away from Crawfordsville. We'd still pay you but you can't expect us to do twenty percent. How about ten for doing nothing for six months?" said Harry.

"How about sticking my left leg up your ass, Harry," said Pres. "I'm saving my right one for your gutless brother Mack. I only wish Jimmy or Sonny or whatever his goddamn name is was here so I could give him my regards, too."

"Now, wait just one minute, young man," said Harry, but he was talking to Pres' back. The door closed and Pres' career in the firm of Hawkins, Hawkins, Hawkins and Hart was over. Harry changed the locks the following day and two days later the gilt "Hart" was removed from the sign.

Marie was not happy to receive the news. "We couldn't live on ten percent." Pres said. "I admit I was wrong. What I did was beyond stupid, but I guess I was expecting more out of Harry. I've done a lot for the firm. I've resurrected the insurance defense business. I didn't mean to cause you or Harry or anyone any harm."

"Can't you apologize to daddy? I'm sure he'd let you stay for my sake," Marie pleaded.

"How could you respect me if I did a thing like that? How could Harry respect me?

How could I respect myself if I knew I wouldn't be working if I hadn't married the boss' daughter, " Pres replied.

"What will you do? " Marie asked.

Pres noticed that Marie had not said, 'What will *we* do.' "Look for another job, I guess, " he said.

"I'm not leaving Crawfordsville, " Marie said.

"That's it? End of discussion? Adios, husband? " Pres asked.

"Look, I didn't get us into this mess, and you could stay here with me if you weren't so full of foolish pride. Daddy will take you back and what's more, he'll not cut your percentage. You just let me talk to him, " said Marie, reaching for the telephone. Pres left the room as Marie began to dial.

"Will you be taking her with you? " Marie asked, pointing to the infamous picture of Pres and the barmaid.

"Marie, I know you don't like me right now. I don't much like myself either, " Pres said, "but, you need to listen to me. I love you. I will always love you. I have absolutely no interest in any other woman, but I can't stay here. I've got to go find work somewhere else and I want you to come with me. "

Marie was silent.

"Alright, when I find a job I'll come get you. You know there are other places in the world than Crawfordsville, Indiana, " Pres said.

The fact was that Pres was more limited in his choice of places to work than he was ready to admit to himself. He knew he disliked big-city practice, with its politics and social obligations, so when he sent out his resumes, he ignored anyplace with a population of more than twenty thousand. He received several inquiries and had three interviews that resulted in job offers. The problem was money. All three firms wanted Pres to take a small percentage with no guaranteed weekly amount. In addition, the trial work Pres craved was simply not available "for awhile." Each firm had a senior partner who was not ready to relinquish the prestige trial work brings "for awhile."

Pres had been staying with his parents in Sellersburg, and calling Marie nightly. She was hesitant when Pres proposed a weekend in Indianapolis.

"Why can't you just come here?" she asked.

"Because you will just try to get me to stay," Pres replied.

"It's been three weeks," Marie said. "I've forgiven you. I miss you. Please come home."

Pres knew that if he did return, he would probably stay. He was broke, he had no job, no prospects and for the time being, no wife.

Marie finally relented, but said she could only stay from Friday night until Saturday morning. Pres protested, but he was secretly relieved. He had borrowed a hundred dollars from his father and he needed to make it last for awhile. The Ho Jo on the west side of Indy was about all there was in his price range, but even twenty-two dollars a night seemed costly.

Their reunion was joyful and passionate. Crawfordsville was not mentioned until Saturday morning.

"Come home, Pres. You know how much I need to be held and loved," pleaded Marie.

"I want to hold you and love you again and again, but I am close to finding us another place where you will be just as happy," Pres lied.

As he was driving back towards Sellersburg, Pres thought about Bill and Enid Walsh. Pres and Marie had maintained a Christmas card friendship with their duplex neighbors and suddenly Pres felt a need to see old friends. He had driven past Paris Crossing dozens of times on the interstate and never stopped. Pres had never even seen the place, but he felt a sense of familiarity with the town from hearing Bill wax rapturously about his bucolic childhood.

It was not hard to find the "Walsh & Son Funeral Home." In cities and large towns, the dead await the grave in surroundings that may be new and prestigious yet sterile and tasteless. In small towns, the funeral homes are always the best old buildings in town. Houses that have learned to contain grief and have made death an elegant passage. "You'll be proud to say your folks stayed with us for awhile" was written under the Walsh & Son sign outside the tall, colonnaded, antebellum structure that was at the heart of downtown Paris Crossing.

"Our guests stay downstairs and we stay upstairs. Business requires us to go downstairs from time to time, but thank God we have never had one of them come up here," explained Enid when Pres asked about living in a home with dead people. "And they never complain, they're always quiet and I never have to worry about what to feed them to eat," Enid continued. "Best of all, unlike most guests, they never stay too long."

Bill and Enid seemed overjoyed to see Pres. Marie was mentioned, but when Pres seemed reluctant to talk about her absence, the topic went effortlessly elsewhere.

"Why not open an office here?" asked Bill. "There isn't another lawyer in town and I've got an office building that just happens to be for sale."

"Bill, right now, I've got about twenty-seven dollars in my pocket. I don't have any clients." Pres' voice broke, "I was doing pretty well until some asshole decided to open his Black Label beer by smashing it across my forehead."

"I want to show you my building," Bill said. "Right now, it's not making me any money at all. I remodeled what used to be a hardware store to accommodate an accountant who lasted about four months. He refused to sign his name to a dishonest tax return and no one around here could figure out why they needed someone who would not file a false tax return for them. There's even a large apartment upstairs where you and Marie could live. If I give you a beer or two, feed you and promise not to raise any more lumps on your head, would you stay the night and see the building in the morning?"

"I would be grateful." said Pres. "Right now I'd be glad to sleep in the yard."

"Of course, we have an ulterior motive" said Enid. "It's been awhile since we've heard one of your songs."

"I have a guitar in my car," Pres said. "Hundreds of years ago, minstrels sang for their supper. The lazy bastards wouldn't hunt a rabbit or chop wood so they had to travel from house to house so as not to sing the same song to the same people and they had to be amusing because if they were not, they would get only the turnips and beets they salvaged after they dodged those nasty vegetables."

"We're having spaghetti," said Enid.

"No one was ever injured by thrown pasta," said Bill and when Pres went to get his guitar, Bill went into the kitchen for beer.

"I wrote this during the so-called oil crisis," said Pres while tuning his six-string. "If you'll remember, alternate

fuels were being suggested and one of them
was methane, which is the title to this song:

"They say by twenty twenty-four
There won't be anymore oil and gas
Well, I have come up with a plan
To save my fellow man
Should this terrible occurrence
      come to pass
Forget about coal
Forget about the sun
We can use our own bodies
To make things run
Fill your coupe with poop
Fill your Subaru with number two
Heat your town with brown
Use your poo-poo
To run your choo-choo

It must be obvious
That our values have to change
What may seem common then
Must now seem pretty strange
Guys will want to marry
Girls with dysentery
Cause you can drive lots
When you've got the trots
Invest in X-Lax
Invest in prunes
Sell your Exon stock
   And buy restroom
    Put your money in inventions
like a pump
  That will go to your tank from your
       rump
Fill your coupe with poop
Fill your coupe with poop."

The office was small, but its front was
all windows, facing Main Street with a view
on the right of people coming downtown and a
view on the left of them going home. The
upstairs was an unexpected delight. Enid had
a taste for design and she had furnished the

apartment with rustic furniture and modern appliances. Bill's sense of history had inspired Enid to use early family photographs to create a montage that dominated an entire wall. "It's sad that I don't know any of these people, but they all contributed to my existence," Bill said.

The next day Bill took Pres into Vernon, the county seat, and introduced Pres to Judge Wensel.

"Would you have any work for a starving lawyer, your honor?" Pres asked.

"I have a real problem getting the local attorneys to do pauper counsel work and I've got money in my budget to at least keep you in cigarettes and beer, if you're interested," the judge replied. "It's mostly dirty work, defending drunks and child molesters, but it will get your name in the paper, and introduce you to the fine folks of Jennings County."

Pres knew that the general public often put lawyers in the same category as their clients. The old adage, "If you lie down with dogs, you'll get up with fleas," pretty much described how people felt about lawyers who represented scum. Nevertheless, Pres needed to be able to tell Marie that he had an income and a place for them to live.

"I've got to think about it," Pres told the Judge. "Mostly, I've got to convince my wife. She's a daddy's girl who spent only about a year away from her dad after her parents divorced, and she hated every minute of it."

"One of the perks to being a Judge is that when you give people advice, they generally listen," said Judge Wensel. "They may not think you know jack shit, but they are usually attentive. You will never be happy living here with your wife unless she wants to live here. She will turn your happy home into Dante's Inferno. You will never draw another peaceful breath."

"The Judge doesn't have a very good track record when it comes to women," Bill said after Pres told Bill about the conversation with Judge Wensel. "He's been married three times, and Enid doesn't think that wife number three is going to stay with the Judge much longer."

"Still, he's got a point," said Pres. "I really like it here and the idea of starting over on my own appeals to me. If I can only convince Marie."

Predictably, Marie was horrified. "I'm not going to live in some rinky-dink place I've never even heard of." Marie said.

"But Bill and Enid love it." Pres replied.

"Bill has never been anywhere else and Enid would follow him anywhere." Marie said.

Both of them were silent as the import of Marie's statement seemed to turn the air into something thick and hostile. Pres finally spoke, "Enid would follow Bill anywhere and you won't venture outside the city limits of Crawfordsville. What does that say about our marriage?"

"I keep coming back to the fact that we had a wonderful life here. I had everything I ever wanted, and you had to go and screw it up with one of your stupid songs, not to mention your obsession with big-titted women," Marie said.

"You're still punishing me," Pres said. "I drove all the way to Crawfordsville, a place I've come to despise, to share the news that I have a job and a place for us to live and you're still pissed about something that happened more than six weeks ago. How many times do I have to say I'm sorry? Can't we just get on with our lives?"

"I am getting on with my life. You're the one whose stubbornness and foolish male pride is standing in the way of our future happiness," Marie said.

"I'm not coming back here," Pres said. "I won't ever practice law with that stupid ass of a father of yours again."

"And I'm not ever coming to Paris fucking Crossing," Marie replied.

As he drove back to southern Indiana, Pres discovered that his balls had returned; both of them were man sized. He also knew that in the male-female conflict, regaining your nuts often meant losing your wife.

CHAPTER ELEVEN:
THE RESTAURANT - THE EARLY YEARS

Pres took Dolly's case. A year later, an hour before the trial was to begin the case was settled in Judge Wensel's chambers. The Indianapolis firm hired to represent Todd's trucking company, had been vehemently opposed to settlement negotiations, refusing to offer more than the cost of Thorney's funeral. The big city defense firm had initially shown up in Vernon with six lawyers. All of them had conspired to put Pres through pre-trial hell.

At first, Judge Wensel was clearly intimidated by the big hitters that had come to his little county. One of them would appear in a Brooks Brothers suit at least once a week to file some type of dilatory motion designed to make Pres' life miserable. Having been in their shoes while defending insurance companies for good old Harry, Pres understood the game and knew the rules. Pres complied with their every request and asked only for a firm trial date. He was beyond going broke. Bill Walsh was Pres' sole source of support these days, as Pres found himself spending forty hours and more a week complying with the stupid discovery requests of the defense attorneys. He was not turning clients down, but Pres had not been in town long enough to attract more than minor real estate and criminal misdemeanor work.

In Indiana, almost every discovery request is granted and it is done ex parte. When the Indy lawyers appeared with their interrogatories, their requests for admissions, and their motions to produce, they always had a comment to make.

"We believe Thorney had an alcohol-related conviction," one of the good suits said to the Judge while filing his motion to produce Thorney's criminal records.

"We think Dolly has had a problem with drugs," said a second suit a week later with a motion to produce Dolly's pharmaceutical records.

This went on for weeks with each request becoming more and more irrelevant. Judge Wensel may have been awed early by prestigious big city counsel, but he was not stupid, and he began to resent the gratuitous and unprofessional comments of the Indianapolis lawyers. It finally became apparent to the Judge that the trucking company's lawyers were using the discovery process to try to get Dolly and her "country lawyer" so exhausted that they would settle for a pittance.

The breaking point came when one of the suits sought a motion to produce Dolly's medical records. "We have it on good authority, your honor, that she has had breast augmentation," he said.

"She's pregnant, you ignorant little shit," the Judge exploded. "Her boobs are supposed to get bigger. Do you also think that she's had a belly implant, cause she sure looks like someone put fifteen pounds of silicone in there too; and what in the fuck does that have to do with the fact that your driver killed Dolly's husband and the father of her unborn child?"

"An operation of that sort reflects on her moral character," sputtered the big city lawyer.

"Get out of my office," shouted the Judge. "Mary Lou," Judge Wensel hollered to his court reporter loud enough so that everyone in his crowded waiting room could hear. "I want you to call the State Board of Law Examiners and ask them to review the test scores of that stupid bastard who's trying to slink out of here. Either they fucked up when they gave him a passing grade, or he hired someone to take the bar exam for him."

When the Judge entered his office early the next morning, he was somewhat surprised to see Mike "cold-hearted" Monroe waiting on him. Mike was one of the managing partners of the formidable legal juggernaut opposing Pres in Dolly's wrongful death case against the trucking firm. Mike had obtained his nickname while representing the driver of an ice cream truck who had turned a school teacher into a mindless, constantly urinating rutabaga. When the jury returned a verdict against the teacher and in favor of Mike's client, Mike's reply to the press was "He got what he deserved."

At age sixty-four, Mike was still a commanding presence. Defying insurance lawyer protocol, he wore his flowing, abundant, white hair in a braid that nearly reached his ass. At six-three and two hundred pounds, he looked as if he could still play strong safety which he did for Yale while in his prime.

"I understand you gave one of my boys a hard time yesterday," Mike said before Judge Wensel could even be seated. "I think you'll understand why it's necessary for me to file this motion," Mike said handing the Judge a document which read:

Motion for Change of Judge

Robert Moore, being first duly sworn upon his oath alleges:

1.   "That he is one of the attorneys representing the Huggins Trucking Company which is the defendant in this cause of action.

2.   That on March eighth (03/08) your affiant filed in this court a motion seeking to obtain the medical records of the plaintiff, Dolly Morris, personal representative of the estate of Maurice Morris, deceased.

3.   That on said date, your affiant was not only denied access to said records, but he was ridiculed by the presiding Judge, to-wit: Reuben Wensel in the presence of several witnesses including the bailiff, the court reporter and several undisclosed lawyers and courthouse personnel.

4.   That the Judge's actions revealed a deep and personal bias against the defendant which would prevent the presiding Judge in this action, the aforementioned Reuben Wensel, from giving a fair trial to your affiant's client, to-wit: the Huggins Trucking Company.

Wherefore, the defendant would respectfully pray for a change of judge and for all other proper relief."

Judge Wensel examined the motion for several minutes without speaking. Finally, he said, "You have every right to file your motion."

"I told my brother, who sits on the bench of the Indiana Supreme Court, as I'm sure you know, that you would recognize the error of your ways," said cold-hearted Mike.

"As I said," the Judge repeated, "you have every right to file your motion. I was out of line and I would have no choice, but to get you a new Judge. You should know, however, that you'd get a fair trial from me, and you should also know that I don't have a brother."

The Indianapolis attorney looked puzzled as the Judge continued.   "I do have a sister.   She married a guy named Fox so you may not have made the connection.   She is the chief enforcement officer and the head of the Indiana Disciplinary Commission.   You and I both know that having a new Judge would only cause further delay.   The new guy would have to get up to speed and fit this case into his or her schedule.   This case needs to be resolved."

"I dictated a letter to my sister last night, and Mary Lou did you put that letter I signed last night in the mail?" the Judge asked, and upon receiving an affirmative reply, the Judge asked to see the copy. The court reporter quickly entered the office and placed the letter on Judge Wensel's desk. It read:

Dear Mrs. Fox:

"At your last judicial presentation, you advised trial judges to report law firms that were using our liberal discovery rules as weapons to coerce settlements for inadequate amounts. You suggested that conduct of this nature might well be against the Rules of Professional Responsibility.

I am presiding over a wrongful death case in which discovery motions have been filed every week for twenty-eight straight weeks. The defendant's lawyers have sought medical records, tax returns, criminal records, high school records, grade school records and correspondence between the plaintiff and her dead husband.

Requests for admissions have been filed, over 120 written interrogatories have been submitted to the plaintiff for her to answer under oath, and depositions have been taken of everyone remotely connected to the case including the head of the Indiana Highway Commission. A deposition was even taken in Japan. To top it all off, last week the defendant's lawyers asked for an exhumation of the dead husband's remains. They want to test for the presence of drugs or alcohol. I haven't ruled on that one yet.

The case is a simple one. The defendant's truck crossed the center line and struck plaintiff's husband's car head-on killing him instantly. It is readily apparent that all of this discovery is being done to harass the plaintiff to such an extent that she will gladly take any amount. The exhumation request is especially vile.

The people of this county don't believe in tampering with their dead.

I suppose what angers me the most is that every time a motion is filed it is accompanied by a gratuitous remark specifically designed to prejudice me. I have been told by these lawyers that plaintiff and her husband were drunks, drug abusers, and criminals. Apparently, these lawyers must think I'm some kind of stupid hillbilly. They forget that I have lived here all my life and I know the plaintiff and I knew her husband. She is and he was both fine young people. Thus, we have even more unethical conduct, to-wit: trying to influence a Judge and lying to him at the same time.

You have no doubt by now noticed that I have not named the defendant's law firm. I wish to discuss this with one of its managing partners first. I don't believe in backstabbing. I won't even do it to a backstabber."

Mike read the letter slowly. When he finished it he smiled at Judge Wensel and said, "Do you mind if I tell you what they call your sister in Indianapolis?" Without waiting for an answer, the lawyer said, "A pit-bull with lipstick."

"That's pretty much what they call her down here, too. Over Christmas dinner she told us she was personally responsible for disbarring forty-eight lawyers," the Judge said, returning Mike's smile with one of his own. "She really likes her job."

"Well, Judge, I know you've got things to do and if you want to give me back that motion, I'll be returning to the big city," said Mike.

"Certainly," said the Judge handing the motion for change of judge back to Mike. "Will I be seeing you again?"

"I don't think so," said the lawyer. "I specialize in trying lawsuits. We had better be settling this one."

To Pres' immense relief, Clarice was born two weeks before the trial was scheduled to begin. The defendant's lawyers, four of whom turned up on the day trial was to begin couldn't help but notice Dolly. Marlene had made some suggestions, but for the most part, Dolly had chosen what to wear. Many women retain fat after childbirth. Dolly did not. She chose to wear jeans and they fit her the same as they did when she was sixteen. Although she was only five foot four, Dolly's legs were long and slim. She was beautiful in a wholesome sort of way. Her breasts were milk-enlarged and deliciously out of proportion to the rest of her slender, lithe body. The rest of her attire consisted of a lacy white blouse and tennis shoes. She wore only a little lipstick. No more make-up was needed.

Pres' recovery target was half a million dollars. This was an obscene amount to expect to receive from a small southern Indiana jury, but Pres knew he had a special client and a once-in-a-lifetime case. As any lawyer will tell you, there is always something wrong with every great case. Either the facts will be against you or the law will not be on your side. The insurance will not be enough, your client will be a pathological liar, or the defendant will be a saint. Try as he might, Pres could find nothing wrong with his case. There were no weaknesses; the sky was the limit.

At the request of the Court, the parties assembled on trial day at 7:00 a.m. The jury was not scheduled to arrive until 9:00 a.m. and Judge Wensel, encouraged by Mike "cold hearted" Monroe's earlier statement that the case needed to be settled, put Dolly, Pres and the defendant's entourage into the now-empty jury room and said, "Now settle this son-of-a-bitch. Forgive my language, Dolly."

Pres started by offering to settle for nine hundred thousand. The defendant countered with an offer for three hundred thousand. Dolly started to cry. Pres took her from the room. The defendant's lawyers took her tears for grief or anger. Pres knew better. Dolly wanted to accept the offer. "I don't want to turn it down, Pres, what if they decide not to offer it again. It's more money than I've ever seen and more than I might ever earn."

"You have to trust me now girl," Pres said. "That offer will never be withdrawn and they are going to offer a whole hell of a lot more before we are done. Please just sit back and watch me work."

Pres countered with eight hundred fifty thousand and the counter offer was three hundred fifty thousand. Dolly sat still. She concentrated on looking at the floor. Pres went down to eight hundred thousand and the defendant's lawyers pissed him off by coming back with three hundred seventy five thousand.

There was a knock on the door and Marlene appeared with Clarice. "It only took her about an hour to drink all that milk you pumped out last night," Marlene whispered. "And she's still hungry," as she passed Clarice over to her mother. Without thinking, Dolly unbuttoned her blouse. For a bit more than an instant, Dolly's left breast was bared and only Pres looked away.

Moments passed. Finally, one of the defense lawyers broke the silence. "You have not responded to our three hundred seventy five thousand dollar offer, counselor," he said. "That's an awful lot of money."

"Its chump change and you know it," said Pres. "I just lowered our offer by fifty thousand dollars and you raised yours by twenty-five thousand. That's disrespectful and exposes your chicken-shit souls. I'm sure that all your mothers suck cocks in leper colonies. Excuse my language, Dolly, but it's time for us to leave. Trial starts in ten minutes."

Pres left with Dolly and Clarice in tow. Marlene caught up with them as they entered the courtroom and took their seats at the plaintiff's table in the courtroom. Marlene had not quite left the room after she delivered Clarice to Dolly and Marlene knew of the three hundred seventy five thousand offer.

"Pres, I know it's not my business," Marlene said, "But, I wonder if you know what you're doing, turning down that kind of money?"

"Marlene," said Dolly, "I love you, but right now you need to shut the fuck up. Pres told me to trust him and so far he's not let me down. Of course, if he does, there will be hell to pay."

Pres started to reply when one of the defendant's minions signaled him to come back to the conference room where the earlier negotiations had been held. "Maybe, we might have some success if you left your client here and we're able to talk lawyer to lawyer," the defense lawyer said.

"Piss on that," Pres replied. "This is her money. This is her life. She is going to see and know everything that goes on." Dolly followed as Pres guided her with his arm and Marlene, carrying Clarice, came along right behind. The room was quiet until Pres and the women were seated. Silence was maintained for effect for a full minute more until the lead attorney for the defendant spoke. "We've decided to make a last offer. I mean it when I say that this is it. It is non-negotiable. We will pay a half a million dollars to settle this case."

Hundreds of thoughts went through Pres' mind in an instant. First and foremost was the certainty that the defendant had more money to offer. Pres knew from experience that no one ever offered the maximum they had authority to spend to settle, but before he had a chance to open his mouth, Marlene said, "We'll take it."

Pres was stunned at first and then he began to laugh. "Gentlemen, my co-counsel probably just cost her sister a few thousand dollars but I guess we have a deal," he said. It was difficult for anyone to be mad at Marlene.

One third of $500,000.00 was Pres' share and he promptly paid Bill and Enid Walsh for back rent. Knowing that he owed them so much more, Pres bought his friends a yellow Olds convertible that had been sitting on a used car lot in North Vernon for at least two weeks. It thrilled Pres to see the look in Bill's eyes when Bill took the keys and saw the car. Pres had fallen in love with the rag-top and he was envious of his friend for receiving such a beautiful car. Unlike most convertibles, this model had four doors and with its top down, it best resembled a sleek racing boat on wheels. Its red leather interior gave it an appearance of decadence and easy sensuality. You knew that if this car was human it would be a woman who would let you have her for a night or two and then leave without a backward glance. Pres asked if he could borrow it from time to time, with Marie still much on his mind.

It seems to be the dream of every small-town, southern Indiana woman, to own a restaurant. Dolly was no exception. The Stop and Shop had closed three years ago but the "For Sale" sign had never come down.

Dolly thought that she could buy the old grocery building cheap and she was right. Its owner, a weasel named Troy Roberts, thought he had a sucker for sure. A young, pretty widow with money was every seller's dream. "I can let you have it for thirty-five thousand," said Troy.

"I'll take it off your hands for five thousand dollars," said Dolly, "and not a penny more."

"I'll prepare the deed," said Pres to a stunned Troy Roberts who had bathed and combed his hair in anticipation of overwhelming young Dolly with his urbane manner and rugged good looks.

"I've got a lot more than that in it," stammered Troy, still wondering why his natural wholesomeness had not ruled the day. A decaying jock, Troy was still able to get into the pants of a former cheerleader or two by reminding her of the twenty-seven points he had scored against Columbus back in his halcyon days.

"Take it or leave it," said Dolly, breaking the silence and turning to leave.

"You've got to pay for the deed then," said Troy attempting to salvage some dignity. Forty-five minutes later in Pres' office Dolly wrote a check. Troy signed the deed that Pres had hastily prepared and the building belonged to Dolly.

Dolly and Marlene did all the work. The walls were paneled with scenes from France. A mural of the Theatre des Champs Elysees was on the east wall. The Arch de Triumph was opposite it on the west. The Eiffel Tower was the first thing you saw on the restaurant's south wall as you entered. De Gaulle walked behind John F. Kennedy's catafalque on the north wall. As much as you disliked the French, you had to admire how they sent their most prestigious citizen to mourn our young prince. De Gaulle, all six-foot seven of him, marched as if in formation, at age seventy, in full military dress. The paneling encouraged conversation and toasts to the French icon with the expensive French wine Dolly provided.

The tables were inexpensively made, but they were covered with lace tablecloths and full linen napkins that would cover even the fattest lap. The silverware was elegant and each place setting had two knives on its right and three forks on its left. The two spoons sat on a napkin of their own just to the right of the knives. A candle, burned just so, with at least one twisted, melted, run down its side, sat in the middle of the table, its wick burned so that it just protruded from the wax. An artificial tulip sat on the tables in the winter. Real red roses adorned the tables in the summer

The wood floor, which had been trodden by many farm feet over the years, was nonetheless in good condition and Marlene had made it her special project. She first washed it with oil soap and then had used polypropheline to bring out its natural swirls and highlight its different colors and tones. When Marlene finished, it was apparent that no rugs would be needed. The sisters had created an elegant French Café in Paris Crossing. Secretly, Dolly had dreamed that the rich and famous people that graced the magazine covers would come to eat at her restaurant.

A name was needed. It was Marlene who suggested the Parley Vous. It was the only French phrase either woman knew and somehow it seemed to fit. The restaurant would be open only two days a week, Friday and Saturday from 5:00 p.m. until 9:00 p.m. There would be no menu. Dolly would cook one meal on Friday and another one on Saturday. If you came, you would eat what she had prepared.   There were no substitutes.   What she had fixed was all you could get.

Dolly had checked out every book the Jennings County library had on French cooking.   Blessed with the patience and innate ability required of every great cook, Dolly found dishes such as Chicken Cordon Bleu no great challenge.   So on the Friday afternoon before serving her first meal, Dolly pounded sixty boneless, skinless chicken breasts into submission.   She then covered each with a slice of Swiss cheese and topped them with a slice of ham.   They were then rolled lengthwise, browned, secured with a toothpick, flying a tiny French flag.   Dry white wine was reduced in chicken stock, butter was whisked in and the liquid was poured over the chicken.   This was accompanied with crepes and asparagus.

Although Dolly had done only a small amount of advertising, over one hundred people showed up to eat at the Parley Vous on its opening night.   Fortunately, ever-optimistic Marlene had purchased lots more chicken, and she cooked while Dolly, giddy with success, waited on people who had driven from as far away as Louisville to eat her food.

"Do you speak?" a customer asked.

"No," said Dolly, thinking that she was being asked if she could speak French.

"Do you understand?" the woman next asked.

"No" said Dolly not understanding.

"Do you comprehend?" asked the woman running out of options.

"No" said Dolly, not comprehending, and becoming impatient to serve someone else.

"I don't understand the meaning of your name," said the bewildered customer.

"You don't understand Dolly?" Dolly replied, now as bewildered as the customer.

"No, I mean the name of your restaurant," the customer persisted.

"Isn't Parley Vous simply a French phrase meaning "Do you understand, or do you speak, or do you comprehend?"

"Oh, sure I comprehend," said Dolly, now determined to get out of the customer's grasp. "I gave the restaurant a French name since its located here in Paris Crossing, do you like it?"

The woman, now completely defeated, merely nodded and stared at her plate.

On Saturday, one hundred thirty customers appeared to eat coq au vin. The chicken vanished from the refrigerated meats department of the North Vernon IGA. This dish was flavored with brandy, mushrooms, onions and salt pork. Garlic mashed potatoes and a small salad completed the entrée. Stubbornly, Dolly adhered to the theme and provided only French dressing for the salad. Some customers complained, but most did not. The food was not only delicious, but woefully under-priced. At ten dollars a meal, Dolly was giving it away. She decided to raise the price for her dinners to twelve dollars per person. Still people flocked to the Parley Vous.

The food was not the only attraction. Dolly and Marlene wore maid uniforms that accentuated their obvious physical assets. Dolly always made it a point to stand to the left of her seated male customers, in order to give them a close-up when she would bend over to deliver the check.

The following Friday, Pres showed up wearing a tux with tails, and he was a passable maitre-de. Bill and Enid Walsh were served early and stayed to help. Over two hundred people arrived. Some stood in line for over an hour, almost all left happy. The boeuf bourguignon was a huge success. Cattle trembled throughout Jennings County.

CHAPTER TWELVE:
NEWS FROM MARIE

Every Saturday morning, Pres drove to Crawfordsville. He and Marie had been living apart for several years and then several years more. She had never come to Paris Crossing. Every six months or so, Pres would ask her to relent and come with him. For his part, Pres knew he could never go back to Crawfordsville. His practice had grown by leaps and bounds. Dolly did not hesitate to sing his praises, and Judge Wensel, when asked, would tell his friends that Pres was the best lawyer in the county. The Judge had a lot of friends.

The time had come for Pres to become confrontational. He had grown tired of having to drive 100 miles just to be with his wife. He had grown tired of being the only one putting any effort in preserving his marriage. Marie still lived with her father, cooked for her father, and cleaned for her father. She was a wife to Pres only when they shared a bed.

Their lovemaking, as usual, was intensive and satisfying for both of them. As they lay smoking, Pres took a deep breath and began. "I want you to come live with me. I have a good practice, a good income and a good life, but I need my wife. I can't come back here, but you can come join me. I don't understand why you won't."

Marie sighed and was silent. "I have loved three men. One doesn't want me. One is my father and one won't live with me. You say you can't live here. Sure you can, but I can't leave here. My father protected me, cared for me and loved me when no one else did. I needed him and now he needs me. His drinking is out of control. I put him to bed every night and it seems as if I take a cigarette out of his hands only just before he sets himself on fire. You can have your bright and shining future or you can come home and try to help your wife survive. In case you haven't noticed, I have a rather healthy sex drive and once a week just isn't cutting it. I doubt if you've become a week-day celibate. So far I have, but I will not do without much longer. I'm young, healthy and for the most part, increasingly horny. I told you long ago that I'm the kind of woman that needs a man. Will you or will you not, be my man? "

So often, we think that we have a secure position and a good argument. So often, we believe that what we say will ring convincingly in the ears of the one we are trying to persuade. Husbands and wives are so emotionally, umbilically connected when they love one another, that each thinks the other will immediately see the other's point of view. Pres was convinced that Marie would succumb to his logic. He was astounded when he realized that she had been formulating arguments of her own.

"Can't you hire someone to come in and look after Harry?" Pres said.

"Is that all you have to say? " asked Marie. "I just finished telling you that I'm thinking about fucking someone else and you can only ask if I can get a babysitter for my dad. I've tried, but Daddy won't have any part of it. I want a yes or no Pres. Are you or are you not going to be my man? "

Pres slowly dressed. When he had finished putting on his shoes, he turned to Marie and in spite of himself, started to cry. He only sobbed at first and then he began to make keening wails accompanied by deep, racking breaths. This lasted for only minutes, but to Pres it seemed to go on for hours. It made no impression on Marie. She sat still, staring at nothing, never looking at Pres. Later, as he was driving back to Paris Crossing, Pres felt disgusted with himself. "You weak little cry-baby" he said over and over as the mile markers flashed by.

Pres called Marie the following day, filled with clever remarks and apologies that would make everything alright. She did not answer the phone then, nor did she on any of the twenty-three times he attempted to call her again. Saturday morning rolled around and Pres decided not to go to see Marie, thinking that would surely cause her to call him. The ploy failed. The phone rang with clients' calls on three occasions but Marie maintained her silence. Pres was confused, concerned and hurt.

As the days passed, Pres became more and more convinced that he should go back to his wife. He told no one of his decision, except Judge Wensel. The Judge listened to Pres quietly. Pres told the Judge everything, omitting only the intimacies. Finally, the older man spoke, "You do what you have to do," the judge said. "You've got to live with yourself. I've never had any success with women. I've never understood them and God knows, I never found one who understood me. So I find myself unqualified to give advice to the lovelorn. I do know you're a hell of a lawyer and you'll be sorely missed by the people of Paris Crossing. You and Dolly are the best things ever to happen to that itty, bitty town."

"I appreciate everything you've said, Judge, and I thank you for being so kind to a lawyer who moved here from someplace else, but I think I'd better go back to my wife," Pres said.

One of the people who had gone out of her way to be nice to Pres while he was in Crawfordsville was Hannah Burke, Harry's longtime secretary. Hannah was childless and had been widowed for over ten years. Her one and only husband, ironically nicknamed "Lucky," had been felled by Lou Gehrig's disease and his brave, mute suffering had given Hannah an optimism she wanted to share with everyone she met. Her favorite saying was "It could be worse." Indeed nothing could have been any worse than watching her big, strong Lucky waste away until near death he bore more of a resemblance to an Auschwitz survivor than to the starting right tackle he had been at L.S.U.

"Prescott, I have just been thinking about you," said Hannah when she heard Pres' voice on the other end of the telephone. "I miss you," she continued.

Pres smiled upon hearing his full name. "Hannah only you and my mother call me Prescott. Anyway, I called to ask you a favor," Pres said.

"I've always liked that name," said Hannah. "It sounds like nobility, and the mountains and snow. Pres sounds mundane, like laundry and weight lifters. What can I do for you, sweetie?"

"You're probably thinking about Sergeant Preston of the Yukon," said Pres. "Hannah, I haven't heard from Marie in over two weeks. She won't answer the telephone. Frankly, I'm worried about her and I need you to go to the house and tell her, now this is important, that I'm ready to be her man again."

There was a long pause on the other end of the telephone. Pres noticed and his lungs began resisting his need to inhale. "Honey, Marie's not here," Hannah finally replied. "You see this place has been going to hell since you left. Clients want lawyers who are willing to go to court and Harry has been continuing everything. I don't know what's happened to Harry, but he seems to have lost something and his clients are literally screaming at him. Mack's too old to do anything. You don't know how much I dread answering the telephone. Anyhow, Harry's been working on Sonny to come back ever since you left and the prodigal son is about to return. Sonny is due back in a couple of weeks. Marie's out there helping him pack and wrap up his affairs. You know how much she loves her 'uncle' Sonny."

"She knows!" Pres thought and then he stammered. "What about Harry? I thought Marie could never leave Harry?"

"Guess who gets to tuck him in; little old me," said Hannah. "Harry wouldn't let Marie get anybody else, so I get to baby sit him every night from 7:00 until he's snoring and then I have to have this place up and running by 8:30 a.m. I'll tell you what; I'm looking forward to Marie's return. Harry's a load. I don't know how Marie puts up with him."

Somehow Pres managed to ask for Sonny's address before hanging up the phone. Late that night Pres finished a song. He put it in an envelope addressed to Marie, care of Jimmy "Sonny" Hawkins at his Portland, Oregon address. The song read:

"There was a ladies man in our town
Jimmy Sonny was his name
He took our young daughters by the hand
And led them down the road to shame."

"Oh, he took out Nellie Ferris
He took her where the lights were dim
She was six days past being twelve years
old
When she had a child by him."

"They took him down to the river
And wrapped an iron chain around him,
They pinned a note to his vest which read
Such are the wages of sin,"
"Hallelujah, mama he's dead
Hallelujah, mama he's dead.
Oh, you don't have to worry bout your
daughters anymore
Hallelujah, mama he's dead."

"Now his body lies in the river
But his soul is burning in fire
Cause I know that the devil's got a
              special kind of hell
For men with the young girl desire."

"Hallelujah, mama he's dead,
Hallelujah, mama he's dead.
Oh, you don't have to worry bout your
              daughters anymore
Hallelujah, mama he's dead."

The munchkins, hog farm pollution, fat free potato chips, George Foreman, water witching, plasma TV, plastic surgery, Farmall tractors, moles, Winston Churchill, legal surveys, Greyhound buses, home brew, cloth diapers, Murphy's oil soap, cobwebs, global warming, whole hog sausage, aluminum bats, bay leaves, mules, the road to the final four, and Francis Scott Key were popular subjects in March.

"Did anybody watch 'Survivor" last night?" Red asked.

"Where the hell are they now?" asked Pres, "La Jolla?"

"I didn't get a chance to see anything," said Bill. "I had to pick up Rudy Montgomery."

"Jesus," Red said. "Did he die?"

"I don't make a habit of picking up the living," Bill replied. "Most people get pissed if you try to put them in a hearse during prime time."

"Am I remembering this right?" asked Pres. "Wasn't there something Rudy did that was really weird when he ran for county commissioner?"

"Don't you remember Ramona?" Bill asked.

"Ramona, goddamn right I remember her. The most luscious piece of ass who ever graduated from Paris Crossing High School." Pres replied.

"Rudy made Ramona place her bridal registry at Big Lots," Bill said.

"Was she going to marry Jerry Van Dyke?" asked Red.

"Jerry would have treated her better than that Fergis guy she married. What an asshole. Fortunately she divorced him six months after they got hitched." Bill replied. "But the reason for Big Lots was that Rudy wanted the taxpayers to see how frugal he was."

"I'll bet she got a lot of rebuilt sweepers, dried flowers and black and white TV's," Red said.

"Speaking of TV's" Doc said, "you mentioned Survivor. It seems to be the newest sensation. I didn't watch it. As all of you know, I don't watch television, but God I miss television."

"I think I know what you mean," said Bill. "Other than news, sports and the Weather Channel, there is nothing else on that is really worth a shit."

"I stopped watching when the stars stopped appearing and singing their theme songs," said Doc. "I think the last one was Carol Burnett when she sang 'I'm so glad we had this time together' pulling her ear. God, she and Harvey and Tim were funny."

"They all had theme songs, didn't they" said Bill. "All of the great ones. Como, "Dream along with me. I'm on my way to a star". Crosby, "Where the blue of the night meets the gold of the day, someone waits for me." Hope "Thanks for the memories". Sinatra, "Put your dreams away for another day", and Durante had at least three "You've got to start off each day with a song", "Inca dinca do" and later on, "Make someone happy."

"Sinatra did something that I really thought was chicken-shit," said Doc. "Frank wrote a song about his wife, Nancy. You remember it. "Nancy with a laughing face." I think it became one of his standards. Anyway, after Sinatra got divorced, he claimed to have written the song for his daughter, Nancy."

"Goddamn it," Red said, "you old guys are all alike. You can't keep your minds on something without thinking about something else. What happened to Rudy Montgomery? How did he die, and what about Ramona? Let's talk about Ramona. I want my subconscious to get involved here, so I can have wet dreams about Ramona."

"Rudy died like most of us will, not with a bang but a whimper. According to his wife, he had just finished taking a late night shit when he came back to bed, coughed a couple of times and went to that big sleep in the sky. She didn't even know he was dead until sunrise, when she rolled over to cuddle and found a cold body instead of a warm husband. He was not merely dead. He was sincerely dead," Bill said. "Doc neglected to tell you that his campaign posters featured a picture of Ramona in a wedding dress with a low cut bodice. Rudy was smart enough to purchase about two hundred extra posters, because many of them were torn down from utility poles and put in barber shops and garages."

"Ramona and Dolly never hit it off, did they?" asked Red.

"At first they did," said Pres. "They seemed to be the perfect complement to one another. Both were beautiful. Dolly was small and Ramona was a tall girl. Dolly's blond hair was in sharp contrast to Ramona's dark, nearly black hair. When Ramona graduated from high school and wanted a job, Dolly was quick to hire her. The Parley Vous had gotten too popular for Dolly and Marlene to handle even with volunteers like Bill, Enid, yours truly and others showing up to help."

CHAPTER FOURTEEN:
DOLLY AND RAMONA

Ramona in a maid's uniform was a sight to behold. Her bra pushed her large breasts up to near nipple level. Indeed, occasionally one or both nips would escape their confines to grin at a lucky patron. Ramona would merely shrug, bow a bit and retrieve her escaping torpedoes with a nonchalant, "Would you like a double order of croissants?"

Dolly had told Ramona to push the croissants, as extras would add two dollars to the bill and Ramona did her job well. The man seated at the table, to whom Ramona's remarks were always directed, could refuse her nothing. Ramona's tips, like her tits, were large and out of all proportion to her performance.

It was the tips that caused the problem. Marlene wanted Ramona to turn them in together with the money Ramona collected for the bill. Almost always, Ramona's tips exceeded Dolly's and Marlene's combined.

"She's putting on a strip show," said Marlene. "Is this a restaurant or a titty bar? When is she going to start doing lap dances in the crepe suzettes? When are the customers going to put their tips in her panties? You're providing a stage she should pay for the use of the hall. It's not right that she should be making more than us simply because she looks like a big, dumb, country slut. You've heard of Toys for Tots? With her, it's tits for tips."

Marlene had a point. Ramona was taking home about fifty more dollars a week than Marlene, and Ramona worked fewer hours. Dolly said, "She's making us money. Maybe we should show some more skin."

"Dolly, look at me," said Marlene. "I'm thirty-two and after three kids I have stretch marks on my eyelids, forearms, ears and breasts. My customers might have pity upon observing my droopy, saggy boobs and give me a quarter towards my, 'Help Marlene get her tits back' fund, but I can't compete on her level."

"Help Marlene get her tits back" mused Dolly. "Maybe we could put that on a label and stick it on a mason jar next to the cash register. Sister, we ought to collect enough nickels and dimes in a month to make those poor things all perky again."

"Dolly, you're impossible," grinned Marlene. "But you'd better take my advice about sharing the tips."

Dolly waited until the last customer had left. She had decided to take a different tactic. As she shared a cigarette break with Ramona, Dolly said, "Mona, how tall are you?"

"Almost six foot," said Ramona.

"Those heels probably make you six-two, don't they?" asked Dolly. "I'm asking because we may want you to dress a little less provocatively. We haven't had any complaints from our male patrons, but their wives want to put shotguns up your ass."

"It's always been that way with me", said Ramona. "Until I met you, I never had a woman friend. I've always been big all over. Marlene tells me she wants bigger breasts. I have these goddamn basketballs. I want some kind of operation where Marlene and I are in the same room laying side by side with tubes attached to our tits, draining all the fat from mine and pouring it into hers. God, how I would like to be small. Every man I meet thinks I must want my bones jumped, without even supper, because I have these big boobs. Women hate me and men just want to screw me. I hate my tits. I hate myself."

Dolly was stunned. "I thought you liked looking slutty", she said. "No, I didn't mean that exactly, I thought you liked wearing the costume."

"I did. I mean I do", replied Ramona. "I'm not very smart, so this is going to sound crazy or stupid, but the same part of me that hates how I look, likes the way men look at me. Besides, I need the money, and the more I show, the less I owe."

"I am going to level with you, Mona" Dolly said. "As you know, Marlene is my sister and I love her dearly. She is more than a little resentful over the fact that your tips are so much higher than hers. Marlene is a good looking woman and a great waitress, but she doesn't have the, how should I put this, raw physical appeal or the willingness to show nipples that you do, and so she thinks a simple solution would be for you to share tips with her. Be a good girl and agree, so that I can stop being a boss, trying to please everyone, and go back to being a cook."

Ramona agreed and at first things seemed to go well. Dolly would later reminisce about how this was her first and last labor relations problem because Ramona was Dolly's first and last employee. Months passed. Ramona seemed compliant and each evening following work, she and Marlene would put their tips in a mixing bowl and divide into stacks, the dollars and coins the two of them had amassed from their patrons.

Ramona took a week's vacation, and then failed to show up for work for another three days. Her absence was explained when an article appeared in the North Vernon Times about a new restaurant that was about to open in old Vernon, the county seat. Its name was "Madamoiselles" and next to the copy was a picture of Ramona wearing the French maid outfit Dolly had purchased for Ramona to wear.

"Damn her" said Marlene when Dolly showed Marlene the paper. "Damn her to hell and back. Where'd she get the money to do that?"

"According to Pres, who made a few calls when he saw it in the paper, her fiancé put up the money" said Dolly.

"Fiancé?" said Marlene. "I didn't even know she was dating anyone."

"Apparently, she had a whirlwind romance with our old friend (emphasis on old) Troy Brown" said Dolly.

"Jesus, Dolly" said Marlene. "He's got to be twenty years older than Ramona, and if he's got so much money, why doesn't he use it to fix his teeth? Who is going to cook for her? What does she know about French cooking?"

Dolly blushed and said, "We've been played for fools, sister. Back when we started the tip sharing business, Ramona suggested that she might relieve me in the kitchen from time to time if I could teach her to cook, so every Monday afternoon for the past several months I've been showing that betraying bitch how to put us out of business. As far as Troy is concerned, he went to college so he could get into dental school."

"You've got to be shitting me" said Marlene. "What did he major in, tooth decay?"

"Louisville gave him a basketball scholarship and he took an elbow from Pervis Ellison in practice his freshman year. That ended his scholarship, his schooling and his dental career. There was a big lawsuit over it but Pres said that Troy hired the dumbest lawyer in Kentucky and Troy ended up with five thousand dollars and a mouthful of dead teeth."

"Can you imagine what kissing him must be like?" said Marlene. "I wonder if those teeth taste as bad as they look, and his breath, Dolly have you ever smelled his breath? It smells like he's been chowing down on weasel shit or barbequed buzzard. Can you imagine making love to him? "

"Marlene, you've made your point" said Dolly. "Why is it I find an overwhelming need to gargle and douche right now? "

There is no customer loyalty in the restaurant business. As Dolly repeatedly told Marlene, and even told Ramona, "You're only as good as the last meal you serve." Novelty and remoteness had allied to give the Vous its stunning debut. Ramona's nipples hadn't hurt much either. Now, there was a new place to eat that was more on the beaten path, and it featured the luscious Ramona.

The effect on the Parley Vous was devastating. On the same Friday of "Madamoiselles" opening just thirteen miles away, Dolly had twelve customers. The next night she had only six. She asked Enid Walsh to take Bill to see how Ramona was doing and Enid was embarrassed to report that Madamoiselles was packed.

"She can't last" Enid said. "Her crepes were soggy and she actually had cheeseburgers on the menu. It said they were served with genuine 'French' fries. "

"Cute" said Dolly, secretly wishing she had thought to do the same with her kids' menu. "Shit" she thought. "If she can steal from me, I can steal from her. I'll add the potatoes and French fried onion rings to the children's menu. Marlene and I will get out of these ridiculous outfits and wear peasant blouses and checkered skirts and we'll cater to families instead of couples looking to get a little after supper. "

The effect was not immediate. Damage had been done to the family trade when Ramona came and she had taken the lovers when she left. Gradually, the families returned, but after two years, Dolly concluded that she was not making any money. A new beginning was needed if her beloved restaurant was to

survive, and Dolly thought she had the
answer.

CHAPTER FIFTEEN:
BILL WALSH

Even as a child, Bill Walsh lived with dead people. His father Frank would leave, usually at night and return with a corpse. They usually stayed three or four days, then they would be gone, but others would arrive. Sometimes there would be as many as three downstairs. On one occasion, following a multi-car, fog-induced collision on the interstate, there were six bodies on the ground floor, occupying every room and the hallway.

Bill was an introverted, shy child whose only friends were the dead. He would name them when they arrived. One was the "Fairy Queen", another was "The Motorman." His mother referred to a long-haired young girl as Rapunzel and Bill asked his mother to read him the fable. This led to his discovery of witches and trolls, evil giants and men with only one eye in the middle of their heads. While Bill and his dead friends would play games in his mind during the day, at night, the once friendly corpses became threatening.

It did not help that his pals would not stay for long. The Good Fairy Glenda, who saved Dorothy, would be replaced by a furious looking woman who would not only eat Bill, but his little dog too. She might be replaced by a man, who looked like Captain Kangaroo, but he would soon depart, and Hitler would take his place. The dead became malevolent.

Then the dreams began vicious, flesh-rending episodes that would end in screams and urination. Monsters covered in blood and reeking with decay took residence under Bill's bed, waiting only for him to nod off before making their hideous appearance. They came from the first floor, shuffling up the stairs, and they crawled up the outside walls to climb into his window, making sucking, chewing sounds. His urine seemed to appease them, for as he awakened from the warmth, which rapidly turned to discomfort, they would melt away, seemingly having accomplished enough for one night, waiting to return rested and ready to tear and dismember his body tomorrow.

Bill's brain registered the fact that the monsters seemed allergic to urine and the moment the first unearthly being appeared to Bill in his dreams, his bladder responded and the flesh-eating beasts would flee. Bill would go to the bathroom, dry himself off, and change pajamas. His parents slept in separate rooms and Bill would drag a blanket into either his mother's or father's room and sleep on the floor. The monsters never came into either parent's room. Bill was a light sleeper and his mind registered dawn with relief. The boy would be fully awake at first light and leave his parent's room usually without being detected. Monsters feared the light and Bill knew he would be safe again until nightfall.

The dead were prepared for their final, earthly exhibition in the basement of the fine old house. The garage and the basement were both under the first floor and the hearse would back down the declining driveway to below ground level where the hearse would be unloaded and the gurney on wheels would transport the corpse to the preparation room. The temperature underground was always sixty-two degrees, which prolonged decay and made the embalming process more leisurely. Air conditioning was still a thing of the future and Walsh's dead, because of the basement, had a reputation of looking good and seldom smelling.

One night, peeing seemed not to drive the monsters away. Bill was about to be disemboweled by a creature who looked suspiciously like his Sunday school teacher when his bladder responded by simultaneously flowing away his fears and drenching his bed. A relieved Bill relaxed in the warmth, knowing it would soon turn cold and miserable, when he heard a shuffling, stumbling creature coming up the stairs. Thump, a foot would fall followed by another, and a muffled curse. The steps were steep, thirteen of them from the first floor where the dead were to the sanctuary of the second floor where Bill and his parents slept, monster-free until now. There comes a time in all of our lives when we become convinced that the monsters will prevail. Evil takes many different forms. It can come in the shape of a beast, a lover, a troll or a friend. Tonight, Bill was stunned to see when he crept to the top of the stairs, that his father was the source of the noise that had terrified him.

"Bill, is that you boy?" his father said. "Get your mother, son."

The stroke that paralyzed the left side of his face gave Frank Walsh an eye that was always open. His lips on the afflicted side drooped and caused drool to accumulate and fall into the handkerchief Frank now always wore around his neck. To Bill, his dad looked worse than any of the dead people his father continued to bring into Bill's house and dreams.

Bill's mother dreaded his first day in school. Her son seemed to spend much of his time clinging to her legs and she was very much aware of how his nights ended in sodden sheets, curled in a ball in her bedroom. Carolyn Walsh felt as if she had been cheated out of a normal relationship with a healthy husband, and now her son was leaving her. She needed so much to help him start to make the transition from home to school, from mommy's boy, to manhood, but she was not getting much in the way of good advice from Frank, who still needed to be in charge.

Frank had gone to grade school in the twenties and in that era, all of the young boys were sent off in short pants. They graduated to knickers around grade five or so and did not get to wear long pants until they entered high school. "The whole idea," said Frank "was to reward them by gradually lengthening their pants to transition them from boys to men."

In truth, Frank had no idea why he had to wear short pants through grade school. He knew only that he had to do it and he turned out "pretty damn good, thank you," so Bill would go to school, winter or summer, wearing short pants. Paris Crossing grade school had farm boys and girls for its students. They grew up tough from working with hogs and tobacco leaves and they came to school wearing practical clothing. Bib overalls were favored by the boys. The girls were not allowed to wear pants so they wore skirts and blouses, but there was nothing fancy or different about their attire. Only Bill stood out. When it got really cold, he was given knee socks which warmed him but made him even more different. Ridicule was his constant companion. He was big for his age, but gentle in his demeanor, and once his male classmates found out that he would not strike back, he was smacked around daily amidst derisive taunts of "Sissy" or the dreaded "Queer."

In the meantime, the dead continued to occupy his dreams. Each night just before going to bed, Bill would drink a full glass of water to ensure his survival. Although the monsters now seemed to be quicker and much more ghastly at eight years old than they were when he was six, they still fled when he peed. Bill's parents were becoming increasingly concerned. When Bill finally told his mother about the daily beatings he was receiving, his father made him a deal. "I'll buy you long pants if you beat the shit out of one of those bullies."

The next day after school, during the long walk home where most of the taunting and striking and shoving took place, Bill picked up a rock and threw it, hitting one of his prime tormentors between the eyes. The boy, a young thug named Harvey Prince, dropped to the ground and Bill sat on his chest. Aiming his blow, Bill struck downward, breaking the bully's nose creating a crunching sound. Blood spewed, and the boy underneath Bill began to shriek and wail for his mother. Bill was so sickened and ashamed at what he had done that he vomited the school lunch's chili onto the bully's face and into his open mouth. Bill's adversary stopped screaming and began to choke on the hamburger chunks Bill had so generously shared. All Bill could think about was the beating he would get from his tormentors the following day and he ran the rest of the way home.

To Bill's immense relief, his well-beaten foe did not go to school the next day. The entire episode had been witnessed by a girl in the second grade who had told everyone how Bill had vanquished his main nemesis, and for good measure, had puked in his mouth. Students from almost every grade, including the god-like eighth graders, had been quick to tell Bill how happy they were that someone had kicked Harvey Prince's ass. The kids that were too small couldn't do it and the kids that were larger would have looked like thugs for picking on a much younger boy. Bill found himself in a most unaccustomed hero's role. The girl who had seen the entire affair was Enid Neilson, who had often been bedeviled by Harvey Prince. She thought Bill was the bravest, most handsome boy she had ever seen.

A phone call from an enraged Lloyd Prince was how Bill's father heard of his

son's triumph. It would end up costing Frank
Walsh seventy-two dollars in medical bills,
but he considered it money well spent.
Bill's mother was horrified by her son's
violent behavior, but she dutifully complied
when Frank asked her to buy Bill a pair of
bib overalls. Bill wore them for eleven
straight days.

CHAPTER SIXTEEN:
BILL AND ENID

For a few days, the monsters failed to appear. One whole night went by and Bill awakened dry, monster-free and well rested. His mother was relieved in no small part, not to have to deal with his pissy bedding. His father thought that a corner had been turned and that his boy was well on his way to becoming a man. In truth, many of Bill's fears had been vanquished by the fact that his house had been dead-free for over two weeks. Frank was getting worried. At breakfast Frank told Bill's mother that if someone didn't die soon, he was going to commit murder so he could put bread on their table. Frank did not need to commit a crime. A murder/suicide involving an unfaithful husband, his mistress, and his wife filled the funeral home the following day. That night, the monsters returned bigger and badder than ever and the one with three heads got close enough to Bill to touch his arm before a pint of urine came to Bill's rescue.

To merely call Enid precocious was akin to saying that Shakespeare could write a little bit. She frightened and at the same time made her parents boastful with her ability to read, comprehend and explain at grade levels far above her own. Most impressive were her social skills. Her contemporaries both envied and adored her. Try accomplishing that in the second, third or any grade in any level of education.

Enid's future husband was unaware that in ten years he would be waiting for her at the altar. Bill knew only that Enid was the one person who paid rapt attention to him. Bill found himself wanting to tell Enid everything, and so he did.

"There are monsters in my house," Bill said.

"There are no such things as monsters," Enid replied. "You have dead people in your house, but they can't hurt anybody, they're dead."

"My dad brings them into the basement and does things to them that turns them into monsters," said Bill.

"What does he do?" asked a fascinated Enid.

"I don't know," said Bill. "But it really seems to make them mad. They wait till after I fall asleep and then they try to kill me."

"Why you and not your dad?" asked Enid resisting the urge to hug, which she knew would distance her from they boy who was too young yet to know the depth of her affection.

"Because I'm the first born," Bill said importantly.

"You heard that in Sunday School," said Enid, making it up as she went along. "But you're not the first born, you're the only born, silly, and that makes a lot of difference."

Bill grinned. For the first time in a while, he felt a sense of relief. The Bible had somehow made him believe that the monsters had meant to kill him because he was their creator's first-born but no, thanks to Enid, he knew that was not the reason. Still his fears persisted. "But what does my dad do to them to make them so mad?" he asked.

"I don't know," Enid replied, "but we're going to find out."

Bill was loved but often not noticed. His presence was registered at suppertime and bedtime but seldom during the hours between. He met Enid just outside his garage at sunset. There was no one in the garage and the outside door was unlocked. Enid had brought a flashlight and they used its glow instead of the overhead light to enter without being detected. The hearse fascinated Enid. "Have you ever ridden with dead people?" she asked.

"Yes," Bill replied, "Lots of times."

Bill was lying. He had ridden in the hearse only once when the family car would not start on a cold January morning and the hearse was needed to take him and his folks to church. "What does it smell like?" asked Enid.

"Leather," answered Bill truthfully, for his father took great pains to insure that his cold, silent passengers had an elegant, final ride. "In there is where he does things to them," Bill said, pointing to the door leading to the preparation room.

Both children were silent as they approached the door. Bill knew that he would never be doing this without Enid. She had given him not only courage but a chance to be brave in front of her. Without thinking about it, Bill was grateful to her. Enid, knowing full well what Bill was thinking, chalked up one more reason why Bill would come to realize he could not live without her.

"Wait," said Bill, losing his nerve. "I'm sure the door is locked and we really shouldn't go in there."

Enid turned the door knob and the door opened easily. The smell of formaldehyde welcomed them, in its unique, disgusting way. Smells do not easily translate. They defy transition into speech or print. The worst of the lot seem to have a sweet foundation, often layered with various types of excrement. If a contest were held, most would agree that hogs produce the most repulsive smelling bowel movements; turkeys come in a close second. Rancid maple syrup poured on top of shit, might capture the smell that assaulted Enid as she stepped into the preparation room.

Enid swept her small flashlight over the room. It was dominated by a stainless steel table. Anatomy pictures covered the walls. There was a drain under the table and various pipes and tubes descended from the ceiling. The floor was rust colored around the drain and the unmistakable smell of blood blended with the formaldehyde in a cacophony of odoriferousness.

Enid's bravery was about to be overcome by revulsion. "Bill," she said, "Come on in here."

"No way," said Bill, peering into the room, assaulted by the same smells that were repulsing Enid. To Bill, the smells were familiar, yet distant. Smaller portions of them had wafted through every room in his house assailing him subtly enough to immunize him from disgust. The smell was not keeping him from entering the forbidden room. It was the sense of trespass into his father's domain and more importantly, it was the fear of learning of his father's dealings with the dead.

They heard a car and Enid retreated into the garage where they hid until it became apparent that the car had passed. They were both full of illicit excitement when Enid left to go home. Bill did not dream of monsters that night. He could not remember dreaming of anything, but the last vision that appeared behind his closed eyes was of the sunburned, pigtailed, blonde girl who had become his best friend.

"I wet the bed," Bill confessed to Enid on the next day's walk home from school. It was not a topic Bill had ever broached with anyone. Young boys fear ridicule even more than monsters, yet Bill knew that Enid would not make fun of him. Their trust was beginning to build as their bond strengthened.

"I used to have a terrible problem with that," replied Enid in that adult manner she had.   "Then I stopped drinking anything after supper and all of a sudden I had dry sheets when I woke up. You should try it."

There was a long pause before Bill replied. "I know that, but I have to pee or the monsters will get me, so I drink a couple of glasses of water just before bed. When I pee, the monsters go away."

Enid grinned.   "When you pee, the monsters flee. You are so cute."

Bill blushed.   "You're making fun of me."

"I am absolutely not doing that," said Enid. "But let's think about this. Do you believe the monsters are real?"

"One almost touched me once, but I peed and it vanished," replied Bill.

"Did you wake up then?" asked Enid softly.

"Yes, at least I think I did," Bill replied.

"Peeing will get you awake in a hurry," said Enid once again in a gentle voice. "Maybe the monsters were only dreams and you knew you were sure to escape them if you woke up, and the quickest way to do that was to wet the bed. What do you think?"

"Maybe," Bill replied furrowing his brow. "But I'm afraid not to pee. What if you're wrong and the monsters are real. Who will protect me?"

"I will," Enid replied.   "But to do that, we've got to see how the monsters are made. The next time your dad gets a dead person, we're going to see what he does to it."

Days passed, then Harold Foy died. It happened on a Saturday at about 5:00 p.m. When his father left in the hearse, Bill called Enid. There was a corner closet in the preparation room that faced the table. It housed the billowy coffin liner that was used to cover unsightly necks, hands or other disfigured areas that the casket would not conceal. The eager girl and the frightened boy, perched in the closet with the door barely open, affording them an excellent view of the alchemy involved in delaying the rot and making, if only for a few days, the dead resemble the living.

The hearse arrived not long after Bill and Enid had secured their hiding place. Frank Walsh was accompanied by Fred Cox. Fred was a big man with few social skills but an unshakeable stomach. On many occasions, Fred had been able to salvage bodies that were so ravaged by violence or disease that Frank did not want to go near them. Once the carcasses were in the familiar surroundings of the preparation room, Frank could handle them. Frank often needed Fred's assistance when automobiles collided or cancer victims lost their long, agonizing fight. Never knowing what to expect, Frank always called Fred when a hearse run arrived and Fred was always ready. Fred called himself the "undertaker's assistant" and managed to gain a small amount of prestige by being one of the first to know about who was recently dead and why. In a small town, death notices are big news and you become important and sought after if you could spread who was dead before the evening newspaper was read.

Fred helped Frank undress Harold Foy. Harold was a small man who had died in his pajamas so the task of removing his clothing was not arduous. Frank then went to work on Harold's mouth. This was a task that Frank performed alone, but he always wanted Fred to stay until the mouth looked just right to both men. The prime consideration was to make the lips meet naturally and it required all of Frank's skill to get it accomplished. If the mouth is closed too tightly, the upper lip will often make the deceased seem to scowl at the mourners. No one wants to see a pissed off corpse. Enid watched Frank's every move, absorbing and digesting, while

Bill remained fearful, vaguely registering how he would be cringing in terror were it not for the presence of the small, brave girl next to him.

When Frank cut the body that used to house Harold Foy, the incision was made on the right side of the lower neck. Bill began to quietly whimper. Enid put an arm, then both arms around him and softly whispered, "It's all right my baby, my love."

Fred left after approving of what passed for a smile on Harold Foy's face, and the body's blood was removed and replaced with embalming fluid. The corpse was then carefully washed and Frank took the stairs up to the kitchen. It was then that Bill and Enid ran from the closet to the outside. Enid was excited and Bill was clearly relieved to escape without being discovered. "You will have sweet dreams tonight, sweetheart. I will be watching over you," Enid said and then she and Bill shared the first kiss of many they would have. It was initiated by Enid and it was awkward, just four chapped lips briefly touching, but it was treasured by Bill for the rest of his life. He did not drink water after supper and neither piss nor monsters interfered with his first, long sleep with a corpse in his basement. Once again, the last picture the camera in his brain displayed was Enid's face.

CHAPTER SEVENTEEN:
THE ROUND TABLE

Howard Johnson, Walter Johnson, Lyndon Johnson, Jackie Robinson, Elgin Baylor, premature ejaculation, billboards on the interstate, Fortune 500 companies, breast reduction, Howard Hughes, Jane Russell, Jane Mansfield, lubricated condoms, why fresh fish should not smell, Dodge trucks, five card stud, and fiddles versus violins were discussed in April.

"What was the first cigarette you ever smoked?" asked Pres to no one in particular.

"Marvels," answered Doc.

"I never heard of them," said Red.

"They came in a red pack and tasted like they had been rolled in a weasel's ass," said Doc. "The only thing they had going for them was that they were cheap. You could buy a pack for a quarter."

"Speaking of taste," said Bill, "why do women taste good and men taste bad?"

"Knowing your filthy mind, I bet you're talking about oral sex," said Pres.

"Guilty," Bill replied. "Just think about how blow job frequency would increase if cum tasted like chocolate."

"Or peanut butter," Red interjected. "Debbie loves peanut butter."

"How about peppermint?" Pres asked, "A woman might perform more if she thought she was freshening her breath."

"Seriously," Bill said. "Ten years ago, no one could have imagined how Viagra would be turning limp meat into dicks of steel. If they can do that, they ought to be able to give us flavorful semen."

"It would have to be low-cal or maybe fat free," Red said. "Debbie's on a perpetual diet."

"Someone get Pfizer on the phone," Doc said. "I think you stupid bastards may actually be on to something."

Red led the race to the pay phone. He quickly found the drug-maker's toll free number and after dialing, he handed the phone to Doc.

"Hello," Doc said, "I have an idea for a new product, but I'd like to talk to a man about it. A woman wouldn't appreciate the concept."

CHAPTER EIGHTEEN:
YOUNG ROB CROSS

Rob Livingston Cross was a grocer's son with doctors for grandfathers. His paternal grandfather had amassed a small fortune practicing medicine eighteen hours a day. Somehow in spite of time constraints, Grandfather George Cross and Grandmother Ellen produced eight children. Doctor George's fortune was diminished by the depression, squandered by his widow and divided into eight parts following Grandmother Ellen's death. As a result, the doctor's children found that their lives of privilege and leisure would be severely affected if they failed to embrace manual labor. Some of Doc's uncles and aunts never grasped this concept. Three aunts married below their stations, for fear of an uncertain, impecunious future. Of his four uncles, two mirrored his aunts by marrying women who they thought would inherit from wealthy parents. The net result of all these parings was marital misery and dysfunctional children.

Only Doc's father Trevor and his uncle Mike seemed to get it. Mike's nickname was "Right." He was a small, muscular man with a tolerance for pain equaled only by the holy men who walked on hot coals and the women who silently gave birth to big-headed children. Mike became a golden gloves boxer when he was twelve and was undefeated when he became a professional at age seventeen. In fact, Mike had been a professional for most of his amateur career. Believing that no one could beat him, Mike had secretly been placing bets on himself to such an extent that at the time he turned pro, he had over twelve thousand dollars in the bank. It was then that Mike started to really get rich. He fought as a lightweight, but he was a middleweight in a lightweight's body and a punch from him to the ribs or solar plexus of an opponent was devastating. Mike was smart enough to direct his punches to the body in the early rounds, waiting patiently until his opponent's hands would come down to protect the gut from the pummeling it was receiving. A punch to the jaw would soon end the match and the legend of "Right" Cross was well on its way.

The purse for Mike's first professional fight was fifty dollars. He was a three-to-one underdog fighting in Louisville against a home town boy named Lou McGraw. McGraw was known as "Louisville Lou" and he specialized in canvas muggings. Lou's forte was to wrestle, clinch, and hold his opponents until they became exhausted trying to escape Lou's bulk. Mike found a bookie, (not a difficult task in Louisville), and placed a ten thousand dollar bet on himself. The bookie was wary. Ordinarily, his maximum bet was five thousand, but Mike looked like fresh meat and the bookie had made a small fortune placing bets on "Louisville Lou."

"I've got to know you can cover" the bookie said. Mike displayed ten one thousand dollar bills. He then cut them in halves, and handed the bookie the left half of every bill. "Those and twenty thousand more had better be in my locker room after I send your boy into dreamland on Friday night," Mike said.

Mike's style was anything but, classic. Instead of bobbing and weaving through the early rounds, Mike would lead with his chin in order to hammer his way into mid-body bone. The first time Lou tried to hold, he took a crushing blow to his left kidney. Because Lou exposed his back when he turned to hold, the referee did not take any points away from Mike, and the fight was essentially over. Lou, to his credit, tried to box for the next two rounds, but bobbing and weaving was not his style and the next time Lou reverted to form and attempted to hold, Mike took one step back and threw an underhanded right that took the breath out of Louisville Lou and most of the people in the arena. It took several minutes for Lou to arise and by that time almost every one was cheering for their new shining star, the "Hoosier Hero, Mike 'Right' Cross." The bookie was in Mike's dressing room as promised and to Mike's surprise, the bookie was smiling. "You impressed the shit out of me when you placed your bet," said Benny the book. "So, I took your money and five thousand of my own and drove to the big joint in Newport and put it all on you. Here's your thirty thousand. Let me know when you're going to be fighting again."

"Next Saturday and every Saturday after that," Mike replied. "I need someone to find me fights. I guess I need a manager. Any ideas?"

"I'm your man," said Benny. "I know every pug and every hustler in Kentucky, Indiana and Ohio and for ten percent; I'll make you a million, so long as you can keep throwing that big right hand."

When he wasn't fighting, Mike worked with his brother Trevor in their grocery store in Madison. Rob, his brother Harold, and their mother Marge all worked there, too. It was hard, time-consuming work. Rob had started when he was five, stocking shelves and making simple sandwiches. He and Harold reported for work after school, and stayed until he, his brother and his mom went home, just before dark. They took sandwiches and chips home with them and that would be the Cross boys' evening, weekday meal throughout their childhood. On Saturday, the store would close at 5:30 p.m. and not reopen again until early Monday morning. If Mike was fighting nearby, Trevor would pack his sons into his wretched Plymouth and the three of them would go see the family hero decimate whomever he faced. Mrs. Cross stayed home. In those days, women did not attend fights. It was considered a sport too brutal for the fairer sex, and men wanted to be sans skirts so they could smoke, drink and act vulgar during the blood sport. Besides, Mrs. Cross had food to prepare for Sunday when the entire family would make up for subsisting on Vienna sausages and hostess cupcakes during the week and would gorge on roast beef, mashed potatoes, gravy and canned peas. When the seasons permitted, the peas gave way to sweet corn, dripping with butter, or fresh green beans, seasoned with ham and cooked on low heat for hours.

Rob's maternal grandfather was Doctor James Christian or Doc Jim as most people called him. He was ancient, but still practicing medicine when Rob was a boy. Both his home and office were in the same four-room house located across the street from Rob and his family. The old doctor loved both his grandsons, but he doted on Rob. Doc Jim had started with Harold, Rob's older brother, trying to prepare Harold for first grade. Doc Jim had abandoned a successful practice in Indianapolis to be near Marge and his grandsons. Doc Jim knew that his organs were gradually shutting down, in direct proportion to the gargantuan amounts of whiskey he consumed daily, and he selfishly wanted help from his family for the dying days to come. He tried to make himself useful in the hope that he would be given care and attention in return. In truth, up until his move to Madison, Doc had been neither a great dad nor a loving grandfather. He had vowed to change and Harold was Doc's first project.

For one hour, every weekday, Doc tried to teach five-year old Harold to read. Harold did not want to read. He was a sweet, loving boy, but he thought that he belonged in the store with his parents, brother and his uncle Mike. After two months, Doc and Harold agreed, with much relief, to abandon their great experiment. Harold went back to the store, and Doc focused his attention on four-year old Rob.

Doc Jim had quite a colorful history. He graduated from Indiana University Medical School in 1897. He joined a practice in Indianapolis that quickly enabled him to display his communicative skills. Doctors, since time began, have had a habit of anointing themselves with god-like attributes. Prominent among them has been an un-willingness among these self-proclaimed intellectual giants to take the time to tell mere mortals why toes hurt or noses run. Usually, those degrading tasks are left to nurses. As a result, patients feel unsure of their diagnoses, often suspecting the worst, believing their doctors would stay around if they had good news and convinced, on the other hand, that nurses were harbingers of death, smiley faces in starched uniforms, disguising malignancy and melanoma.

Doctor James Christian wanted to be a surgeon. The doctor who interviewed Doc Jim noted his desire for surgical training, but saw in the recent graduate a skill that no one else in the twelve-doctor office possessed. Doc Jim could relate to people. He had none of the aloofness so common to healers. Doctor Christian actually spoke to nurses in a friendly, non-condescending manner. His hopeful interviewer took Doc into the adjoining hospital where Doc Jim spoke to patients, looked into their eyes and on one occasion, held an elderly woman's hand, causing her to burst into tears and causing him to hug her for several minutes until her sobbing stopped and she said,

"Thanks Doc, I guess you knew I really needed that."

Doctor Christian sat in on as many patient consultations as time would allow and followed the other doctors on their hospital rounds. Doc Jim's job was to humanize his fellow physicians, and he did his job well. Patients and their families were so grateful for the unaccustomed attention that word spread throughout Indianapolis of the caring physician. Soon, Doctor Christian was sitting in on consultations with not only the sick, but the rich and famous who needed their imagined ills diagnosed and their faux pain appreciated. Although there was some jealousy among the other doctors upon learning that patients were insisting upon Doc Jim's presence throughout the entire course of their treatments, most of Doctor Christian's fellow physicians appreciated being rid of the need to be kind and compassionate. "I'll be the healer, and Jim can deal with the bullshit," was the often expressed sentiment among Doc Jim's colleagues.

In the next few years, Doctor Christian counted among his patients Woodrow Wilson (who really was sick), Eli Lilly, Winston Churchill's mother, and James Whitcomb Riley. At that time, Riley was certainly the best known Hoosier in the world and one of the country's most popular poets. Strangely, Riley spent most of his life living in hotels, lodging houses, or with friends. He never married, and although he called Indianapolis his home, Riley was seldom there. He needed company, and for that matter, so did Doc Jim. The two men didn't exactly hit it off at their first meeting.

Riley was seriously ill in 1910 and after meeting his lung specialist, Doc Jim came into the famous poet's room. Without even introducing himself, Doc Jim began to recite, "The Passing of The Backhouse."

Riley was lying on his side when the doctor began to recite. The poet never moved throughout the six stanza outpouring. When Doctor Christian finally stopped after, "I'm now a man, but none the less I'll try the children's hole," there was silence for almost an entire minute. Finally Riley spoke. "I did not write that crude, offensive drivel. I do not know who you are. Get out of my room."

Stunned and embarrassed, Doc Jim fled. He had long been an admirer of Riley and when Doc Jim learned of the poet's presence in the hospital, he had brushed up on Riley's works, memorizing the risqué "Backhouse" which Doc Jim hoped would impress and amuse his sick hero.

Two days passed. The poet's condition improved, but not his disposition. Doctor Christian was urged to work his magic on the surly Riley. Shaking and sweating, Doc Jim entered the poet's room with a bottle of Jack Daniels, two glasses and a basin of ice. Riley watched warily as the doctor arranged the anti-temperance display on a table next to the poet's bed.

"I earlier asked who you were," Riley said. "I no longer care; just pour that Tennessee Sunshine."

Doc Jim did as he was told. Riley drained his glass in seconds and stared at his doctor. Jim followed suit and poured. Riley again gulped his drink down and silently challenged his companion to do the same. Jim complied. Two more drinks were poured and consumed. The bottle was showing signs of exhaustion. Not a word had been spoken until Riley asked for another and casually asked if the doctor could guarantee more, once the nearly drained supply was no longer capable of dispensing joy. Doc opined that he could probably find more where that came from and opening his satchel smilingly and smugly, produced a large bottle of

Kentucky whiskey known for its bite. The locals lovingly called it "Old Snake Shit." Doc Jim only knew that the nearly depleted Jack had cost him five dollars and the bottle of three-month old, snarling, pissed-off brown venom that he was about to open cost only a buck fifty.

The doctor poured the Jack into his glass and the nasty into the glass of the poet, a fact that Riley silently observed. Doc Jim downed the last of the Tennessee whiskey while Riley sullenly sipped the vile brew that passed for sour mash.

"I must leave now to urinate," Doc Jim said in the pompous, precise manner the truly drunk adopt to disguise their ability to no longer function. As he arose, the room became rebellious. The floor rose when his left foot went to meet it and fell when his right foot sought purchase. The door to the toilet rolled first to the left, then to the right and when entry was finally achieved, the stool rolled backward. Doc Jim tried to chase it, holding his cock which was now spewing piss, in spite of the fact that the doctor had it gripped tightly between the thumb and forefinger of his left hand. The ceiling then started to roll and the lights dimmed and brightened as they neared and then retreated from the doctor's head.

The stool appeared as a place of repose, a sanctuary where thoughts could be gathered and sobriety reclaimed if only Doc Jim's head could rest upon its porcelain rim. The fact that the doctor had sprayed urine in every direction en route to the toilet, and upon its floor and walls, no longer mattered. Indeed, the left hand that had been holding his dick now joined the doctor's right hand in supplication, seeking the water-filled bowl, for a far more serious problem had begun to arise. From deep within the doctor's gut, Tennessee Sunshine had combined with today's lunch of a bacon, lettuce and tomato sandwich. The morning's coffee had awakened, together with rye toast and a glass of orange juice. Long forgotten meals of eggs, pork chops, onions, and peas stirred and came alive. Most of the liquid and near-liquid escaped from the doctor's mouth, but an alarming amount spewed from his nose. Doctor Christian made one valiant leap to capture the stool before the deluge, but it swerved to the right, and he slipped on the pee-soaked floor, hitting his right eyebrow solidly on the left side of the porcelain rim. Head injury blood, in typical copious amounts, joined with the vomitus lumps, bile and urine to create a tableau in which the now unconscious doctor was the centerpiece.

"Nurse!" Riley yelled again and again until one finally appeared. "I think I may have a dead man in my bathroom." The poet sipped his drink and gleefully watched while the nurses, housekeepers, and doctors all viewed the scene with revulsion. When one of the younger nurses began to gag, a housekeeper turned the nurse around and pushed her outside the room. "I've got enough slime to remove my dear. No more puke is appreciated, thank you," the housekeeper said.

Doctor Christian was not seriously injured, but he was bloodied and bowed. In addition, he stunk, his right eye swelled and closed and he had a headache that throbbed with every heartbeat, as strands of barbed wire paused between beats and serrated new globs of brain tissue when his heart beat again. The pain was nothing compared to the humiliation. Doc Jim barely remembered being stripped and lowered into a tub, but one thing pierced through his alcoholic fog. The nurse who undressed him was young and attractive and she clearly found him to be contemptible and repulsive. One positive did come out of the evening. The young doctor and the old poet became friends.

"Mrs. Christian," Riley said into the telephone. "This is James Whitcomb Riley. As I'm sure you know your husband has been helping to cure me from a malady that has been inconsequential but persistent. He has succeeded and I am told that I shall be released from the hospital in a few days. Unfortunately, your talented young husband has come down with what is being called here as the "Old Poet's Flu" and he asked me to call and tell you that he will be spending the next night or two here."

Doc Jim, lying in a bed that had been brought into Riley's room, was still too drunk to talk even though hours had passed since his spectacular fall. Still the young doctor heard and was moved by Riley's kindness.

"You'll not like the way he looks when you next see him." The poet continued talking to Betsy Christian. "He was not handsome to begin with, but he slipped in some water while tending to me and that and the fever caused by the flu caused a fall which gave him quite a shiner. He asked me to call before they gave him a sedative and he's resting quite comfortably now. He told me to tell you that he'll call you in the morning. Good night, my dear."

CHAPTER NINETEEN:
BEAU JACK

To understand the making of Rob Cross, it is necessary to continue to focus on the two most important men in his young life: Mike Cross (even Rob called him Uncle Right), and Doc Jim. Rob wanted to emulate both of his heroes. In the fantasy world minds of kindergarten children, anything is possible. Rob saw himself pummeling boys who brutalized girls then salving the tender legs of the always grateful damsels. Rob would next tend to the bully and the beautiful girl would express her gratitude. A warning would be given to the thug who would slink from the scene, leaving Rob holding, kissing and looking at the underpants of the girl of his dreams. This was as far as it went. Rob thought that seeing a girl's panties was as good as it got.

By October of 1941, Right Cross was a wealthy man. His record stood at 78 wins, two defeats, and four draws. Seventy-one wins were by knockout. He had never been knocked out or even knocked down. He no longer fought every week. In truth, he was not in very good shape. Trevor and Marge had begun making and selling sandwiches and their business was booming. The boxer was a sucker for the ham salad which, in spite of the name, contained no ham. It did, however, contain lots of fat and lots of calories. The concoction was made with coarsely ground bologna, chopped hard-boiled eggs, thinly sliced sweet pickles, and mayo. Right Cross liked cheese with his, so ever day two pounds of ham salad with American cheese was made separately, and every day the boxer made himself four sandwiches on white bread which he washed down with buttermilk.

In August, knowing he would have to lose twelve pounds to fight as a lightweight again, Right Cross moved up a division and fought a middleweight named Irish Tony Malloy. At forty-two, Malloy was no match for the younger Right Cross; but the fight lasted for ten long rounds and the two men did little but lean on one another for the last five. The crowd displayed its contempt for the out-of-shape, floundering pugilists by booing so loudly, Right Cross could not hear the ring announcer and learned of his victory, only when the referee raised Right's hand. He decided to forego his usual victory lap, choosing instead to flee to his dressing room as vegetables began to fly. Malloy hesitated for a moment before making his exit and took a tomato in his ear. A blood lust seemed to seize many of the men when they saw the tomato hit its target, and heavy objects began to fly ring-ward. A potato, a rutabaga, several turnips and even a shoe were flung in the unfortunate Malloy's general direction. A melee might have ensued had not the referee, who was also getting pelted, drawn his revolver and fired it into the air.

When the Japanese attacked Pearl Harbor on December 7, 1941, Mike "Right" Cross joined the navy the following day. He looked forward to using weapons, as opposed to relying on only his hands. How easy, it appeared to the boxer, it must be to win with a gun or a grenade.

Mike's recruiter swelled with pride when Mike appeared. "Guess we won't have to worry about winning the lightweight championship from those army bastards with you on board, will we sailor?" the recruiter gleefully inquired.

"I'm joining to fight the fucking Japs," replied the boxer. "I don't want to hurt another soldier and keep him from joining in on the fun."

Sidney Walker was two full years older than Mike Cross, and by the time Mike entered the navy, Sidney had fought twenty-two more times as a professional than had Right Cross. Sidney's professional name was Beau Jack and he was the top lightweight of his time. A Georgia boy, Jack learned to fight in brawls organized by white men who would put several blacks in a ring and have them fight to see who would be the last man standing.

Bobby Jones met Beau Jack at Augusta National where Jack worked shining shoes between fights. The southern aristocrat and golf god was impressed by Beau Jack's fighting ability and gave Beau Jack money for formal boxing training.

From May 20, 1940, through December 30 of the same year, Beau Jack had sixteen professional fights. He lost three of his first six. His formal boxing training had let him down. Bobby Jones was a gentleman and he wanted to mentor a pupil who would jab, dance and dazzle his way to pugilistic success. Beau Jack tried to please his benefactor, but the fighter had a difficult time becoming a boxer. His sixth fight, a rematch of fight number three with Jackie Parker, ended just as the first one had, with Jack dancing and jabbing his way to a sound beating. Following that fight, Beau the boxer disappeared and the brawler reemerged. Using his great upper body strength, Jack started swinging when the bell sounded and stopped only between rounds. Beau Jack won his next ten fights, seven of them by knockout. He went on to become the lightweight champion of the world.

Beau Jack was called into service in 1945 and he served in the army, his boxing career on hold, for ten months. The military seemed not to know what to do with the famous black fighter. During World War Two, most Negro soldiers were given menial tasks to perform, reflective of their role in the white-dominated society that was America in the forties. And so, the great Beau Jack was sent to Fort Benning, Georgia, where he was to learn to cook.

Mike Cross embraced his new occupation. He had never before seen the ocean, nor had he been any further west than Saint Louis. In January of 1942, an excited Right Cross sailed out of San Francisco on a destroyer bound for the South Pacific. Mike was well liked by both his officers and his fellow seamen, although the enlisted men would have preferred a less enthusiastic shipmate. Mike's eagerness to please made him the example his officers used to demonstrate how things should be done "in this man's Navy."

Gradually, Mike's body responded to its owner's new demands and the different types of fuel it was being provided. Navy chow was wonderful, plentiful and nutritious in stark contrast to Mike's grocery store grub. Basic training had been shortened in the Navy's haste to fill the void caused by the loss of the seventh fleet, but its rigors were a shock to the fleshy Right Cross. There is a process, more mental than physical that both athletes and the merely athletic go through on their way to fitness. After a while, the body seems to desire and crave pain. Fifty push-ups are no longer enough. A five-mile run seems inconsequential. Muscles rebel and scream while they harden and grow. Tendons stretch and sometimes pull, but their elasticity is needed to support the growing muscle mass and so pulls are viewed as progress and ignored or even welcomed. By February, Mike was doing 100 push-ups, 100 sit-ups and fifty squats, twice daily. In addition, he ran everywhere. He had lost fifteen pounds. He was a lightweight again.

The ensign aboard Mike's destroyer was from Covington, Kentucky and he had seen Mike

fight in Cincinnati and lose against a local
boy from Newport, who looked to be no match
for the mighty "Right" Cross. It was a
four-rounder, during which the upstart landed
three blows to every ten savagely delivered
by Mike. The judging was on a round's won
basis and at the fight's conclusion, the
referee ruled it four rounds to none in favor
of Mike "Right" Cross. The judges
disagreed both voting that Mike had won only
one round and the Newport kid had won the
rest. The result was a split decision and
Mike had lost. When the decision was
announced, screams of "fix" filled the air,
and the referee who worked the bout, together
with the judges, quickly made their exits and
did not reappear to work any of the bouts
that followed. Typical of the way boxing was
in those days, the referee found future work
hard to come by while the judges were in much
demand.

"That was so unfair," the ensign said
after discovering the boxer now under his
command was Mike "Right" Cross. "Wasn't
there anything you could do?"

"Sir," said Mike, "there are no
appeals in boxing. The trick is to know in
advance when you are going to get screwed.
That fight had a stench about it from the
beginning. That was only the kid's third
fight. You don't put inexperienced boxers in
against maulers like me. He should have been
fighting someone who was also in the ring for
the third time."

"But Mike it looked to me like you were
toying with him," the ensign said. "Why
didn't you just deck his ass?"

"There were two times when I had him in
trouble." Mike said. "In the second round
when I hit him clean with a left to his ribs
and in the fourth when I connected again with
the same hand to the same ribs."

"Why didn't you finish him off?" the
ensign asked incredulously.

"I had nothing to gain by it," answered Mike. "Besides, I felt sorry for the kid. I had a hunch that if the fight didn't go the distance he might have ended up in the Ohio River."

"What do you mean you had nothing to gain by it?" asked the ensign. "Didn't a defeat like that hurt your title chances?" Mike laughed, "Excuse me sir, but you don't know jack shit about the fight game. I never had any title chances. The only way you get those is by fighting tough guys. I never had a fight against anybody who was worth a flying fuck. I fought pushovers and has-beens, guys I knew I could beat. I had no desire to get hurt. That's strictly for champs and losers. I ain't either one."

"What about the big purses?" the ensign asked. "How did you make any money fighting bums?"

Mike laughed again. "The biggest purse I ever got was two hundred dollars. The way I made money was by placing bets on myself."

"But who would take your bet?" asked the ensign. "Why would anybody want to bet against you if you were fighting marshmallows?

"Sir," explained Mike, "there are people who would bet that a butterfly could whip a bumblebee's ass if you give them ten-to-one odds. Besides, I was cautious, I didn't have any money on myself when I fought that kid from Newport, and I never bet against myself. That would have put me in the same bed with thieves and I am pretty picky about who I sleep with."
"Was that the only loss on your record?" the ensign asked.

"Oh no," Mike replied. "Do you remember a fighter named Jackie Parker? He was one hell of a fighter who was supposed to be on the way out when I was booked to fight him last year. He damned near killed me. I won the last round because he was arm weary

---

142

from beating the shit out of me for the first five, but I only had three hundred on that fight, so I didn't get hurt too bad."

The war passed uneventfully for Rob's uncle Mike "Right" Cross. There were some in that terrible theater who never heard small arms fire. Mike helped man a big gun which seemed always to be directed toward a Jap position on some hill on some piss ant island. The blows to his ears in the ring had eliminated Mike's ability to hear whispers or the cooing of doves. The guns diminished most of the rest of the sounds so that for the rest of his life, Mike needed to face friends and lovers to hear even loud-spoken praise, shouted instruction, or passionate moans.

Mike's ensign became a captain, and in 1945, both men found themselves stationed in Pensacola, Florida, waiting for the war to end. One evening in March, the captain burst into Mike's quarters. "Guess what, me Bucko? Beau Jack is in the Army and the powers-that-be want him to fight some exhibitions to amuse the troops. I volunteered your sorry, white Navy ass and the admiral is beside himself. After I told him of your prowess, the admiral is convinced that you can beat that Army colored boy."

Mike was stunned. He knew that exhibitions between brawlers seldom remained "fights for fun." It was impossible for down and dirty fighters like Right Cross and Beau Jack to put on boxing demonstrations. In truth, they were pit bulls, not house cats. There would never be hisses and swats for them; only growls and lunges for arteries, brains and vital organs. "Captain," Mike said, "I can't fight him. He'll kill me. This guy is for real. Don't you remember me telling you about champions and losers? He's as good as it gets and if I get into a ring with him, I'll become the loser I vowed never to become."

The captain just smiled. "You're not fooling me Mister Right Cross. You're every bit as good as that Negro. Remember, I saw you fight. You just never had your chance for a title fight, but now I'm going to see that you get one. After you pummel Beau Jack, the whole fighting establishment will demand that you get your shot at greatness. Besides, what do you have to lose? It's only an exhibition. That colored Army boy will not be expecting a Navy lightweight to hit him as hard as I know you can. You get his attention you get noticed by some very important people. The admiral is already lining up some of his most influential friends to see the Navy's own contender, Seaman First Class Michael "Right" Cross."

The fight was to take place in six weeks at Fort Benning. Mike, resigned to his fate, trained frantically. To his surprise, he seemed stronger and quicker than he had been in years. Mike needed sparring partners and at first, they had not been hard to find. The men who worked below deck, the hull techs and boiler techs, were by nature hostile and aggressive from being confined to close quarters in the heat and dim light and they were eager to volunteer. One by one they fell. The lumbering heavyweights were easily dispatched and all were vanquished in the same manner. Hit a dozen times before they were able to uncork their wild, ugly swings, the massive strong men were quickly exhausted and fell when Mike's fist found its way into the fat between their hearts and their navels.

The next cracker jacks eager to trade blows with the boxer were the Irish and the Irish wannabes. The big men had been like punching bags to Mike and he had used them to reinforce his shoulder and arm strength. In addition, a rusty fighter, one exposed to the civilized world, will sometimes question the need to punish and disable his opponent. A left to the liver once strongly swung, will slow when it nears its target. Golfers, baseball players and field goal kickers all suffer from "contact flinch" as their minds question the need to swing or kick as far as they had originally planned. The flinch occurs just before contact and it is nearly always disastrous. Mike knew he had flinched just before he gut-stuck the engine room heavyweights. He knew there was no need to crush the breastbones of stationary targets. He needed to test himself against big men, but he needed the Irish lightweights to help him remember to brawl and be quick, just like Beau Jack.

His first lightweight volunteer was a tough little shit named Malloy. To complicate matters, Malloy was a southpaw with boundless energy and a love for contact. When the bell rang, Malloy ran at Mike, swinging wildly before clinching and pounding lefts to Mike's ribs. Malloy's skull was below Mike's and the Irishman's head rose swiftly, seeking Mike's chin. Anticipating the move, Mike shrugged out of the clinch and stepping backward for balance, then forward for power, put a left uppercut into Malloy's esophagus. No "contact flinch" occurred. Mike's left hand buried into his opponent's throat and for the first time in his life, Malloy confronted his mortality. The Irishman could not breathe and his eyes widened with fear as they began to hemorrhage from lack of oxygen. A corpsman with a pen knife created a breathing hole and Malloy survived, but the fight had been witnessed by hundreds and Mike was out of sparring partners. No one else wanted to test their manhood against the boxer and Beau Jack waited while Mike trained alone. The fight was in ten days.

Beau Jack was bored. The great fighter expected to learn to kill when he entered the Army. He wanted to slay his country's enemies with guns or with his bare hands. Instead, the Army was teaching him to make thick pork chops edible and rabbit taste like chicken. When word came down from his officers that a boxing match was to be arranged, the champion welcomed the news. Even though it was only to be an exhibition against a nobody, it was better than chopping radishes. The great Beau Jack began to run and shadow-box when he learned that he had only days to train.

The ring in Fort Benning had been hastily erected outside in the parade grounds. Although it was an Army fort, the Navy had bussed nearly two thousand sailors to the compound in hopes of seeing Navy beat Army. The soldiers were three thousand strong and out-shouted the sailors as the ringside introductions were being made. The referee was a Marine imported especially for the occasion. His instructions were broadcast throughout the fort and it was clear that the Marine loved the microphone. "It is indeed ironic," he intoned, "that the pussy branches of our great armed forces have asked a mean-assed Marine to referee your little fight."

The crowd began to boo and shout. "Sit down and shut up, you horseshit smelling cocksucker" was one of the more imaginative shouts directed toward the smiling Marine, whose ring announcements followed.

"On my left, wearing navy blue, who I could beat with one hand on my dick, is the pride of the Navy, Mike "Right" Cross." The sailors' cheers were thunderous. Mike came into the ring wearing his crackerjack hat and he doffed it to his naval admirers.

"On my right, wearing army green, who I could beat while screwing his sister, is the lightweight champion of the world, the pride of the Army, the great Beau Jack. Will the boxers come to the center of the ring?"

Both fighters came forward. Beau Jack quietly asked the Marine to raise his hands. When the referee inquiringly complied, Beau Jack threw a thunderous left hook that sent the Marine crashing to the floor. "You shouldn't be talking about my sister," Beau Jack said to the prostrate Marine. At first, the crowd fell into a stunned silence; then they went berserk, wildly cheering as the Marine was carried from the ring.

"We don't need us no referee, do we boy?" Beau Jack asked. "We'll jab and dance and pretend to hurt each other and then go drink some beer. How's that sound?"

"Sounds wonderful champ," Mike replied. "I just want to tell my grand kids how I once got into the ring with the great Beau Jack."

There are times in everyone's lives when we want minutes to last for hours. Your first real embrace, the smile on your baby's face, the celebration when the home run wins the game in the last inning. Mike Cross felt the same elation and joy, the sense of never-ending fun, as he spent the next twenty minutes of his life sparring with the champion.

The match was set for four rounds. In round one, Beau Jack was the dancer and Mike was the stalker. The champion danced and jabbed while Mike plodded trying to land a big blow. In the second round, Mike was the bobbing and weaving butterfly while Beau Jack was the plodding slugger stalking his prancing foe. A slightly off-target uppercut thrown by the champion would have beheaded Mike. The breeze from the blow raised the hair on his head. Mike grabbed the champion in a clinch and said, "Jesus, Beau Jack, you would have killed me if you'd have connected with that last one."

"I didn't plan on hitting you, boy," said the champ. "Now let's let them have a show in these last two rounds. I'm going to pretend to hit you like I hit that jive-assed Marine and you are going to fall, all right?"

"Let's give them their money's worth, champ," replied Mike, and a wild easy right thrown by Beau Jack hit Mike squarely on his left ear. The punch did not hurt, but Mike went down, thrilling the Army contingent. From that point on, until he died thirty-three years later, Mike "Right" Cross was deaf in the ear the champion barely touched.

Mike was unconcerned about his hearing loss at the time. After all, his ears had failed him for years and one more hearing level loss seemed inconsequential. Mike was still having the time of his life and when he picked himself up off the canvas and answered the bell for the fourth and final round, he was already mourning the loss of the moment. He wished somehow that there would be another time in his life when he would feel as complete and at peace as he did at that moment.

"Your turn now boy," said Beau Jack as the fighters touched gloves in that strange gesture of peace, in the midst of violence, that precedes the final round. Although Mike could not make out the works spoken by the champion, he knew their import when Beau Jack dropped his left hand, making him vulnerable to, of all things, a right cross. Mike threw it, but flinched prior to contact, so as to make the punch sting but not hurt. Beau Jack fell on his ass, to the delight of the Navy.

For the remaining two minutes, Beau Jack pursued Mike, swinging wildly, pretending to be enraged about being dropped by a Navy nobody. When the bell sounded and the fight was declared a draw, Beau Jack embraced Mike and shouted into his damaged ears, "I ain't allowed to have a beer with you in the enlisted mans' club. Seems like I can fight your white ass in front of thousands of people, but I can't sit down with you to have a drink."

"I have six cold ones waiting on ice in my tent," said Mike, "and three of them are yours. Follow me, champ."

Rob Cross went to medical school to learn how to cure his grandfather's alcoholism and to restore his uncle's hearing. Both men died before Rob could help.

Beau Jack died just short of his seventy-ninth birthday in 2000. Following his discharge, he returned to box again in December of 1945. He would fight for another ten years, but he would never regain the title he lost to Bob Montgomery in 1944. The great Beau Jack went back to shining shoes. Other than box, it was all he knew how to do.

CHAPTER TWENTY:
DOCTOR ROBERT CROSS

Rob met Julie Hearter at Butler University when both of them were seniors. Julie was dark and small with seductive eyes and a hoarse, sensual voice. She was also Einstein-smart and fearless. Julie asked Rob out on their first date and ordered meals for both of them at the Russian Café on Maryland Street. She also ordered the wine, which she later admitted had been a failure, but Rob didn't care. He was not used to strong, intelligent women and he was thoroughly impressed and titillated by Julie's self-assurance. As he ate his veal, Rob realized that he was falling deeply in lust with his diminutive companion. When Julie suggested that they should have a nightcap in her room, Rob's penis sprang to attention. Were it not limbless, it would have saluted. As every man knows, erections vary from tepid to raging. Rob's was a flaming, heathen, blue steel wonder. As the waitress began to clear the table, Rob ordered coffee, stalling for time, trying desperately to make his hard-on go away. He tried thinking of his mother, the Virgin Mary and Eleanor Roosevelt, but nothing helped to soften the iron rod that seemed to protrude several feet from his jeans, threatening to burst his zipper and levitate their table.

"Rob," Julie said, "I think I know what your problem is."
Rob was thunderstruck. How could Julie know that every ounce of his blood had left his head and descended into his dick? Somehow, both his upper and lower extremities, had also drained downward, upward, and inward, engorging a member which was now the size of an elephant leg. Rob knew that everyone in the restaurant had to be watching. His humiliation was complete. He contemplated

feigning death. Out of desperation he blurted, "Julie, how about some dessert?"

"I am not asking you to go to bed with me, so you don't have to worry about turning me down," Julie said. "I'm not promiscuous. As a matter of fact, I'm a virgin and I plan on staying that way until my wedding night. Does that relieve your mind? I just happen to have a decent Cabernet back in my apartment and I thought I would show you what we would have been drinking, if I had ordered correctly."

An unrequited erection does not drop unceremoniously. It takes time for a dick to get the message that it will not find happiness in the warmth of one or more of the soft, perfumed, slick female openings that earlier seemed to be so available. Rob's cock ever so slowly began its descent. When the chocolate cheesecake arrived, Rob's erection was down to the size of an inverted bowling pin. He ate slowly.

Julie stood up. "I'll walk myself home," she said.

"Please sit down," Rob pleaded. "I have been stalling, but it's not because I don't want to be with you for a while back in your apartment. I can't get up right now, because I have a physical problem."

Julie sat back down. "What is it Rob?" she asked.

Rob reddened as he whispered inaudibly, "I have an erection."

Julie replied, "You need a collection? Is that what you said? Listen Rob, if this about money, I invited you. I'll pay for the meal."

"No," Rob said, "you don't understand. I have an erection." Once again Rob's volume was muted so that the last four words diminished, dwindled and evaporated before they ever had a chance of penetrating Julie's left ear which was only inches from Rob's mouth.

"Did you say you were having a reaction?" Julie asked. "What are you saying? What is going on? Are you allergic to chocolate?"

"Goddamn it Julie, I've got a hard-on," Rob blurted in a voice that now turned heads and further deepened his embarrassment.

Julie was silent for a moment and then she slid her chair over to Rob's side of the table. Lifting the tablecloth, Julie stared at Rob's source of embarrassment. Rob thought seriously about sawing through his wrists with the butter knife. Finally, after what seemed like one hundred and twelve billion years, Julie dropped the tablecloth. "I always thought erections were bigger than that," she said.

Rob's cock dropped faster than a whore's panties. Ridicule will do that to a dick. Men think a lot about the size of their penises. Most would trade a college degree for a ten-inch wonder rod. By age sixteen, over eighty percent of the boys in the United States have used tape measures, rules and yardsticks, pushing the beginning end deep into dick stems, to achieve respectable measurements. Negative comments about cock length, especially from women, can alter a man's future. Imagine Buffalo Bill as a young man being told that he had a puny penis. The resultant blow to his ego would likely have turned him into Rabbit Bill or worse. He might even have become the legendary Needle Dick the Bug Fucker.

"Rob," Julie said grinning, "I was only kidding. Actually, you had a nice little tent going down there."

"Julie," Rob said, hating her now, "I'm sorry if I embarrassed you, and right now I'm sorry I ever met you."

"Oh poor little Robbie," Julie said, still smiling. "Did bad old Julie hurt him's feelings? Tell you what, Julie will kiss you and make you feel all better."

Rob stood up. "I'll race you to your apartment," he said.

Julie looked approvingly at Rob's pants as the tent began to reappear. "Okay, let's do it," Julie said. "But no fair, it looks like you've already got a two-foot lead."

Rob beamed. Julie was forgiven. His confidence was restored.

Rob and Julie continued to date up until their graduation. Their relationship was difficult to describe. They were not really lovers, even though male hands became intimate with soft female breasts and inner thighs, and female hands willingly transformed hardness into sticky tumescence. They were mostly one another's rock. Everyone needs a quiet place. Rob thought that Julie was the smartest person he had ever known and the least judgmental. Julie thought that Rob was funny and clever and God help her, she thought Rob was the most wonderful man in the world. She was hopelessly in love with him. Her emotions terrified her. Julie was staying in Indianapolis to pursue her dream of becoming a physical therapist. Rob was bound for Lexington to attend medical school at the University of Kentucky. Rob's assurances that they would burn up the highways to be with one another were of little solace to Julie. She knew they would have eighty-hour work weeks and long, painful separations. She knew that she could survive and that her love for Rob would only grow stronger. She doubted that Rob felt so intensely about her. Visions of short-skirted, long, white nyloned legs attached to tight little asses haunted her. Julie knew the nurses at U.K. would love to get their hands on Rob.

A woman knows when her man is finding pleasure between the legs of someone else. She does not require an intercepted phone call, a strange pair of panties, or scratches on her man's back. She doesn't need to find different colored hair in all the wrong places, phone numbers in pockets or dried semen on shirttails to tell her. Her man will admit his unfaithfulness by failing to call, by not coming to see her and worst of all, by lying. Rob called Julie often and on each occasion, he told her he missed her and would be coming to see her soon. Never did he tell Julie he loved her and only once, two months following their separation, did Rob come to see her. On two occasions following Rob's visit, Julie had excitedly told Rob of her intention to come to Lexington. He could never quite find the time to see her.

"Julie, you know how much I miss you and want to see you, but they are working me to death down here. It's work twenty-four hours, sleep six, and then do another twenty-four. You know how it is. When I do get a day off, all I want to do is sleep. Thanksgiving's coming surely they'll let us see each other then."

It would be two years before that occurred, long after the phone calls ceased and the promises of tender reunions faded. Only then would they see each other again at the Holiday on Ice show in Indianapolis on October thirty-first, 1963.

CHAPTER TWENTY-ONE:
THE ROUND TABLE

Neil Armstrong, mashed potatoes with chicken gravy, Donna Reed, cut worms, warts, coleslaw, Hollywood Henderson, cutting Viagra pills into four pieces (so you can at least stop peeing on your shoes) fortune cookies, fat free potato chips, Old Spice, atomic clocks, Newfoundland dogs, Benny Hill, Carol King, chain saws, DVD players, Readers Digest, wicker furniture, the smell of cat urine, obesity, the sacred area between a woman's ass and her vagina. Ben-Gay, and Doppler radar were only a few of the topics that were discussed in August, 2000.

"Tattoos and body piercing," said Bill. "What is with that? I passed a strip mall in Terre Haute with that sign in front and I wanted to stop and suggest to them that they change it to read: Your one-stop self-mutilation store."

"A tattoo on a woman's leg of a butterfly, or a rose on her back, is very sensuous," Red volunteered.

"I don't disagree," said Pres, "but it's really out of hand. I have seen photos on the internet of women with hands tattooed on their breasts and one woman had Al Pacino tattooed on her ass so that she could always sit on his face.

"I read a story on the internet about this woman who had a stud in her tongue and lightning struck it," Red said.

"Goddamn it, Red," said Doc, "You can't believe that internet shit. Anybody can put anything on there they want. I could write an article about how you can painlessly cut your balls off using only scissors and duct tape and some damn transsexual wannabe will believe it."

Red's feelings were hurt. Being in the company of educated men every morning was a privilege he cherished. Each evening, he would tell Debbie of his contributions to the breakfast conversations, never failing to embellish his part in the tale-telling and knowledge sharing that were as much a part of his breakfast as the cigarettes and eggs.

"It was on the BBC," Red replied importantly. "The lightning bounced off a bridge and hit her in the face. She ended up with blisters on her mouth, and feet and she couldn't speak for three days."

"Look Red," Pres said patiently, "I suppose it could have happened, but why hasn't lightning struck any of the men or women who wear earrings, or navel rings or genital rings, for Christ's sake? That would make a better story. Woman's labia welded shut by melted iron."

"I am getting bodies of people with rings in the god-damnedest places," said Bill Walsh, "I had an uncircumcised old man who had one through the tip of his foreskin. Wouldn't that cause an infection if he pissed into his incision?"

"Probably not," said Doc. "A healthy person's urine contains no harmful substances. As a matter of fact, primitive women used to pee on their children to cleanse them. Childbirth can be a pretty messy and unsanitary business and urine was used by Eve and a lot of women who came after her, to clean up their blood and waste-sodden newborn."

"After telling you that," Doc continued, "I doubt if any of you want to be given a short history of body piercing which I just happened to learn when I took a course in anthropology."

"Why the fuck would you pay money to learn about that perverted shit?" asked Red, clearly astonished.

"Go ahead and educate us," said Pres. "I wonder why I order runny eggs. Every goddamn day one of you repulsive bastards will bring up some topic that will make the egg-slime resemble placentas or semen or puss, and how and why would you remember crap like that?"

"Well," said Doc, obviously delighted by the reaction, "in the first place, Red my boy, it might help you know that there are other things in this world than women's bodies or expired driver's licenses. As for you my lawyer friend, can you imagine the courage it must have taken for that first man to wipe the shit off the shell that came out of a chicken's ass. And to then crack it and suck the mucus it contained. If you get nauseous listening to tales of afterbirth, you have never been really hungry and maybe you should have Clarice hard-boil your eggs from here on in. You remember all the words and music to 'Splish Splash I was taking a bath', Why does it surprise you that I remembered something important?"

"Look, Doc," Bill Walsh said, "I realize that these other two under-educated assholes don't care to listen about why I am hearing tales from my fellow merchants of death about nose, nipple, penis, tongue and pussy rings, but I am, and besides I've got to get Buddy Willis ready for viewing."

"What happened to Buddy?" asked Pres.

"He fucking died," answered Bill. "What would I be doing with him unless he was ready for eternity? You know it's not that life is so short, it's that death is so long."

"You know what, Bill?" Pres replied, "Sometimes I think you took smart-ass lessons. If it wasn't for Enid, most of us would have stomped the shit out of you long ago."

"Body piercing started about 5,000 years ago," Doc began as if he had never been interrupted. "Kids today are not doing anything new. First it was the ears, and then the nose. The Nez Perce Indians who saved Lewis and Clark's asses got their name from the French words which meant, 'nose pierced.' I don't remember much about lip piercing except pictures I saw as a kid of African women who had these enormous lips. These were all done to enhance the appearance. So was the Prince Albert piercing."

"The what?" asked Red.

"Prince Albert was the husband of Queen Victoria of England," Doc replied. "Men wore extremely tight pants back then and your cock had to be held on one side or another so it wouldn't repulse the fairer sex by bulging in the middle of the pants in an unsightly manner. To correct this problem, Prince Albert and many noblemen of the era had their foreskins pierced to allow their dicks to hang on a hook on the inside of their trousers."

"You've got to be shitting me," said Red. "What would you do if your dick was on a hook and you started to get a hard-on?"

The mike on Red's shoulder squawked at him in a language incomprehensible to anyone not in the business of law enforcement. The female voice on the other end droned in a disinterested monotone. "One, four, twelve, this is one, eight, twenty-two. We have a fourteen hundred approaching on two five zero. Do you copy?"

"Fucking bicycle riders," Red said to the table as he rose to leave. "No offense Pres, but you people disrupt traffic and aggravate the local rednecks when they have to slow down to pass six or seven hundred of you. There's just something about people having a good time that pisses off people in their pick-ups trying to make a living. We get these bike groups that come through here eight or nine times a year and I have to guard them like a shepherd does sheep, to make sure road rage fueled by Budweiser doesn't tempt Billy Bob Joe into sending a Schwinn to the promised-land. "

August in southern Indiana is the cruelest month. Farmers' dreams of profit are often doomed by the cracks that appear like so many z's in the parched fields. The red lines in thermometers move up to the ninety-degree line by ten in the morning and do not stay there long, usually edging up to ninety-six or so by three in the afternoon. The darkest and the coolest hours are just before dawn; by four a.m., it is a frosty seventy-six degrees. Those unfortunate enough to be out in the heat of the day walk like mourners, shuffling heads down, trying to shield heads from the merciless summer sun.

It is the humidity that demoralizes and eviscerates. Fog envelopes all but the high ground in the evenings, turning into steam in the mornings. The slightest exertion opens pores that soak clothing with stink no deodorant can mask. The fastidious, of whom there were few in Paris Crossing, bathed two or three times a day. The rest, knowing that when everyone smelled bad no one could distinguish his stench from that of his friend or spouse, bathed only once or less a day. What was the point?

Tempers flared. God was cursed, and the revivalist preachers, smelling the blood of the lamb, began to pitch their tents. They seemed to appear out of nowhere. There had not been a fervent, God-fearing gathering in North Vernon for months. No histrionics had been heard in Louisville or Madison since August of the preceding year. The tents seemed to appear everywhere at once and the fervent prayers punctuated by "Hallelujah" and "Praise Jesus" filled the evening air of every hamlet, city and crossroads. Pres claimed that the same men and occasional woman spent their winters selling orange cleaners on television or Mazdas on big city car lots. "When they pass the plate, do you have any idea where the money goes?" Pres asked. "I'm sure that a few aren't charlatans, but my guess is that most of them line their silk pockets with nickels for Jesus."

August was also fair time. The local newspapers featured pictures of pigs and fair queens, and you could usually distinguish one from the other. "Doesn't Four-H stand for head, heart, hands and hogs?" Bill Walsh asked. Homes that were unlocked most of the year had their doors securely bolted during fair season when the carnival workers arrived. They were an odd lot. The men appeared to have stepped out of the pages of a Steinbeck novel. The women had big hair and bigger breasts and were frequent patrons of the Parley Vous where they could smoke with impunity. Clarice thought they were disgusting and she loudly complained about the lipstick stains left by the carnival women on cups, spoons, and the filters of their discarded cigarettes.

The bicycles which had begun to appear in small numbers during the first warm days of spring, now passed through Paris Crossing in ever-increasing numbers. It seldom rains in August and fall semesters have yet to begin. The people who organize cross-country bicycle trips recognize August's advantages and schedule more trips during the month than at any other time of the year and so the cyclists flock to the back roads of southern Indiana in August.

Although Paris Crossing is not on any major cross country route, cyclists from Indianapolis, South Bend, Fort Wayne and Chicago, seeking a rural experience, often passed through on the way to the challenging descents and climbs into and out of the Ohio River valley. The local pedestrians would view both bike and owner with benevolent amusement. "Where did you start from?" and "Where are you going?" the locals would inquire, cigarettes in hand. "You mean you've already biked twenty miles and you're going to go another forty in this heat?" they would marvel, shaking their heads at the foolishness of it all.

The modern bicycle is sleek and energy efficient, the really good ones are costly. If you have the money, Trek will gladly build you the same bike Lance Armstrong rides. In this, cycling is unique. You could buy Tiger Woods' clubs but you would probably find it difficult to use them. You could buy Jeff Gordon's stock car, but where would you race it? Armstrong's bike, on the other hand, could be ridden by anyone almost anywhere with none of the difficulty an amateur would encounter trying to use Tiger's equipment. In fact, riding Lance's bike would likely improve the performance of even the sorriest cyclist.

Cliff Noble owned a Trek. Although it was not as sophisticated as Armstrong's, Cliff's bike contained many of the same components. It was a brand new twenty-two hundred alpha series which Cliff had purchased two months before he embarked on the week long, five-hundred mile trip which would take him through Paris Crossing. Cliff's wife and teenage girls were thrilled by his decision to get his sedentary, over-sized ass off of his Lazy-Boy (aren't they well named?) and on to the narrow arrow that passes itself off as a bicycle seat on a road bike. Cliff was forty-five and fat, but he wanted desperately to be slim, to want his wife and girls to be proud of him, and to be proud of himself again. He had trained for two months for this trip and he had lost twelve pounds, but when the trip began, only his balls, the cord running back to his ass, and his asshole itself fit upon the seat. His cock was in a knot forward of the arrow and the left and right sides of his ass were hams suspended in air, each rising and falling in rhythm seeking purchase on the minuscule bicycle seat. Great pools of sweat collected, chaffing his scrotum and his rectum. The pressure upon his genitals and prostate created a condition known by bikers as "numb dick," not to be confused with "limp dick," which is a problem usually cured by pharmaceuticals or the genital caress of a loving woman.

Before starting out that morning, Cliff had wisely hydrated by drinking nearly a quart and a half of water. The theory is that you will not have to urinate no matter how much water you consume on days when the heat is extreme, because you will lose the water through your pores. God knows Cliff had sweat buckets. By 10:30 in the morning, his Polo top and padded Cannondale shorts were sodden. The top dried in the breeze generated by Cliff's pedals, but the shorts stayed wet and the rash that was at first a minor irritant mutated into flesh that felt as if it had been flayed with whips and rubbed with salt. Cliff had to stop every five miles for a few minutes, dismounting from a bicycle seat he knew had been designed by the Marquis de Sade, to pull his wet shorts away from his pitiful ass. Trying always to be cool, Cliff pretended he had stopped only for a drink from one of the three water bottles he had attached to his bike, so the riders that passed him by would not suspect he was dying from a terminal case of red ass.

Worse than the pain, was the fear of failure. His wife and kids were so proud of him for going on his great bicycle adventure. He knew that they were planning a hero's welcome for him when he came home after completing the seven-day, five-hundred mile trip.   Cliff also knew that his wife would reward him with open legs in lieu of a medal, and that was one treat Cliff did not want to miss.   "I am so proud of my big, strong lover," he imagined her saying as she wrapped her legs around him and showered his face with sloppy, passionate kisses.

The most urgent thing confronting Cliff as he neared Paris Crossing was his need to pee.   The air temperature was eighty-seven degrees.   On the black-top it was close to a hundred.   In the corn, standing tall as a man, it was one hundred fifty degrees.   The rows were planted close to each other.   Dense vegetation absorbs sunlight and breathes it back into the environment, creating intense heat.   None of this was known to Cliff as he viewed the corn.   Nothing else seemed to offer a modest man a place to pee in privacy. Seeing a gap in a row, Cliff put his bike down by the side of the road and headed for the corn.

Red had been asked by the sheriff, who had been asked by the Indiana State Police, to take special care of this group of bikers. It seemed that the governor's daughter and oldest grandson were among the group of two hundred who would be passing through Paris Crossing.   Pre-arrangements had been made so that the "special package," as the State Police put it, could be easily identified. The progeny of the highest ranking official in the State of Indiana had bike jerseys with basketballs on them, a different color for every day.   The governor's daughter had wanted tops emblazoned with the State seal or a cardinal, the State bird.   She was quickly overruled by her father who feared that both emblems would make her and his grandson, his precious Bubba, too visible and too vulnerable.   The governor did not want Bubba, exposed to the jeers and missiles of the Southern Indiana crackpots who had never voted for Bubba's grandfather.

Red was driving a county highway truck. Its bed contained bananas, energy bars, Fig Newtons, potato chips, Gatorade and three five-gallon jugs of ice and water. Pres had helped Red stock provisions for the bikers, vetoing Twinkies and hot dogs. "Why potato chips?" asked Red. "Some of these people will have over-hydrated enough to wash the salt down to dangerous levels." Pres replied. "You combine that with sweat depletion and you're looking at a serious problem. Organs start to shut down. Our bodies need salt. Potato chips are otherwise nutritionally worthless, but they are a great way to give us a salt fix."

Red could not help but admire the body of the governor's daughter. Biker's clothing is more designed to protect than enhance. As a matter of fact, most of the attire appears to have been designed by geeks for geeks. Good looking women somehow manage to escape from the confines of their attire and look wonderful in overalls or mud wrestling arenas. The first daughter's legs were long and muscular and her padded shorts rounded her perfect ass. Red spotted her as she entered Jennings County and he was determined to watch her bottom as it lifted and fell and tilted right to left until she left his jurisdiction. "I love my job," thought Red to himself.

There were six state policemen on the trip guarding Bubba and the governor's daughter. They occupied a Cadillac Escalade. The armed men trailed along closely behind their charges. Bubba would tire early and his little bike would be ridden by the cop who had lost the coin toss. The theory was that the cop on the bike would ride next to the first daughter and take a bullet for her if that became necessary. The seat on Bubba's bike would be raised, and the designated cop would try desperately to stay up with his strong-legged protectee. To her credit, the governor's daughter wanted nothing to do with her bodyguard and so the policeman on the boy's bike would fall behind, knees rising to chin level as he tried desperately to maintain dignity under ludicrous conditions.

Red was in his patrol car, just in front of the Escalade and only a few yards back of the magnificent ass of the governor's daughter, when he saw someone entering the corn about a mile in front of him. Red turned on his light and his siren. Rural policemen have an intimate, almost sexual relationship with their lights and their sirens. Viagra was never needed following a chase or an arrest.

The bikers scattered and the Escalade hastened to follow the patrol car. The unfortunate cop on Bubba's bike commandeered a pick-up. The state police, convinced that Red had detected some threat to the governor's family, drew their guns and ran after Red as he entered the corn field.

Cliff had fallen to his knees and was apparently unconscious. He also had a death grip on his dick. Red saw nothing but a man near death from hyperthermia. Using his enormous strength, Red draped Cliff over his shoulders, and carried the unfortunate biker out of the suffocating inferno. The guns of the state police were quickly holstered and replaced by cameras as Red emerged from the corn carrying a man who appeared to be trying to piss in Red's ear.

Red gently lowered Cliff to the ground and hurried to the bed of the county highway truck. Lifting one of the five-gallon buckets of ice and water, Red returned to the stricken biker and poured the half-frozen mixture on Cliff's head, neck and torso. Cliff quickly revived. He would finish the tour.

Red was not aware of the cameras flashing as he emerged from the corn, nor was he aware of the proximity of Cliff's dick to the entrance of his ear canal. Pride surged through Red as he thought of the impression his heroics would make on Debbie. Their relationship had been suffering. She had even, in a way, questioned his manhood. This would show Debbie what kind of a man she married, thought Red.

CHAPTER TWENTY-THREE:
DEBBIE COX

The Hoosier Dome was not big enough to contain the joy and elation Debbie felt when she learned she was pregnant. She and Red had never practiced birth control and it had been nearly seven years to the day since they had first started having sex. Debbie said she knew exactly when conception occurred, because she started vomiting while in the throes of one of her typical strong orgasms. "I knew something was different," she confided to Clarice. "A good come never made me sick before."

Clarice never knew what to make of Debbie. Clarice was in awe of her friend's sensuality. Clarice had been raped when she was just in her teens and she viewed sex with the wariness of an often beaten puppy. She longed to be cuddled, but she was frightened of the pain and repulsed by the mess. Debbie reveled in the exchange of bodily fluids.

For the first six months of her pregnancy, Debbie spent every waking hour either vomiting or thinking about vomiting. Wonderful smells of coffee brewing, bacon frying and perfume became putrid. It was as if her nose, which had never before betrayed her, had now acquired rancid sensors which overpowered those that detected pleasant smells. Thankfully sleep brought relief as did chocolate and making love to Red.

Debbie was on top and her eyes had rolled back into her head so far that only the whites showed. She was in the second month of her pregnancy and she and Red had made love nearly every night since she had conceived. Suddenly, while coming, Debbie's cheeks filled with the most of the box of chocolate covered cherries she had been consuming for the last ten hours. She attempted to turn her head and dismount, but

Red had other ideas. Unaware of Debbie's distress, and about to come himself, Red used one big arm to reseat Debbie and he used the other to turn her lips towards his for that blissful orgasmic kiss. Volcanic, projectile vomiting spewed from lips that Debbie had tried unsuccessfully to close. Cheeks can only hold so much and when they finally succumb, their surrender is complete.

Half-digested chocolate and maraschino cherries are not nearly as tasty the second time around. Mixed with stomach acids, they acquire a yellowish tinge and sulfuric smell when refluxed back into a burning esophagus. Debbie lowered her head in an attempt to spare Red as best she could, and he, sensing the onslaught, moved quickly enough to escape with only a few spatters on his neck and chest.

Red had not quite finished showering when he saw Debbie through the translucent door. "I'm almost done honey, " he said.

"Are you mad at me? " Debbie asked pathetically.

"No, " replied Red, genuinely meaning it.

"I know you didn't get to come, " Debbie said. "Do you want me to finish you off? "

Red opened the door. Debbie looked and smelled like a shit-stained waif. Red stepped aside Debbie entered the shower clutching the odiferous bedding about her. As Red watched, Debbie dropped the sheets and turned on the water, intending to wash both herself and the bedding. A wave of tenderness nearly brought him to his knees. "Darling, " Red said, "you need to get some rest. I'll come twice tomorrow. Where are the clean sheets?"

In spite of the morning sickness which seemed to last until the moon lost all its face, and the bloating, swelling, bleeding, and constant need to pee, Debbie was happier than she had ever been. She felt strangely creative, as if she knew she had a masterpiece in her womb. Debbie believed she and Red had made a baby who would be special. She would help her child become another Bach, Einstein, Margaret Thatcher or Elvis. Debbie started and finished hard books such as Silas Marner, Moby Dick and Heart of Darkness. She had always been a voracious reader, but her taste had been confined to novels of romance and mystery. She wanted to be smarter. She wanted her body to absorb knowledge and through osmosis, impart what she was learning into the formative brain of the special child inside her. Red wanted a football player or a prom queen. Debbie wanted an artist who would become a university president and later be elected to the United States Senate. She would give birth to a nine-and-one-half pound beautiful girl whom she named Edna, after Edna St. Vincent Millet.

Edna was three when Red heroically emerged from the corn. Two days before Red saved the life of the beleaguered bicyclist, he and Debbie were in the male-superior position. Red was only seconds from coming when Debbie roughly inserted an index finger into his anus. Red's climax was delayed as Debbie searched for his prostate. When she found it, Red's response was intense. Wave after wave of pleasure poured out of his penis. Without speaking a word, Red stalked out of the bedroom and into the shower. He did not emerge for nearly an hour. Debbie was asleep when Red dropped heavily into bed, making noises intended to awaken Debbie and provoke an argument. Debbie lay stiff and silent although she had been fully awakened by Red's sighs and his bed turns from right to left and back again. Finally Red spoke, "Don't you ever do that to me again."
"OK," Debbie replied. "Good night."

Red was seething. "Only queers do things like that and I'm no goddamn queer."

"OK," Debbie replied again. "I'm sorry if I offended you. Good night, for Christ's sake."

Red was silent for a moment and then he erupted. "Did you do that because you think I'm a fag? Where do you come up with such things? Have you done that to other men? Did you go to bed with queers before you married me?"

Debbie reached for her night stand and picked up Steinbach's Grapes of Wrath. She had continued reading classics hoping to be able to converse with Edna about literature in the very near future. Tonight, however, she was more grateful for the book's heft than its content as she brought it down forcefully upon the left side of Red's head. It was the first time either of them had struck the other and it stunned them both. "Holy shit," Red said.

"Have I got your attention, sweetie?" Debbie said. "I certainly hope so because you need to listen very carefully. Am I too much woman for you? Are you man enough for me? These are two very important questions I'm going to be thinking about in the next few days. Sometimes I think I married a little boy. Now be honest with me. Our future depends on it. Did you enjoy my little digital intrusion?"

"You can't understand," Red whined. "Men have to be men."

"Answer my question," Debbie commanded. "Be a man. Do you think I'm going to go around telling everyone I know about how big Red likes it up his ass? Don't you trust me? Don't you know that nothing the two of us do willingly is perverted or queer? Look closely, darling," Debbie said pulling the sheets off her body. "Don't see a dick, do you? What are you afraid of, you big baby?"

"Yes," Red whispered.

"Yes what?" Debbie demanded.

"Yes it felt good," Red stammered.

"Well guess what," Debbie replied. "There may be hope for us yet, but there's one more thing you brought up that needs to be discussed. Your little remark about my going to bed with other men, homosexuals even, did not go unnoticed. Have I ever asked you about the women you bedded before we were married?"

"No," Red replied quietly, sensing the importance of this exchange, wishing he had kept silent.

"First of all," Debbie said, still angry, "nothing I did before we were married is any of your goddamn business. I am a one-man woman. I have never been unfaithful to you. I will never be unfaithful to you and if that's not enough for you that's just too fucking bad. I will tell you that I never stuck a finger up a man's ass before and apparently I'll never do it again; now goodnight."

Debbie, exhausted by the confrontation, fell quickly asleep. Red awakened her a few minutes later saying, "I guess maybe you could do that again sometime."

Debbie was only half awake when she muttered, "Goddamn it, Red, I'm trying to sleep. It's one thirty. Stick it up your ass."

CHAPTER TWENTY-FOUR:
THE RESTAURANT

Dolly needed a gimmick to resurrect the "Parley Vous." She had considered everything. She could prepare Mexican food and she thought of renaming the restaurant, "Dolly's Hot Tamale." She was also pretty good at cooking Chinese and "Dolly's Rice So Nice" became a possibility. Shamelessly, she even considered combining both cooking cultures and calling the restaurant "Delores Wong's."

Dolly and Pres had taken a long Sunday morning bike ride to eat breakfast at a Bob Evans in Scottsburg. When they asked to sit in the smoking section, they were politely told that there was none. Their waitress told them that the owner had emphysema and he was blaming cigarettes. "He couldn't even come into his own restaurant," she explained.

Soon thereafter, most of the fast food chains banned smoking in their establishments. Dolly had found her niche. Signs appeared and a newspaper ad trumpeted that the Parley Vous was a place where you could still have a cigarette with your cup of coffee. Dolly stopped serving an evening meal and concentrated on breakfast and lunch. The profits soared. Any restaurateur will tell you that the first two meals of the day are where the real money is made. It doesn't cost much to buy eggs, to brew coffee and make toast. Hamburger, buns and potatoes for french fries are also relatively inexpensive compared to the prices people will pay for them. Dolly was not in the restaurant business for the money. Pres had helped her invest wisely. She was worth over a million dollars. But she did need the social contact. As a matter of fact, Dolly was lonely. In addition, she was beginning to dislike her future. Each morning, she would eavesdrop on the conversations the three educated men and Red would have and Dolly would lust after knowledge. In addition, she began to lust after Pres. Their bike rides became more frequent.

Pres was working on a new song and he sang the chorus to Dolly as they crested the long hill near Midway.

"Whiskey and women have robbed me of my wealth.
Women and whiskey have stolen my health.
I'll die before I'm forty and I'll burn for my sins.
But the saddest thing of all is that I'd do it again."

Pres stopped singing and he and Dolly paused for a cigarette in the shade of an enormous catalpa tree that stood near the beginning of the long driveway that led to the Porter home. This was a familiar spot to most of the bikers who came through the area. The hilltop was a place to relax for a moment and the big tree offered enough shade to cool a dozen or more cyclists when the large groups came through.

"Clarice has a crush on you," Dolly said.

"What is there, a thirty year age difference?" asked Pres bemusedly.

"I didn't say it was serious," Dolly said. "But I can see the attraction. You're a nice man and you like women. That's quite a switch for Clarice. You're still in love with Marie, aren't you?"

Pres paused before answering. It was late August and he could hear the catalpa worms chewing as hundreds of them feasted on the large leaves overhead. The worms were ugly and black when they first began to perform their yearly ritual, then the chlorophyll in the leaves turned them ugly and green. The worms would strip the trees bare, eating until they were too fat to stay aloft. They would then drop to the ground where they would be harvested by cuckoos and bass fishermen.

"My nephew Harold turned orange from overeating carrots when he was a youngster," Pres mused aloud, thinking of the catalpa worms.

"You are the strangest man I've ever met," Dolly said.
Pres seemed surprised by Dolly's remark.

"You don't believe me?" Pres said. "Take a look at your urine the next time you eat asparagus."

"You are so full of shit," Dolly replied. "I don't know why I put up with you."

"I don't know if I am or not," Pres said finally, answering Dolly's question. "It's been ten years since I've seen her."

"Have you been faithful to her?" Dolly asked.

"Are you making a pass at me?" Pres asked.

"Mount up, asshole," Dolly grinned, throwing her right leg over her bike. As she pedaled away, she thought that she could probably fall in love with the lawyer, but she treasured their relationship too much to endanger it. "I might sleep with him, though," she said to herself, picking up the pace as if she needed to get some distance between herself and her sexuality.

The day after Clarice went away to college, Dolly put a "For Sale" sign in front of the restaurant. She wanted to go to college. She wanted to be smart.

Dolly also felt loyal to the town that had been good to her. Most of all, Dolly wanted to preserve her restaurant. She wanted it to continue to be the gathering place for the community. She wanted her "old men" to have a place to go. There were inquiries, but most were about the apartment upstairs. Four months passed with no offers when Troy Roberts, Jennings County's eternal stud, reappeared.

"Dolly, I'm going to do you a favor," Troy said smugly, his eyes focusing on Dolly's breasts. "I've got a buyer for this place if you're willing to sell it on contract."

Pres was unimpressed with Troy's proposal when Dolly asked for the lawyer's advice. "Dolly, this place is worth more than that, and the down payment is far too small. At this rate, it will take the buyer twenty years to pay you off. You do what you want to do, but this is not a good deal. By the way, who's the buyer?"

Dolly tried to avoid going on the defensive. She had sought Pres's advice and she had known in advance that he would not approve of the terms of sale. Nonetheless, Dolly badly wanted to sell the restaurant and she began the explanation she had been rehearsing for hours.

"The buyer is a young guy from Columbus who has been running the restaurant at the Marathon for the last two years. Troy tells me that this guy can cook and wants a chance to have his own place. I met him. His name is Jimmy Fountain."

"Troy is a scumbag. When he dies, his wife will have to pay pallbearers to carry his sorry ass," Pres vehemently replied. "Don't do it, Dolly."

Dolly was silent for nearly a full minute. When she did speak, her eyes gripped Pres's eyes, daring the lawyer to look anywhere but directly at her. "In case you haven't noticed, my clientele isn't getting any younger. We started smoking because our parents smoked, our friends smoked, our movie star idols smoked. It was cool then. It's considered gauche and dumb now. I care about you. I care about Doc. I care about Bill Walsh, I even care about our dumb ass deputy sheriff. I care about our little town, most of all though, I care about me. I want all of you to have a place to go. This buyer will keep the restaurant open for all of you and for Paris Crossing and I can go to college without feeling like I have abandoned you. Is that understandable?"

For once in his life, Pres was unable to think of anything to say.

CHAPTER TWENTY-FIVE:
RED'S THOUGHTS ABOUT DEBBIE

"I really do love her. I wish she would shave under her arms more often. She thinks she's smarter than me. Her breasts are starting to sag. She can't drive worth a shit. How many men did she sleep with before she married me? She is so hot. I wish she wasn't so hot. I am so lucky that she is so hot. Do I satisfy her? Did her other lovers satisfy her better than me? She is a really good mother. I am surprised that she is a really good mother. I hate the rock music that she plays on the radio. Why does she have to dress like a slut or a farmer all the time? Does she even own a sensible blouse and skirt outfit? Doesn't she know that other men are looking at her? You would think she'd start dressing like Clarice. Doesn't she realize that she's a mother? I wish she'd put her Tampax in the garbage can outside. She is not a very good cook. She is too hard on Edna. She is letting Edna rule this place. She is spoiling Edna. I want to fuck Debbie all the time. I don't want it as much as she does. She never says excuse me when she farts or belches. I'd put the toilet seat down after I pee, if she would put it up after she sat on it. Why can't she crap without a magazine and a cigarette? Doesn't she know that shit and tobacco combined smell like burning assholes? Doesn't she know that I'm going to be the next person to follow her into the bathroom? Doesn't she care? Does she love me? Nice girls don't act like she does in the bedroom. I don't think I married a nice girl. I'm too hard on Debbie. I get a hard-on just thinking about Debbie. I'm so jealous. I have nothing to be jealous about. I can't stop remembering that other men have fucked my wife. Maybe other men haven't fucked my wife. Why won't she talk about it? I don't want her to talk about it. I do want her to talk about it. I wish I would have married a virgin. Maybe, I did marry a virgin. Maybe, I'm the only man she has ever been with. Maybe, all her talk and whorish behavior in bed are only because I turn her on. Maybe the Pope is Jewish and Lassie is a Vietnamese pot-bellied pig.

DEBBIE'S THOUGHTS ABOUT RED

"I really do love him. He's too fat. He smokes too much. I wish he'd pay more attention to the impression he makes on other people. He comes across as an overweight Barney Fife. He should argue with me more. He shouldn't let me have my way so often. He is such a good man. I should be happy that he's my husband. I'm not happy at all. I hate this little hick town. Red could easily be a state cop. He has no ambition. He will live here for the rest of his life. This is not such a bad place to live. The people are nice enough. It is a wonderful place to raise Edna. Why do I want to make love so much? I want it more than Red does. He almost seems relieved when I'm on my period. He is a good lover. I wish he would take the initiative more often. If he had his way, he would always be on top. I've certainly taught him a thing or two or a thousand. The problem is that I make him jealous whenever we do anything that is not just a simple screw. I don't know what to do about that. Why can't he understand that I couldn't be unfaithful to him if I hadn't even met him? He should have married a virgin. The two of them would do man on top every Saturday after Lawrence Welk. He should have married Clarice.

Heddy Lamar, the Spruce Goose, Listerine, Jerry Lee Lewis, Homer, Arnold Palmer, wisteria, bandanas, fortune cookies, helium, gypsies, the Fox television network, Rapunzel, Dick Clark, the Righteous Brothers, LaBoheme, Oscar De La Hoya, Pat Conroy, Sonny Liston, Dick Trickle and the Palmer House were just a few of the topics discussed in September, 2000, as the men at the table were joined one day by Marvin Hinkle, the high school band teacher from North Vernon. Pres has been praising the rock group "Queen."

"I agree with Pres," said Marvin. "Just look at the effect "Queen" has had on sports music. Before Queen came along, the sports world musicians would play the same old shit, most of which would sound like the themes from Michigan or Notre Dame. My pep band plays three Queen songs: "We are the Champions," "Another One Bites the Dust," and the ubiquitous "We Will Rock You." We are not the only ones. Go to any sporting event in America where there's music whether it's canned, live or a goddamned organ, and I'll bet you money, marbles or chalk that you'll hear at least one Queen anthem."

"Not to mention the fact that Queen wrote and performed the greatest rock and roll song ever written," said Pres.

Marvin knew what was coming. It was not the first time he and Pres had talked about Queen. "Pres, I do not know how you can call 'Bohemian Rapsody' a rock and roll song," the music teacher said. "Use American Bandstand's definition; it hasn't got a great beat and you can't dance to it. It may be brilliant. It certainly is different; but it ain't rock and roll."

"I know, it's only rock and roll but I like it," Pres sang, ignoring the music teacher's comments. "The Stones had so many great rock and roll lines."

"What about Gordon Lightfoot?" Red asked.

"Gordon Lightfoot? When did he ever write a rock and roll song?" Pres asked condescendingly.

"Why, you hypocritical snot," Marvin said to Pres.

Red spoke, rather than sang, one perfect, haunting stanza from "The Ballad of the Edmond Fitgerald."

"Does anyone know where the love of God goes?
When the wind turns the minutes to hours?
Now all that remains are the faces and the names
of the wives and the sons and the daughters."

The table turned silent. "That's poetry," Doc said.
"Most good songs are poems set to music," Marvin said. "A cigarette that bears lipstick's traces. An airline ticket to romantic places."

"That must be really old," said Red.

"I had a class in college entitled 'Love, loyalty and loneliness', said Marvin. "It was about the songs that came out of World War Two. 'These Foolish Things' was one of them. 'I'll Be Seeing You' was another. These songs contained poetry. The vocals were mostly done by females and you can hear the heartbreak in them as the women try to deal with the uncertainty of wartime, and the realization that their young husbands might never return."

"You'll never know just how much I love you," Pres began to sing.

"You'll never know just how much I care."

Clarice came out from the back and the old men in the restaurant sat silently as Pres finished the haunting ballad.

"I'll be go to hell," Marvin said. "You can actually sing."

"Of course I can sing," Pres declared defensively. "I've been singing all my life."

"But not well," Marvin replied. "Like most men our age, you've been impersonating Elvis and your impression of the King sounds like he should have been called the jack or maybe the trey of clubs, but you did a good job on that incredible love song."

"I want drugs. I need drugs. I love drugs," Pres began singing and slaughtering the Elvis standard.

"Enough," Marvin interrupted. "If Kermit the frog had been born in Mississippi, you would have his voice down pat. Goodbye gentlemen. I have a band to inspire," Marvin said, rising from his chair.

Clarice went back to the kitchen, but not before she kissed Pres on the forehead. "You have a beautiful voice, sweetheart," she said.

"Don't call me sweetheart unless you mean it," Pres said, smiling.

"What makes you think I don't mean it, darling?" said Clarice with a smile of her own as she looked back over her shoulder, tossing her hair in a feminine gesture that was foreign to the men in the restaurant.

"What in the fuck was that all about?" asked a stunned Red.

"Well, it was obviously not about your sorry ass," said Doc. "If I didn't know better, I would guess that the snow queen has the hots for Pres. Bless her heart, I think Clarice is horny.

Red was horrified.

CHAPTER TWENTY-SEVEN:
JIMMY FOUNTAIN

Everyone liked Jimmy Fountain. His parents worked a small acreage farm owned by Purdue University. They grew corn and beans in the summer and raised hogs year round. Jimmy was their only child. In most farm families, the male children joined their father in the fields at an early age. The girls stayed in the house with their mother and learned to cook for their men.

Melody Fountain was not your ordinary farm wife. She and Al had been married for a little over a year when Jimmy was born. Melody was on a tractor when she went into labor. She was back in the fields two days after she gave birth to nine-pound Jimmy. Melody loved farming, and she was not about to give it up to become a full time mother. When he was an infant, Jimmy was taken to his grandmother's house every morning at seven and returned home around six every evening. Warm plates containing marvelous combinations such as chicken and dressing, sausage gravy and biscuits, Salisbury steak and mashed potatoes, and cornbread and beans accompanied the young farmer's son when he returned home every evening to his loving and affectionate parents.

Grandma Grace was something of a local character. She had never been married and no one in Bartholomew Count had any idea as to the identity of Melody's father, although everyone knew that Grace was well off. She did not give birth until she was thirty-six. She had been a television local celebrity and seller of used cars. An attractive woman, Grace had posed for Playboy. "Women of the Midwest" was the title of the pictorial. Grace was on page seventy-seven where she proudly and defiantly bared her breasts. Most gas stations and barber shops within one hundred miles of Columbus prominently displayed Grace between the bank calendar and the Indiana basketball schedule. Grace's breasts were off-center and faced a little left and right instead of forward. The smiling visage of Isaiah Thomas on one side and a leering, arctic fox on the other looked sideways toward her turgid nipples.

Everything changed when Melody was born. Grace had given birth to her best friend. She had searched for attention, companionship and love and had found all three gestating inside her. When Melody married and moved five miles down the road, Grace went through some difficult times getting used to the emptiness inside of her heart and inside of her little house.

Melody did not get pregnant just to please her mother. While she was always a compliant, eager-to-please child, Melody's motives were selfish. Her husband could use another farm hand and when Jimmy was born, Al was ecstatic. He envisioned easier days and long winter trips with Melody to Fort Myers while their boy looked after the farm.

Jimmy followed Grace like a devoted dog. At first, the young boy feared abandonment when his parents left him with Grace. Jimmy had to have the only other adult he knew in sight and within arm's reach. For the first three weeks, Grace cleaned, did her laundry and cooked with Jimmy cradled in her left arm. His right hand grasped the sweatshirt Grace continuously wore and he would not release it until he napped beside her in her narrow bed.

Children are shallow, fickle and insecure for good reason. You never know when you are three or four if your favorite adult might vanish. If that occurs, you cling to what you have left. If you are abandoned again, you may never fully recover. Grandparents, uncles and aunts help soothe

the transition from parents to the uncaring environment of first grade.

Because he was small, and because that "hussy" Grace was his grandmother, Jimmy was treated contemptuously by his male counterparts. His teachers and the young girls of the first and second grades doted on him. He was smart and nice looking, which pissed off nearly every boy in Bartholomew County Elementary. Jimmy was jostled on the bus, teased hard in class and treated roughly on the playground. A favorite diversion for boys was to exchange blows to each other's shoulders. No matter how hard he tried, Jimmy could not deliver as much pain as he received. He would turn two or three times during the day to give one or other shoulder some relief. He would not cry or even flinch when the blows were struck, but by the end of each day, his arms would dangle as he ran home, unable to be raised beyond lap level, barely high enough to eat. Even as an adult, Jimmy drank by lowering his head to his glass, barely raising his hands.

Because of his vulnerability, Jimmy was often placed in what passed for elementary school "protective custody." Instead of going out for recess, Jimmy spent his break time in the school building, free to roam as a trusted student. One day outside the principal's office, Jimmy overheard an elaborate plan to trap Hubie Crow into admitting that he was behind the scheme that spread horseshit over the front porch of the school's most despised teacher. After school Jimmy caught up with Hubie, a five-foot eleven-inch, two hundred fifteen pound giant, who had spent eight years just getting to fourth grade. Hubie was surrounded by adoring sycophants, who craved attention from their fearless classmate. Over the last three years, Hubie was rumored to have stopped up the school toilets, placed several pigs in different classrooms overnight, and last, in an act of genius, ignited a bag of horseshit which he had placed on algebra teacher Homer Craft's front porch. After ringing the doorbell, someone (Hubie?) yelled "Fire" and the unfortunate Mr. Craft had tried to put out the lighter fluid ignited blaze by stomping on it with his slippered feet. Shit flew everywhere, to the delight of the twenty or so junior and high schoolers crouched in the shadows.

"Hubie," Jimmy said in a voice almost too small to hear. "Hubie," Jimmy repeated, "I heard something I think you should know." Dick Frist, the main member of Hubie's entourage, swung a roundhouse right toward Jimmy's swollen shoulder. Before the blow could fall, Hubie struck Dick in the back and Dick ended up swinging through air before landing on his ass.

"What have you got for me, short stuff?" Hubie asked, picking Jimmy up so that their faces were inches apart. Jimmy's heart raced. Hubie had never bothered him. A true bully picks on those smaller than he. Hubie delighted in beating the piss out of juniors and seniors, especially those who represented the institution he despised. Football players, basketball heroes and class officers gave the belligerent, blood-lusting, fearless fourth-grader a wide berth.

"Come up with an alibi for last Friday," Jimmy said in almost a whisper. His lungs had used every other particle of oxygen to keep up with his heart which was doing handstands, aerobic dancing and breast strokes.

"Get out of here, the rest of you," Hubie said to the faithful four who gathered up the sullen Dick Frist and reluctantly left knowing that they were only as important as their hero wanted them to be. Jimmy told Hubie of the plot the faculty had hatched. "Not that I'm saying you had anything to do with it," Jimmy said. "I just wanted to warn you that the principal and the superintendent are out to get you."

The alibi worked and Hubie again escaped unscathed. He remained in school for only two more years, but they were the happiest twenty-four months Jimmy had ever experienced, for the word was out. Hubie had made sure that everyone knew better than to ruffle a hair on the head of Jimmy Fountain. The unmolested Jimmy Fountain grew. It was as if his tormentors were forced to release the heavy hands which had pushed down on the top of his head. Unfettered from his cranial burdens, by the time Hubie quit coming to school, Jimmy was the tallest boy in his class. He was the center on his junior high basketball team. His folks could only attend a few of his games, but Grandma Grace came to every one. It would be the only year Jimmy would make the team. His enthusiasm and energy were his best qualities, but being athletic will never be as good as being an athlete. Jimmy stopped growing at five-foot eleven-and-a-half and the gifted boys on his team spurted past him.

Each evening during the school year, when his classes were over, Jimmy would spring across the railroad tracks that adjoined the south end of the school property and cross the state highway that ran in front of Grandma Grace's home. Once there, Jimmy and Grace began communicating in the common language of food. Children cannot speak on an adult level, and adults come across as pathetic imbeciles if they attempt to scale down their vocabularies and use the latest kid slang. Alternate languages are abundant and rewarding. Fishing, baseball, clothing, shoes, golf, hair, are all subjects that can vanquish the awkward gulfs and silences. Music and movies used to fit into the common language category, but the Beatles could not relate to Snoop Doggy and "An Officer and a

Gentleman" had nothing in common with "Dumb and Dumber".

"What are we going to fix tonight, Grandma?" Jimmy would ask as he burst through the door. Over the years, Jimmy had learned Grace's cooking methods by osmosis. The comfortable words in the vocabulary of food were soothing and reassuring, quail gravy, oven-browned potatoes, spaghetti and meatballs, and best of all for a southern Indiana boy, corn on the cob, locally pronounced "roastinears."

"Stuffed mangos," said Grace, stubbornly refusing to yield to the northerners who insisted that what she called mangos were really green peppers.

"Come over here," said Grace. "Look at those beauties." Grace had cut the tops off the peppers and scraped out the seeds and membranes from their insides. Seven big, fat green peppers were bobbing and weaving in boiling water. From one frying pan came the smell of whole hog sausage, and onions were frying in olive oil in another. Rice was boiling on the back burner and the oven was turned to three hundred fifty degrees.

"Open that can of tomato sauce over there darling, would you please?" Grace asked while she drained the grease from the sausage skillet. Jimmy watched intently while Grace added the cooked rice to the meat, then added the un-drained onions and topped the mixture with the tomato sauce. The wondrous smell of the garlic Grace had minced earlier was blended into the mixture, as were small amounts of cumin and chili powder.

"You need to add the spices last or their flavors will be absorbed and diminished. It's the same thing with the onion. If you fry it in meat grease, it will take the flavor of the meat and you might as well just be eating another quarter pound of stringy meat," Grace propounded as she

cooked. Jimmy was rapt, but he tried not to
let his Grandma know. He would pretend to
look out the window as she spoke. Sometimes
he would look at his shoes or the Wyeth print
of the kelp fisherman Grace incomprehensibly
had hung over her stove. Jimmy was going
through the "men do this and only women do
that" phase of his life with its often-
malignant repercussions. At age twelve, it
is better to be dead than to be thought of as
being feminine.

"Try not to chop onions," Grace
intoned. "Slice them thinly if you must.
Let them be themselves. God meant for us to
eat them raw and to have them make our
sinuses burn, our eyes tear and our pee smell
strong. They cleanse and purify."
Jimmy helped Grace hold the mango pot as she
used tongs to pull the green peppers out of
the boiling water. She carefully drained
each one and set them upright in a large
baking dish. Grace then filled each pepper
with the meat, rice and tomato mixture and
put them in the oven. "This will only need
to cook for forty five minutes," she said.
"Then we'll take it out, cover the peppers
with mozzarella and bake for twenty minutes
more. Now it's wine time, my boy."

Grace poured a large glass of Chianti
Classico for herself and a smaller glass for
her grandson. She then placed the glasses on
a round Coca-Cola tray and the two of them
moved into the living room in a ritual they
would repeat throughout the remaining days of
Jimmy's childhood. There were two easy
chairs in the room. They faced one another.
A small table was at the right side of one
chair and another table sat on the left side
of the other. On each table was a book.
Beside each table was a floor lamp. Jimmy
took his place in his chair as Grace placed
the small glass on the table next to Jimmy's
chair. Jimmy opened *Watership Down*. He was
on page thirty-seven. Grace disdained

bookmarks. "Reading requires memory. Without memory, each time you put down a book you would have to start at the beginning when you picked it up again," Grace had proclaimed. "Learning how to memorize is one of the side benefits of reading. If you can, remember the number of the last page you read."

There was no television in Grace's home. She read voraciously and feared the distraction. On her table was volume one of the Manchester classic, *The Last Lion: Winston Churchill*. Grace did not confine herself to great books. In fact, she would read anything that had a good-looking cover. Her Bartholomew County library card was swollen with different titles. Dozens of the little yellow cards were filled with irrelevant due dates as Grace returned nearly each book within two or three days. The Manchester book would be an exception. It was a daunting six hundred and eighty-four pages and it was about one of Grace's heroes. She paused after each page, not wanting the book to end too quickly. It took six days for her to complete.

Because he was the son of farmers, Jimmy's summer months were not filled with long days of leisure. While his city friends enjoyed pond fishing, baseball and Marco Polo, Jimmy and his parents would rise before dawn. He would feed the hogs and weed beans or sucker tobacco. Grace insisted that Jimmy help her prepare supper, so the hard work ended at four when Jimmy would watch and listen as his grandma prepared supper. Wine and a book always followed at five and Jimmy and Grace would deliver supper at six.

One August, two weeks before school was to start, Grace told Melody and Al that Jimmy needed a geography lesson. Grace claimed to be a direct descendent of Daniel Boone and she often invoked the name of her famous ancestor as an excuse for her wanderlust.

Grace wanted to drive to the west coast and back and she wanted her grandson along to educate and to keep her company.

Al protested at first. "Goddamn it Grace, I know he's yours in the winter but he's got hogs to take care of and machinery to help me get ready for harvest."

"Goddamn it yourself," Grace replied. "When was the last time you were out of Bartholomew County? When were you ever out of Bartholomew County? I'm giving your son a chance to see this great country of ours. You and Melody took care of things before Jimmy was born and you can do it again while Jimmy and I have ourselves a little fun. The child needs some time away from those fucking hogs."

"Grace," Al protested, "when are you going to start talking like a grandmother instead of a sailor?"

"When those fucking hogs sprout wings and fly," Grace replied.

CHAPTER TWENTY-EIGHT:
CHEESE SALAD SANDWICHES

Grace pulled off Interstate 57 at Cairo, Illinois. She wanted to show Jimmy where the Ohio River flowed into the Mississippi. Unfortunately the confluence is not easy to see and after an hour of trying to determine which water was what, Grace pulled over and told Jimmy to drive. She had been behind the wheel since six in the morning and her back had turned into a rebellious sore which no amount of seat adjusting could comfort. Jimmy was doubtful. "I'm only fifteen. I don't have a driver's license. I've never driven a car," he protested.

"You've been driving a tractor since you were ten. This is the same only easier," Grace said, pulling Jimmy out of the passenger seat and lowering it so that she was able to lie with her head nearly resting on the back seat. Jimmy reluctantly got behind the wheel. Grace closed her eyes. "We are on State Road 62. Take it to I-55 and go south on the interstate until you come to the rest area just this side of Arkansas. Pull over there and we will have lunch." The motor noise on her Ford Fairlane V-8 told her that the big engine was in gear and ready to roll. Within minutes, Grace was fast asleep.

Grace had prepared fourteen cheese salad sandwiches the morning before. The recipe was one of Jimmy's favorites. It called for sharp shredded cheddar cheese, sugar, pickle relish, diced hard-boiled eggs and lots of mayonnaise. Grace added a small amount of minced garlic and a couple of sprinkles of "Frank's Red Hot Sauce" and mixed all of the ingredients. She spread the mixture on poppy seed buns. They would have the sandwiches, together with the chips and colas Grace had bought at the Shell when she stopped to gas up just north of Marion, Illinois.

Grace was not just well off, she was downright wealthy. No one knew just how she had acquired her fortune. Rumor had it that she had sold her charms to the highest bidder. No one dared ask Grace herself. She was as intimidating as a linebacker with rabies.

Grace knew how to stay rich. Cheese salad sandwiches instead of Big Macs would save her plenty. God knew the gas for this trip was eating her alive.

Jimmy pulled into the rest stop filled with pride. His Grandma had cautioned him to drive no faster than sixty miles an hour. For a time, Jimmy heeded her admonition. Then traffic began to push. Semis filled his rear view mirror, urging him to do sixty-five, seventy or even eighty miles an hour. Jimmy sensed approval from the drivers of the big rigs as the powerful Ford responded to the increasing pressure being exerted by Jimmy's right foot. He still remained in the slow lane, uneasy about passing, but he kept up with the vehicle in front of him. He was a driver. He was an interstate driver. He was a man.

It was ninety degrees. Grace spotted a picnic table in the shade. She carried the picnic basket with the cheese salad sandwiches and napkins. Jimmy brought he paper sack with the chips and sodas. Grace had neglected to bring a cooler, so the Doctor Pepper was tepid and the sandwiches were melty warm. They were also delicious.

They hit Interstate 40 west of Memphis and took it across Arkansas until they got to Fort Smith. Grace was educating as she was driving. She spoke of Sam Walton. She told Jimmy about the bitter, state name pronunciation debate, and how nearly half of the populace wanted the state name to be pronounced "Are Kansas," and she spoke of her love for her friend "Babe" who was born in Fort Smith.

"Come in with me," Grace commanded as they pulled into a generic motel with a Denny's next door. "How much is your cheapest double room?" she asked the balding, semi-clean desk clerk. He fumbled through several sheets of paper before replying. "I could let you have one for thirty-five dollars, but it ain't got no color TV."

"That's too expensive," Grace replied. "Come on, Jimmy."

"How bout I let you have it for thirty?" the clerk said before Grace and Jimmy could make their exit.

"I'll pay twenty," Grace said, "but I want to look at it first. Give me the key."

"Look, lady," the clerk said, using his hand to brush hair that belonged on the left side of his head forward so that it partially covered his right eye. "I'm trying to make a living here. Twenty don't even pay for the air-conditioning in that room."
"Why didn't you tell me the room was air-conditioned?" Grace said, smiling. "I'll pay twenty-five provided it passes my inspection. Now may I please have the key?"

Over supper at Denny's, Grace asked, "Did I embarrass you?" While the room negotiations were going on, Jimmy had pretended to be engrossed by the post-card rack. "No, I mean I guess I was," Jimmy replied. "I felt sorry for that guy, even though he was a dork."

"Just remember, my dear grandson," Grace replied "this is America. We embrace capitalism. A fair price is what a buyer is willing to pay and what a seller is willing to take. We found that price. There is no shame in trying to reach an agreement that is fair to both parties. Are you going to eat the rest of that meat loaf?"

Grace sipped wine as she started Stephen Wright's wild and wonderful *Going Native*. Jimmy stared at the television, too tired to read. Both were in their beds and by nine, both were asleep. Jimmy awakened once near three in the morning to pee. Briefly, he thought of the cheese salad sandwiches. They had been in the car all day and most of the night. The heat had not lessened. Neither of them had thought to refrigerate or even bring the sandwiches into the air conditioned room. Grandma Grace's wonderful cheese salad marvels would be spoiled by now.

The "Welcome to Oklahoma" sign appeared in their windshield at five forty-five a.m. at the same time as the "Welcome to Arkansas" banner could be seen in their rear view mirror. It was already eighty degrees.

We are all exhilarated when we cross borders. The elation and anticipation of wondrous new vistas, combined with the intoxication of dawn to excite Grace's passenger. Grace had a tale for every mile of the trip and so Jimmy learned of the migrating despair of Steinbeck's dust bowl "Okies" the great land rush, and the wisdom of Will Rogers. Eventually, the boredom of Interstate 40 overwhelmed them as they drove deeper into the Sooner state and Grace's history-geography lessons began to lose their luster. Twice Jimmy interrupted her to ask about the meaning of the mysterious "Do Not Drive Through Smoke" signs that appeared every thirty miles or so on Oklahoma's portion of the Interstate. "Are you just supposed to stop?" Jimmy asked. "What if no one behind you stops?"

"You ask such hard questions," said Grace as she gassed up west of Oklahoma City. They were now on the mother road and Route 66 had brightened her spirit and renewed her enthusiasm for education through travel. "Go get us some chips and soda and we're going to solve those questions and more when we eat our cheese salad sandwiches at the next rest area." They were just east of Texas when they pulled over. It was ninety-three degrees when they sat down at the picnic table. Jimmy could think of nothing but bacteria decomposing. He visualized maggots forming.

You can tell a lot about a person by watching them eat. Eating is the only sensuous act commonly performed in public. Grace was not a fastidious eater. She had half of her sandwich devoured before Jimmy had even un-wrapped his. Jimmy watched Grace, expecting her to begin writhing in agony at any minute. His mother had warned him of the certain, agonizing death he would endure if he consumed food contaminated with un-refrigerated mayonnaise. The words botulism and salmonella were not in common usage, but "spoiled" embraced both of these terms and many others. Jimmy tentatively bit into his sandwich. He was starving. Breakfast that morning had consisted of an overripe banana and a glass of warm orange juice plucked from the pathetic breakfast buffet.

Grace had taken a pillow from the back seat of the big Ford and to Jimmy's embarrassment, had stretched out on top of their table. Jimmy studied his Grandmother's face, concentrating on her throat and mouth from which the poisonous vomit was certain to spew. He listened for the beginnings of the volcanic, stomach rumblings that would be harbingers of the runny, convulsive expulsions that would be certain to bring Grace's knees to her forehead. He spotted the women's room about two hundred feet away and silently searched for a trucker that might be willing to help him take his shit- and puke-sodden grandma to a place where she could at least be cleaned before a hearse took her away.

Jimmy looked down to see that he had eaten nearly all of his sandwich while he had envisioned Grandma Grace's earthly exit. To his great surprise, Grace still lived and was snoring in no visible distress. Jimmy stared at the remains of his cheese salad treat and thrust it into his mouth. As he slowly chewed, he envisioned his classmates and how even those who had treated him like a butt-scooting dog would mourn his passage. He hoped Danielle would cry and regret not giving him a valentine in the fourth grade when he had sent her candy kisses in a box with a lace-trimmed heart. Self pity quickly changed into self preservation. Seizing the opportunity, Jimmy silently took three of the remaining sandwiches and tossed them into the trash. Only one was left. Ten minutes passed before a fart that passed from Grace's ass was loud enough to wake her and disgust the parents of three Mennonite children at a nearby table.

Grace arose from the table's top and when her feet hit the ground, she farted again. The children were delighted. Their parents decided to pray.

Grace let Jimmy drive to Amarillo. She had too much to say to concentrate on the highway. She let Jimmy know that Texas was the only state to enter the union as a sovereign nation. She spoke of Sam Houston, Jim Bowie, and Davy Crockett, who was immortalized in two states, Tennessee and Texas. She sang Crockett's composition in her deep rich voice:

  "Farewell to the mountains
  Whose mazes to me
  More beautiful fair
  Than the eye can see.
  Farewell to the land
  Of the savage and wild.

The land I have loved as a father his
child.
The wife of my bosom
Farewell to you all.
In the land of the stranger
I'll rise or I'll fall. "

"Davy wrote that just before he left
for Texas to die in the Alamo, " Grace said.
" I have often thought that it takes either a
hero or a fool to fight another man's
battles. What do you think? "

"No man is an island, " Jimmy replied,
and it was then that Grace remembered why her
grandchild was so special.

They spent the night in Tucumcari in the
Blue Swallow Motel. They found a buffet and
gorged themselves on fried chicken, meat loaf
and peeled shrimp. "Don't waste stomach
room on salads or healthy shit when you can
get double portions of the main event, "
Grace cautioned. "Mashed potatoes and gravy
and baked beans are the only non-meat items
that are permissible, and for dessert, select
cream cakes or pies, preferably those that
contain chocolate. "

The Blue Swallow was a landmark on Route
66. It had only fourteen rooms, but all of
them were clean and comfortable. Jimmy felt
like one of those beetles that gorged itself
until it was too fat to cling to the dead
armadillo it had discovered lying beside the
road. The room was mercifully air-
conditioned. When Jimmy closed his eyes at
eight-thirty, it was eighty-seven degrees
outside. He thought briefly about the last
cheese salad sandwich, covered in foil and
lying in a paper bag on the back seat.

They were on the road by five-thirty in
the morning. Jimmy was driving, filled with
the adrenalin the beginning of a new day
brings, especially when you are traveling

through unfamiliar territory toward unknown destinations. They each had a sweet roll and coffee for breakfast, and the big Ford had its belly filled with twenty-four gallons.

The scenery finally had a western air about it and Grace spoke of Pat Garrett and Billy the Kid. From the map, she read of towns with Spanish names and she told her grandson of the Hoosier who authored 'Ben Hur' and later became the first provincial governor of New Mexico. Jimmy was in Gallup, just east of Arizona, when they stopped for gas. He brought a package of peanut butter crackers and a Milky Way while Grace was paying for gas, pop and chips. "There's a rest stop just inside the state line where we'll eat. It's only about twenty more miles," Grace said. "Do you think you can put off eating your favorite sandwiches for a few miles longer?" Jimmy mustered a grin and said, "There's only one left. While you were napping yesterday, I just kept on eating. I'm sorry. They just taste so good."

Grace frowned. "I wish you would have told me. What will we do for lunch today?"

"I bought some crackers and a candy bar," Jimmy said. "I'm all set. You can have the last sandwich. I apologize for being such a hog."

"Speak not of those filthy animals," Grace said. "Your mother may have married a pig farmer, but my grandson will be an astronaut, or a senator. I'll give you half a sandwich for half of your Milky Way, deal?" Jimmy nodded glumly. The bitter taste of bile began to invade his throat, where it would take residence until Jimmy took his first bite. From there the fierce harshness would move into the back of his nose where his adenoids used to hang. As Jimmy pulled out of the service station, he could visualize his death from eating spoiled food. The thought of puking his intestines out of his mouth and nose gave way to a plan that just might ensure his survival.

The rest stop heralded their arrival into Arizona. It was twelve-nineteen and one hundred degrees. As the two of them opened their car doors, the heat slapped them viciously. Energy which had been stored, waiting for release, retreated from the onslaught. The first foot touched the blacktop eager to walk, stretch and escape the confinement necessitated by automobile travel. The second foot knew better than to hurry. When it touched the road, it lingered, questioning the need to leave the cool interior. Both feet seemed reluctant to participate in the act of standing. Asses hesitated to leave seats. Arms which had been poised to help asses arise, became limber and sullen. Somehow, Grace and her grandson made it to the picnic table carrying their lunch, but it was not without effort. Arizona will do that to you. "This is where they ought to put all the prisons," Grace said. "And none of them should be air conditioned. A week or two in an Arizona jail would have all of those child molesting, raping, sons of bitches pleading for a noose."

The chips, candy, crackers and remaining cheese salad sandwich were placed in the middle of the table. Grace opened Jimmy's Doctor Pepper and handed it to him. She then opened her Pepsi and carefully tore the sandwich in half. As was her custom, Grace sat facing away from Jimmy in order to rest her back against the hard, unyielding picnic planks. She stretched her long legs and without waiting for Jimmy, put all of her half sandwich in her mouth and chewed it furiously. Not more than thirty seconds had passed before she was devouring her part of the Milky Way. Jimmy sat across from his grandmother facing her back. He stared at the ground searching, until he saw exactly what he needed. As usual, the ground under the rest area picnic tables teemed with foraging insects. Jimmy quickly crushed a black ant between his thumb and forefinger and placed it on top of his part of the sandwich.

"Jesus," Jimmy exclaimed. "Look Grandma, it must have fallen out of that tree."

Grace turned around and looked at the dead ant. "Well," she said, plucking the ant off the sandwich, "are you going to eat that or not?"

"I can't eat that, it's nasty."

Grace removed the top piece of bread and folded the bottom to recreate the sandwich effect on a smaller scale. She offered it to Jimmy. "What if ant guts soaked through into the cheese?" Jimmy said. Grace looked her grandson in the eye as she put the cheese salad sandwich in her mouth. After it was devoured, Grace climbed to the top of the table and was asleep within thirty seconds.

Grace began to shit in earnest at mile marker 235. There is a rest area there thirty miles east of Flagstaff. She had a puny crap after awakening from her nap just across from the New Mexico line. When she was away from home, Grace would shit four or five times a day. The first stool squat seldom satisfied. Occasionally, the second shit was the blessed "double flusher" that produced smiles and contentment, peace and harmony, and an almost orgasmic relief. Most of the time, however, one trivial shit followed another until one day ended and the next one began.

Graces' bowels had been muttering for miles. At first the noise was gentle and amusing. Farts soon followed and just as robins tell us that spring is near, farts are harbingers of shit. "Grandma," Jimmy complained, rolling down his window, "you're vile."

Grace left the 235 rest stop reluctantly. The car was parked only fifty or so feet from the restroom, but by the time Grace returned to the big Ford after her ass had spewed a quart or two of hot brown water, she was ready to shit again. Knives were inside her bowels searching for ulcerated flesh. They probed and poked and sent bile into Grace's throat and acid into her nose. Grace could only pat her ass dry. Wiping with the cheap, rough rest area tissue was out of the question. "Jimmy, I think we should stop for awhile. Grandma has a severe case of the trots."

It might have been the cheese salad, the ant guts, or even the Milky Way that reduced Grace into a shitting, shivering, crying, old lady. "I wanted to show you the Grand Canyon, the London Bridge, the lost mules of Oatman, the Hearst Castle, the Columbia River, the Corn Palace, the Custer Battlefield and the Badlands, but I have nearly crapped myself to death," Grace said after she and Jimmy spent two days at a dreary MasterHost Inn just east of Flagstaff. "Take me home, boy. I can't stand being sick and away from home at the same time." Jimmy was only too happy to comply. Sharing a bathroom with a respected elder can change your perception. The awe and reverence are diminished by the sight of a spattered toilet bowl and the smell of defecation that chokes the feeble efforts of the exhaust fan. Driving home, Jimmy vowed never to eat another cheese salad sandwich, and he never did. What's more, they were never on the menu during Jimmy's brief tenure as owner of the Parley Vous.

CHAPTER TWENTY-NINE:
THE ROUND TABLE

Starlings, banana bread, the Fortune 500, Morley Safer, Moslems, Saddam, the Hunt for Red October, cocoa, laminated flooring, Sean Penn, Radar Reddleman, Sadie Hawkins, Coleman Hawkins, Fat Boy Slim, Vincent Price, satellite radio, the meaning of the work "efficacious", why birds' feet don't freeze in the winter, crop rotation, John Dillinger, Galena, Illinois, and Sylvester Stallone a.k.a Rocky Balboa were only a few of the topics discussed in October, 2000, along with the "My childhood was harder than yours" theme, which reappeared more and more frequently.

"Did you ever see any corn in your stool?" Doc asked.

"I try not to look at my shit," said Pres. "One flush and it's gone before I stand up."

"You ought to pay more attention to it," said Doc. "It can tell you a lot about the state of your health, and you always need to be on the lookout for blood."

"Why do I sit here day in and day out, listening to you disgusting old farts?" asked Red.

"I haven't said a word," said Bill. "But to reply to your question, Doc, no I've not seen corn in my stool. For that matter, I've not seen radishes, nor have I seen pork chops, or Aunt Jemima pancakes nestled down among the turds. And what kind of question is that anyway? Am I deprived because I'm not passing niblicks?"

"Elephants can't digest corn," said Doc. "Trainers often feed corn to elephants anyway because it gives them a full feeling and when feed gets too expensive, corn will do the trick for a day or two. The corn kernels will show up in the elephant's dung more or less intact."

"Where in the fuck are you going with this?" asked Bill.

"And who really gives a shit?" asked Red.

"I can't believe you just said that. The elephants give a shit. Haven't you been paying attention, you dumbass," Pres said, grinning at Red.

"When we were little guys, before dad had the grocery store, we were just dirt poor," Doc continued. "Harold and I would look for mushrooms in the spring and when the weather got warmer and the circus started to tour southern Indiana, we would get on our bikes and see if we could find an elephant."

"Look," Bill said, "rather than hearing the rest of where this repulsive tale is certain to end, I will concede that your imagined childhood was tougher than mine, even though we had to fight rats for our bread."

"We had to battle rabid possums," said Pres.

"The old man drooled," Red said. "Mom would buy a chicken or a roast or turkey and while he carved it, he would drip spit on it. The rest of us couldn't eat it."

The remaining three were silent and embarrassed, knowing that their foolish, poverty embellishments had caused their young friend to join in with a revelation that was truthful and too intimate to share. Doc broke the silence.

"The object was to check the elephant shit for corn. Most of the time, we struck out, but every now and then, Harold would see the gold shining in the brown and we would use a tea strainer to retrieve the kernels. Sometimes the manure would be fresh, and the green flies would be swarming around our heads. The ankle flies would join in and bite and as if on cue, the mosquitoes would surround us. On many an occasion, Harold lost so much blood that he fell face first into the hot brown. Somehow we prevailed in bringing enough corn home for mom to clean and using chicken claws and potatoes, she would make a chowder that almost didn't taste like elephant shit."

CHAPTER THIRTY:
THE RESTAURANT

Jimmy Fountain had succeeded at the Marathon mostly because of what he had learned from Grandma Grace. Good gravy was the solution to almost every culinary puzzle. Jimmy's eggs featured a side of gravy, as did his steak, chicken, pork chops, and hamburger. People flocked to taste what would be covering their mashed, fried and baked potatoes, for Jimmy liked to tease. On each table would be placed a large gravy bowl that would arrive with the entree. Jimmy had read that chicken gravy complemented chops and so he would often serve it with the fried potatoes that accompanied his thin, small pork chops. "Put catsup on the potatoes and then cover them with gravy," Jimmy would tell the children who accompanied their parents to the Marathon and later to the Parley Vous. He would grin with satisfaction when he would observe the parents eating their potatoes covered with catsup and gravy.

Hot-dog gravy was his own invention. He fried bacon until it was crisp. The bacon was drained, crumbled and set aside and Jimmy then sliced hot dogs into one-inch pieces and browned them in the bacon grease. He added flour to thicken and poured milk into the mixture to produce a creamy gravy which he topped with the crumbled bacon. Jimmy recommended that his "killer, artery clogging delight" be served over a baked potato. He was quick to recommend that butter and sour cream not be added. "I would not be happy if you died before you paid your bill," Jimmy would often say. "Besides, you might cause me to lose some customers if they saw you writhing in cardiac arrest before they placed their orders."

He used round steak to make his Beef Stroganoff and chicken broth instead of beef broth. Jimmy's roast beef hash consisted of the usual left over meat, cooked diced potatoes, sautéed onions, celery seed and paprika. What distinguished Jimmy's hash was the canned milk he added to the mixture which he poured and let stand for a half hour. Every cook is tempted to stir his creation, but this was one dish that had to fry undisturbed over medium heat until the edges browned and the smell told the trained nose when it was crisp just before it burned. The hash was never turned in the skillet, but was served on the plates with the brown side up. Jimmy cut narrow strips of sharp cheddar which he placed on the sides of each plate of hash. The diner was encouraged to place some or all of the cheese on the hash. The pungent melt accentuated the beef and the entire concoction hit the palate with a decadence akin to sexual arousal.

Ultimately, it was his success that led Jimmy's abrupt departure from Paris Crossing. Willard Frey had inherited millions of dollars from his tobacco-baron father. In addition to the cash, Willard had acquired real estate from his dad consisting of three horse farms near Ocala, Florida and a magnificent ruin of a hotel in Louisville pompously named "The Majestic." Willard had grandiose plans for the stately old palace. He had closed it shortly after his father's death and carpenters, plumbers, decorators, painters and electricians had been prowling the empty rooms for seventeen months. Willard had wisely done nothing to the exterior, thereby preserving the ante bellum plantation look that had caused Theodore Roosevelt to gushingly proclaim it "The Crown Jewel of the South." Willard planned on a June re-opening but it was already mid April and he was in need of a chef. Willard estimated that he had read over a hundred resumes and sampled the fare of some of the nations' finest cooks. So far, Willard was unimpressed. No one seemed to get it. While the guest rooms were to retain their elegance, each named after a former Derby winner and each containing a portrait of the horse for which the room was named, the restaurant was to feature simple fare. All the cooks who had auditioned for Willard had fed him uppity food like goose liver or pheasant. One Frenchman failed his audition by suggesting that preparing corn beef hash was beneath him. And so when Willard overheard one of his plumbers positively gushing over the roast beef he had eaten in Paris Crossing, Willard was quick to react. Within two hours, Willard was savoring meat loaf, mashed potatoes and gravy and baked beans lovingly prepared by Jimmy Fountain.

Enormous wealth was not the only thing Willard had inherited from his father. The younger Frey possessed knowledge of economics that surpassed even that of his legendary dad. The Majestic was a downtown hotel and Willard had not failed to notice the new Holiday Inns and the like that were being built along the interstate highways. Willard knew he could not compete with their convenience, but he could host conventions. His Citation Conference Center could accommodate eighteen hundred people. These people would need to be fed and Willard's plan was to provide his conventioneers with hearty meals at only slightly inflated prices. He would rent his rooms at reasonable rates so as to attract the large gatherings he so coveted. He would then provide his guests with meals that were deliciously prepared, but inexpensive to provide. Most restaurateurs are content with a fifteen to twenty percent net profit on every meal they serve. Willard wanted twenty-five and if he kept his menu simple, he figured he could get it. As he finished his meal, Willard asked his waitress if he could see the cook. Willard had found his chef.

The only problem was that Jimmy was not interested. "Mister Frey, I just bought this place a year ago. I can't just walk away from it. Besides, Dolly did me a favor by selling the restaurant to me on contract. I owe her. How can I go now? I've still got mouths to feed."

Willard was not dissuaded by Jimmy's remarks. In fact, Willard was impressed by Jimmy's loyalty to Dolly and his desire to stand by his word. Willard knew that Jimmy would be just as loyal to him if Willard could only convince Jimmy to come to the Majestic. "Let's talk some more about it when you are not so busy. Could you be in my office tomorrow around eight in the morning?" Willard said holding on to Jimmy's arm.

"No, I can't," Jimmy replied. "I open at seven."

"What time do you close?"

"When the last customer leaves."

"I'll wait," said Willard. It was a little after eight in the evening. Jimmy did not sit at Willard's table again until nine forty-two. Willard had been counting the minutes.

"Can you get me a copy of your contract?" Willard asked.

"Mister Frey," Jimmy protested, "I'm glad you like the way I cook, and I'm flattered that you want me to cook for your restaurant, but I just don't think I'm your man."

"Let me be the judge of that," Willard replied. "And how can you turn down an offer that I've yet to make? All you know right now is that I want to hire you. We haven't begun to discuss financial arrangements and without looking at your contract, I can't tell if employing you is even feasible. I know you are not interested, but I waited nearly two hours to speak with you. Please be courteous enough to show me your contract."

Willard knew how to press the right buttons. Jimmy had been taught to be courteous to even the rudest of people. He went upstairs and returned shortly with the contract in hand. Willard read it quickly. Its terms were about what he expected. The former owner, one Dolly Morris, had been eager to sell. There were no liquidated damages and the default clause provided only that in the event of a breach, the seller was to "be restored to full ownership and the buyer would have no further right or interest in said real estate." "Piece of cake," thought Willard.

"Here is my offer," said Willard, handing the contract back to Jimmy. "My lawyers hate it when I don't put things in writing, but we will do that later. I will write you a check today for twenty thousand dollars. We will consider that earnest money. In addition to that, I will pay you a salary of five hundred dollars a week. Of course you will be eligible to participate in both our health care and our pension plan, and you will be given a company car to drive provided you don't mind having a ceramic horse's head for a hood ornament. It's my trademark. It's supposed to look like Secretariat, but I think it looks more like Whirl-A-Way. What do you say?"

Jimmy was stunned. He was as frugal as his Grandma Grace, but there the financial resemblance ended. Grace had money. Jimmy had none. He was a miser out of necessity. He made only a hundred dollars a week working at the Marathon. He was a little better off at the Parley Vous, but only because he lived upstairs.

"Oh, and I almost forgot," Willard said as if he had read Jimmy's mind. "Your meals will be furnished and a hotel room will be yours. I want you to live close to your job."

"What about my contract?" Jimmy said. "What about Dolly? I gave her my word."

"Your contract says that if you default, Dolly gets the restaurant back," Willard said. "It doesn't say you can't default. Besides, I'll have my lawyers talk to her in the morning, and if she wants a little money, I'll take care of her."

"Really?" Jimmy brightened. "You'll take care of Dolly?"
"I'll take care of her," Willard repeated. "Now do we have a deal, kid?"

Dolly was living in Evanston, Illinois. She was only weeks away from completing her second semester at Northwestern. The knock on her door at 9:00 p.m. alarmed her. She was still a small town girl. Living alone in a big city had been both exhilarating and terrifying.

"Who is it?" Dolly said to her triple-locked door.

"We're lawyers representing James Fountain," came the reply. "May we see you?"

"No," said Dolly. "Go away."

A brief silence ensured followed by a more authoritative voice. "The other lawyer," Dolly thought.

"Mrs. Morris, Mr. Fountain has an offer which I think will be of interest," the other voice said. "He wants to give the restaurant back to you and give you some money."

"Take it up with my lawyer," Dolly said.

"Ma'am, we would be glad to do that." It was the voice of the first lawyer again, "but we've had a long drive up here from Louisville and both of us need to be back at work in the morning. With your permission, if you'll open the door just a little, I'll hand you this document and maybe if you'll call your lawyer and read it to him we can complete our business and not have to bother you any more. We'll wait out here on your porch."

Dolly unlocked the dead-bolts, but left the chain lock attached. Both lawyers were wearing ties and sport coats. The younger of the two handed Dolly a one page document. A check was paper clipped to it. Dolly closed the door and quickly engaged the dead-bolts.

Dolly was certain she had awakened Pres, even though he denied it. She apologized for her intrusion and then explained the reason for her call. "It's entitled Release", said Dolly, referring to the document.

"That little son-of-a-bitch," said Pres, referring to Jimmy Fountain.

Dolly read the Release. Pres was silent at first and he repeated, "That little son-of-a-bitch. What is he doing with big city lawyers?"

"Pres, what am I going to do. I don't want that restaurant back again," Dolly pleaded.

"I was afraid this would come back to haunt you, Dolly," Pres said. "I told you when you only asked for a five hundred dollar down payment that you were only asking for trouble. Five hundred is a hell of a lot easier to walk away from than five thousand."

Dolly was furious. "I don't need a goddamn lecture," she said. "I need a lawyer to tell me what to do."

"I'm sorry," Pres said. "I didn't mean to sound so sanctimonious. It's just that I hate telling you that there's nothing you can do. Fountain doesn't even need a release. He can just walk away. You keep everything he's paid and you get the restaurant back."

"Then why does he want me to release him for the sum of one thousand dollars from any and all obligations created by a certain contract between the parties, etc." said Dolly.

"It's just neater," said Pres. "It eliminates any future controversy. I would want a release too if I represented Fountain. Do you suppose Grace is behind this? Jimmy sure as hell can't afford a thousand dollars, let alone two Louisville lawyers who had to drive all the way to Northwestern University. I'll tell you what, let's just see. Tell them you want five thousand to sign."

Dolly was smiling as she once again opened all but the chain lock on the door. "My lawyer says I can't sign for less than five thousand," she said.

"In that event, would you please return the release and the check?" said the lawyer with the big voice.

Dolly handed the two documents through the narrow space, closed the door loudly and slammed the locks into place. "Well Pres," Dolly said to the phone, "I may have just lost a thousand dollars, but..." The knocking returned. Dolly re-opened the dead locks. She was handed a check for five thousand dollars together with the release.

"Mrs. Morris, if you will just sign your name on the line where I have placed an x and initial inside the circle where I have crossed out one and written in five thousand, we can be on our way," said the younger lawyer.

Dolly reluctantly complied, and the lawyers left. "I'll be damned," said Pres. "It must have been Grace, but I don't understand why. Do you want me to put the Parley Vous back on the market again?"

"Let me think about it Pres," Dolly said, "Why do I feel like I just got screwed without being kissed?"

The two lawyers drove three blocks to the stately Holiday Inn in downtown Evanston. After checking in, they walked to Pete Miller's Steakhouse. They were quite proud of themselves. Mister Frey had given them authority to pay as much as ten thousand dollars. He was concerned about a claim of tortuous interference but the release his lawyers had obtained, should afford him ample protection. The lawyers ordered steaks and an eighty-dollar bottle of wine.

As Willard Frey's lawyers celebrated in Evanston, Pres found it difficult to go back to sleep in Paris Crossing. Why had he not made Fountain's lawyers come to him? Why had they settled so quickly? Why had he settled so quickly? Did he do a bad job for his client? The phone rang again at two-thirty in the morning. Pres had just drifted off into an uneasy, guilt-ridden sleep. A familiar voice was on the other end. Marie began by singing in a voice that trembled, "Hallelujah momma, he's dead."

CHAPTER THIRTY-ONE:
HOLIDAY ON ICE

Rob Cross had been seeing Ginger Watson off and on for several months. She was from Indianapolis and her parents were both professors at Butler University. Ginger was an undergraduate at UK majoring in English Literature. Rob had met her at a pizza place where she was sitting at a table across from his. She had been laughing and Rob was in a bad mood. Happy people can piss off the sullen and Rob fumed while this child dared to be gleeful in the face of his gloom. Rob was determined to put her in her place and then he began to soften. He supposed it was because of the guttural, sensual way she laughed. He envisioned her making the same sounds in bed, and in spite of himself, he began to smile. She didn't seem to be with anyone in particular and when he asked her to join him for a glass of wine, she happily came to his table.

In mid-October of 1963, Ginger invited Rob to spend a long weekend in Indianapolis with her at her parents' house. "My folks have great tickets to the Holiday on Ice show at the Coliseum. Jinx Clark will be performing. Don't you just love her? "

Rob didn't much care for ice shows, but he did like Ginger and he needed a break. His third year in med school was so exhausting that he was seriously thinking about dropping out for a while. So he found himself in Ginger's big Pontiac, headed for Indy on October 31, 1963. It was a Thursday evening and thanks to the time difference, both of them had been able to complete their classes before they had to head north. With any luck, they would be at Ginger's parents' home by 6:30 p.m. in time for supper with her folks and show-time at eight-thirty at the Coliseum.

Rob had not been back to Indianapolis since he had last seen Julie following their graduation from Butler in 1960. Driving towards Indianapolis brought back memories of Julie. Rob had treated her like shit. He knew it was unrealistic for them to continue in a relationship that was doomed to fail because of the distance. In addition, Rob knew he was not in love with Julie in 1960 and he was looking forward to meeting new women and having new relationships. Yet he had not had the guts to tell Julie how he felt. He had cruelly strung her along. He hoped she was happy, and yet at the same time, he hoped she still thought of him, because in the three years since they had parted, he had not found anyone he had cared for as much as he had cared for Julie.

Ginger's parents were overly joyful, overly cheerful, and overly happy to meet Rob. It was a reception he had become accustomed to receiving. Young male medical students are America's equivalent of European royalty. Mister and Mrs. Morrison had moved into the guest room for the night so that Rob would be comfortable in their bedroom. Breakfast would be awaiting him at whatever time he awakened, Mrs. Morrison told Rob, and nervously asked him how he liked his eggs. She also hoped that Rob liked lasagna, the dish they were about to have for supper.

"Mrs. Morrison," Rob began.

"Helen," she insisted.

"Helen," Rob continued. "I have been subsisting on college food for so long that whatever you put in front of me will be gratefully appreciated."

"See Helen," said Harold Morrison, "I told you he'd be no different from us."

Ginger glared at her father. "Would anyone like a drink before we eat?" asked Mister Morrison. "How about it Rob, would you like a Schlitz?"

"I'd love one," said Rob.

Rob and Ginger got to the Coliseum just before the show was to begin. Ginger was disappointed in the seats. They were clearly not the best in the house. The box seats across from them in Section C on the lower level had the best view and Ginger silently bemoaned her father's penurious nature. Rob seemed not to care. His stomach was filled with pasta and beer and he was fighting sleep. The show was entertaining, but juvenile and he kept nodding off, once startling the five-year old next to him with a snore that sounded like the last gasp of a dying mule.

"Do you want to leave?" Ginger asked. It was eleven p.m. and the show was winding down. "One reason why my folks put you in their bedroom is because they are in the room between us."

"So if we are going to make out, it's the car or nothing; right?" Rob asked.

"You've got it, sweetie," Ginger said, kissing Rob on the nose. "And I'm ready for some loving."

CHAPTER THIRTY-TWO:
MINNIE AND GOOFY

Brenda Hanson and Tom Meeker were the quintessential "cute couple." People smiled when they walked by. In addition to her pleasing features, Brenda had large breasts dominating her one hundred seven pound, five-foot-two frame.

Tom was Troy Donahue handsome. In addition, he had a non-threatening "aw shucks" smile which rarely left his face. He was six feet eight inches tall. When they entered the Coliseum, dressed in their Halloween costumes, they were greeted with cheers and laughter. Tom was wearing a Goofy costume and Brenda was dressed like Minnie Mouse; both carried their tails over their shoulders.

The wonderful, old ribald joke had to occur to more than a few of the spectators as they viewed the cartoon-costumed couple; Mickey has sued Minnie for divorce. During the proceedings, the judge tells Mickey, "I cannot find any evidence to support your allegation that Mrs. Mouse is insane."
Mickey replies, "I never said Minnie was crazy, I said she was fucking Goofy."

Smoking was permitted in airplanes in 1963. You could smoke in many college classrooms, and at all bowling alleys. You could even smoke in your hospital bed. Cigarette machines were everywhere. At sporting events and entertainment venues, smokers huddled in the aisles happily puffing away. Smoking was forbidden while patrons were in their seats, but during intermissions, smokers fled to fill the concession areas and rest rooms with their poisonous, blue haze.

Even though it was Halloween, there were only a few people in the Coliseum who were wearing costumes. By intermission, Brenda and Tom had shed their Goofy and Minnie heads. They were hot and they were cold. Ice shows and hockey games have a way of freezing the feet and suffocating the head. Thermostats are raised to fend off the cold, but ice stays close to the floor, and those patrons in expensive, ground-level seats are left wanting thermal socks and fur-lined boots.

Because of the way they were built, Brenda was mostly cold and Tom was mostly hot. He fended off the cold by resting his feet on Goofy's head, wrapping Goofy's droopy ears around his ankles. Minnie's head was of no help to Brenda. It was much smaller and Minnie's ears were erect and stationary. Brenda stood at intermission and told Tom she was going to look for hot chocolate. Tom wondered if anyone was selling ice cream.

Brenda and Tom had been "introduced" by Butler University's legendary coach, Tony Hinkle. Coach Hinkle was well liked by almost everyone. He was an affable, gregarious man with a playful nature. "Shelbyville," he said to Tom on a practice day when Tom couldn't seem to make a basket. "Get your mind off basketball for a minute and come over here."

Tom had graduated from Shelbyville and although Coach Hinkle had a hard time remembering names, he always remembered where his players went to high school. Your school became your name. Tom went to where Coach was standing. At coach's side was a cheerleader.

"What's your name?" Coach asked of Brenda. When she told him, Coach said, "Shelbyville meet Brenda. I just wanted the best looking tall guy to meet the prettiest little gal. Say hello Shelbyville." Tom did, turning beet red in the process, and

Coach said, "Now go put some balls in the hoop, so maybe you can impress Brenda."

Brenda called Tom the next day. It was her idea to see the ice show and dress for Halloween. It took the two of them several days to find costumes that fit. In the end, Brenda's mother had to sew on patches to lengthen the legs of the Goofy costume. The Holiday on Ice show was their first real date, but the costume search had gotten them acquainted. Brenda was rapidly coming to the conclusion that she really liked Tom. Tom was feeling the same way about Brenda. Both were wondering about sexual positions and the size of apertures and organs.

Below section C was an area shielded by a blue curtain. Tom raised the edge and peered in. Brenda had found her chocolate but it had not been hot for at least forty-five minutes. She swallowed it anyway but she had started to shiver and couldn't seem to stop. Her feet were freezing.

"I've got an idea," Tom said, gently guiding Brenda towards the curtain. "Let's go in here and get you warm."

Behind the curtain was a small storage area illuminated by a bare bulb. Under the bulb was a ladder that appeared to have been positioned to facilitate bulb replacement. Tom picked Brenda up and placed her on the top rung. They were now at eye level with each other. Tom took off Brenda's shoes and socks and placed them on a lower rung. He then put one of her feet under each arm.

"This should do the trick," Tom said. "Of course your feet will smell like my pits, but at least you'll be more comfortable."

"I'm sure my feet smell like garlic popsicles as it is," Brenda said. "A little sweat juice should make for an interesting combination."

Minutes passed in silence as awkwardness set in. The crowd above was beginning to stir.

"Feel better?" Tom asked.

"Much better," Brenda replied.

Tom gave Brenda her shoes and socks and after she put them on, she impulsively leaped, putting her arms around Tom's neck and her legs around his waist. They kissed. The ladder fell sideways overturning a bottle of propane gas just as the audience burst into applause at the re-emergence of the skaters. Neither Tom nor Brenda knew that the valve on the propane tank ruptured, sending the highly flammable gas in search of a flame. Neither of them smelled the gas because someone had neglected to place an additive in the gas to give it a warning odor. Besides, they were busy.

"Let's get out of here," Tom said. They were more than a quarter of a mile away from the Coliseum, locked in their third embrace when all hell broke loose.

CHAPTER THIRTY-THREE:
DISASTER

The following words appeared in the
November 1, *Indianapolis Star*:

"October 31, 1963, will forever be
ingrained in the memory of the people of
Indianapolis. That night an explosion ripped
through the Indiana State Fairgrounds
Coliseum, claiming the lives of 74 people and
injuring nearly 400. It was one of the worst
tragedies in Indiana history."

"It was opening night for the Holiday
on Ice show with more than 4,000 spectators
on hand. Propane, being used to keep pre-
popped popcorn warm, was leaking from a
faulty valve. At 11:04 p.m. an explosion
sent bodies flying nearly 60 feet. A second
blast took place a few minutes later, caused
by heat rising and air rushing into the
vacuumized (sic) area. The victims were
either severely burned or crushed by
concrete."

Both Rob and Ginger were spared. The
first explosion knocked them down and
immediately enveloped them in an almost
impenetrable fog as portions of the ice
vaporized in the intense heat. Flames
followed the bodies into the air, leaping
nearly to the top of the enormous ceiling.
The second, more intensive, concussion
occurred while they were still on their hands
and knees hesitant to arise. Fortunately,
they were seated near an exit, and Rob
grabbed Ginger's arm and pulled her to her
feet. The two of them made it outside before
thousands of hysterical men, women and
children clogged the escape routes, injuring
many more in their panic-stricken exodus.
Rob stopped. "You go home," he said.
"I've got to stay."

Ginger looked at Rob not comprehending what he had just said. "Let's go Rob," she said. "This place may blow up again and again and burn to the ground." Her voice was tinged with hysteria.

"I'm a doctor," Rob replied. "There are people in there who need me."

"You're not a doctor," Ginger said. "You're a third year medical student and I need you. Don't you realize that if you go back in there, you might not come out? Please Rob, come home with me."

"Take the car and go," Rob insisted. "Your folks will be worried sick. I'll call as soon as I can. I'll catch a ride to your house." He tried to escape with a simple kiss, but Ginger clung to him and he could feel her legs trembling. After a few moments, the screams and sounds of human suffering began to intensify and Rob was able to extricate himself from Ginger's arms. Rob was the only person attempting to enter the Coliseum. "Let me through, I'm a doctor," Rob shouted over and over and an old priest who had been attempting to exit, turned and grabbed Rob's hand. "Let us through," the priest joined in, raising their co-joined arms.

It was difficult to tell when they made entry. There was the fog and there were the dead and injured. "I forgot who I was there for a minute," said the priest, looking at Rob, but addressing his remarks to no one in particular. "When you've only got a little bit of gas left in your tank, you try to save what you have. How did you get here so fast?"

"I was inside, the same as you," said Rob, "and a woman wanted me to forget who I was."

As he examined the carnage, Rob began to wonder why he had not gone with Ginger. The priest left Rob to comfort and pray for the living, and beseech God to accept the souls of the dead. He knew what to do. Rob was a healer without tools to heal. Morphine was what the living needed most. Pain was the killer. Shock bore the blame for the deaths of the badly injured, but it was pain that pulled shock up like a sheet over the mind and body, bringing the blessed nothingness of a coma. The sheet is covered by a blanket as the coma deepens and the mind hides, fearful of the return of pain. The fine line between unconsciousness and the final coma is easily crossed. "Death caused by shock," reads the certificate, but it is pain that pulls the plug.

Rob went from person to person, rearranging limbs so as to make broken bones more comfortable and pulling dead people off of the living or off of the other dead. As he reached down to check the condition of a young woman who was lying on top of a large man, her left arm lifted and encircled his neck. Her eyes were closed and her voice was just above a whisper, but Rob heard Julie say, "Did you come back for me?"

For years afterward, Rob felt real guilt about what happened next. Instead of staying, and trying to help others, Rob cradled Julie in his arms and rushed for an exit, once again shouting, "I am a doctor" as he placed Julie into the first ambulance that arrived on the scene. "Aren't you staying, Doctor?" the ambulance driver inquired.

"I've got one I think I can save," Rob said. "I don't know about the rest. Now I want you to drive to Methodist as quickly as you can."

In 1963, Methodist Hospital was one of the premier health-care facilities in the Midwest. A massive structure located at the intersection of Sixteenth and Capital, its great yellow bulk served to reassure the sick

and the injured. Rob used the radio in the
ambulance to speak with Ginger and with
Julie's parents. It did not take long for
the intern on duty to unmask the third year
med-student. In fact, after answering some
preliminary questions, Rob revealed his
status. The intern seemed not the least
concerned about Rob's pretense and permitted
Rob's presence during Julie's examination.

"All I can tell you for certain is that
she has sustained a concussion," the intern
told Julie's parents in Rob's presence.
"She is unconscious, but just barely. She
seems to know that Rob is with her. She
tried to keep Rob from leaving the room by
grabbing him by the hand. She didn't want to
let go. I've attempted to isolate a specific
area of injury, but quite frankly, she hurts
all over. It's my guess from what Rob told
me that she may have been thrown into the air
by the force of the blast and her landing was
cushioned by the poor bastard she landed on.
We have her on a mild narcotic; anything
stronger might precipitate a slide into a
real coma. She is comfortable. She is
stable. It is necessary for her to regain
consciousness so she can give us some
indication as to what areas we need to x-ray
and treat. It would be my suggestion that
Rob be permitted to be with her because she
responds to his presence and I think she will
come out of it more quickly if he continues
to talk to her and hold her hand. The
quicker she comes out of this, the better off
she will be. We have hundreds more coming
in," the intern continued. "I'll be back
to see Julie again when she is conscious or
in three hours, whichever comes first." He
took off at a trot and Rob turned to go into
Julie's room.

"Not so fast you son-of-a-bitch,"
said Julie's mother, grabbing Rob by the arm.
"If anyone is going to talk to Julie and

hold her hand, it's going to be me and not the lying bastard who broke her heart."

"I deserved that," Rob said. "You go see your daughter."

"It's not that we don't appreciate that you saved Julie's life," Mr. Hearter said, looking at the ground.

"I'll wait here," said Rob. "Go in there and bring her back."

Rob dozed and then called Ginger again. It was nearly two in the morning and he had hesitated to call, but the phone was answered on the first ring by Ginger's father. "Honey," he shouted to his wife, "you and Ginger pick up the other phones. We have a hero on the line."

An *Indianapolis Star* reporter had taken a photo of Rob carrying Julie out of the Coliseum. It had made all three of the television stations. "Before we get off here, I just want to tell you that we're damned proud of you, son," gushed Ginger's dad.

"Can you come here now?" Ginger asked. "You must be exhausted and I want to hold you so bad."

"They need me here right now," Rob lied without knowing why. "There are hundreds of injured people here and they need all the help they can get."

"I love you, Rob," Ginger said.

"That's sweet," Rob replied, unwilling to say more, unwilling to hurt more. I'll try to be there in time for breakfast."

The next voice Rob heard belonged to Julie's doctor who was shaking him awake.

"Get up Goddamn it," he said. "Why haven't you been in there with her?"

"Her folks didn't want me in there," Rob replied.

"I got the story from her parents. She's worsened," the intern said roughly. "You carried her out of the fire, but you may still have killed her with your neglect.

I told you what would save her, but you caved in to avoid an argument? What a pitiful excuse for abandoning your patient, doctor. If she dies, it's your fault, asshole. "

Julie lived another three hours and then died in Rob's arms. The cause of death was listed as shock, but Rob knew it was pain. When he didn't return to the room, Julie thought he was running out on her again. The pain which had been dulled by Rob's presence returned to induce the coma which pulled the covers up and over Julie's eyes.

Rob and Ginger were married in 1965. Rob quietly mourned Julie every day for the rest of his life.

Following the disaster, The *Indianapolis Star* filled many of its pages over the next few days with stories of hope and pain.

A relief fund was formed to aid people facing weeks and months of hospitalization. By the end of November, more than $58,000.00 had been donated.

The Holiday on Ice issued ticket refunds.

A young couple was arrested for soliciting money by going door to door falsely representing they were children of Coliseum victims.

Fingers were pointed at the Discount Gas Company for failing to include a warning agent which was supposed to smell like dead animals.

On November 22, President Kennedy was assassinated. The great Coliseum disaster was relegated to the back pages and vanished shortly thereafter.

CHAPTER THIRTY-FOUR:
HALLELUJAH

Pres had not heard from Marie for two years. "Marie, where are you?" he said.

"Right now I'm in Crawfordsville in the Montgomery County jail," she replied. "I killed Sonny and it seems there are laws against that even when you shoot a man who is trying to rape you. I want you to be my lawyer."

Pres sat on the edge of the bed trying to get his breath. Finally he spoke. "Rape? What do you mean? Marie, haven't you been living with him?"

"Never in the same house in Portland and never in the same house in Crawfordsville," Marie replied. "No one knew we were lovers except you and even you don't know what's been going on for the past two years. For all you know, I've been faithful to my husband, although I doubt if you've been faithful to me."

"Are we still married?" Pres asked. "I never received any papers, but I assumed you had divorced me long ago."

"I wondered about the same thing," Marie answered, her tone softening. "So you didn't divorce me either. This must be my lucky day."

"When did all this happen? What is your bail? Where is your dad? Why hasn't he bailed you out?" Pres said in a rush.

"I killed Sonny about two hours ago," Marie calmly replied. "They have not set my bail and Daddy is indisposed. Are you going to represent me or not?"

"Why do you need me, Marie? Can't your father handle this? Even an incompetent drunk should have no trouble getting you off if no one else knew you had been regularly screwing the man who raped you," Pres angrily replied.

"For reasons unknown to me, the police seem to doubt that I killed Sonny while he was raping me," Marie replied. "You see, I shot him in the back of the head. I am about to be charged with a serious crime, and I need a serious lawyer. Who better to defend my honor than my husband?"

"Ok, Marie," Pres said, "I'll come see you and try to see what I can do about getting you out of jail, but I don't know how I can defend you when I don't believe you. Have you given a statement to the police?"

"I'm telling you the truth," Marie said. "Even whores can be raped, and don't give me that bullshit about not being able to help me because you don't believe me. My daddy is a lawyer. I'm married to a lawyer; the man I killed was a lawyer. You hypocrites would defend Hitler, and no, I have not talked to the police. I've absorbed some knowledge just by being around you bastards."

"I'll be there at nine tomorrow, but don't expect me to bail you out. Your father can do that. He has more money than Midas," Pres said.

"Thank you, my darling dear," Marie replied in a voice that sounded sincere to the bewildered Pres. "I look forward to seeing you. Bring me a blanket. It's cold in here."

The first thing Pres noticed was Marie's breasts. She had surgically enlarged them to a delicious voluptuousness that was truly breathtaking. "How do you like them?" Marie asked, looking in both directions before lifting her sweater. She had previously removed her bra and it was lying on the arm of the chair on which she was seated. "I call them Curley and Moe."

"Put your sweater down," Pres gruffly commanded. "Someone might see."

"Wouldn't you like to touch them first?" Marie asked. "You can't believe how soft they are. I can hardly keep my hands off them myself. Are you going to be my lawyer?"

Marie removed her sweater entirely and then slowly put her bra back on, nestling each breast separately in what appeared to be double D cups. She pirouetted twice before replacing her sweater with her back turned to Pres. "Have you missed me baby?" she said. "I've sure missed you."

Marie was not in the general population. In fact, she was in a room just behind the Sheriff's office that afforded her privacy and permitted visitors a keyless entry. The door to her room was closed, but no one, not even the Sheriff, dared enter without her permission. The door to her "cell" was locked from the inside. Harry Hawkins was still a force to be reckoned with in Montgomery County. Harry knocked before saying, "Honey, it's your daddy. Are you decent?"

Pres had not seen Harry for a decade. During that time Harry appeared to have aged by at least a decade times two. Harry's eyes were slits. Below each of them rested the headless bodies of old jaundiced mice. Harry's lower lip protruded in the middle and drooped on each side, creating drool trenches. His alabaster hair had not thinned, but it had acquired a nicotine tint. Harry had gained about fifty pounds of unhealthy fat and his belly had succumbed to gravity. From the front it was impossible to tell if he was wearing a belt. Harry took a serious pull from his unfiltered Camel and focused on Pres. As the old lawyer began to speak, Pres realized that Harry was drunk. It was only eight in the morning, but Harry was ten-thirty p.m. drunk. In his cigarette-free hand, Harry carried a handkerchief that he held to his face to sop up the spittle.

Pres suspected that it was also employed to mask the unmistakable smell of Jim Beam ineffectually disguised by Scope.

"You must excuse me, son," Harry said, "I've been up all night. It seems that my cousin tried to rape my little girl and she is accused of killing him."

"Daddy I did kill him," Marie protested.

"It's hard for me to believe," Harry said. "He was my idol, my law partner, Marie's own cousin. What got into him? He deserved to be shot, but goddamn it, I loved him," Harry blubbered, unleashing snot, tears and saliva.

Pres looked on with disgust. Marie viewed her father through eyes filled with compassion. "Still her daddy's girl," Pres thought as Marie arose and hugged her father from behind, her arms failing to circumnavigate his massive belly.

"What am I doing here?" Pres asked when Harry's thunderous sobs slowed to whimpers. "It was only yesterday when I thought I was divorced. It's been years since I left the law firm. I didn't think either of you cared if I lived or died and I sure felt the same way about you, Harry."

"You still love me though, don't you darling?" Marie interrupted before Pres could finish "At least just a little?"

"Look, son," Harry said, attempting to achieve sobriety by enunciating slowly and emphasizing vowels. "We have ourselves a crisis here. Your wife may be charged with murder for killing a man who was trying to rape her. You are the perfect man to defend her. Not only are you the aggrieved husband, but you are one hell of a trial lawyer. My cousin is dead and I grieve his loss, but I have to protect my baby. She is all I have left. Marie and I were up all night and both of us regret the way you were treated before you left. You take care of my girl and you

name your price. The law firm is yours, and
I think Marie is yours too if you can help us
out of this mess. Am I right baby? "

Marie nodded coyly. Sitting behind her
father, she crossed her legs a la Sharon
Stone to briefly reveal her panty-less,
hairless, pudendum and stuck out her tongue.
"Pres knows I want us to be together again,
don't you darling? "

Pres felt as if all of the oxygen had
been removed from his body. Marie's wanton
invitation instantly replaced logic with
lust. Pres's brain knew that his dick was
now in charge. "Tell me what happened, "
Pres panted while Marie smiled and began to
lick the chocolate from a Snickers bar.

"I don't remember much, " Marie said as
she continued to perform fellatio on the
candy bar. "I awakened to find this man on
top of me and I shot him. "

"Where did you get the gun?" Pres
asked without taking his eyes from Marie's
mouth. Somehow her lips seemed fuller, her
tongue longer.

"It was under the bed, " Harry said.
"I gave it to her a couple of years ago.
She had some son-of-a-bitch peeking in her
window and I told her to shoot the bastard if
she ever saw him again and to keep the gun
where she could reach down and blast his ass
without having to open a drawer. "

"Didn't you tell me he was shot in the
back of the head?" Pres asked.

"Apparently, " Marie said. "At least
that's what they tell me. I don't remember
where I shot him."

"She must be suffering from some kind
of post-traumatic problem," Harry
volunteered. "Didn't you have trouble
remembering what happened to you after you
were hit in the head with that beer bottle
while singing that song about Veedersburg? "

"You had to bring that up didn't you?" Pres said instantly furious. "Both of you turned your backs on me after that."

"If I recall correctly, sweetheart, it was your decision to leave me and it was your behavior that caused our separation," Marie said.

"I'm sorry if that brought up bad memories," Harry said. "I only mentioned it to remind you how an event like that can mess up your mind. We're due in court in five minutes. Marie is about to learn what crime she is being charged with and how much it is going to cost to get her out on bail. You need to enter your appearance as her lawyer."

As they entered the courtroom, Pres was struck with its unfamiliarity. Old counsel tables had been replaced and moved. Sterile, straight-backed chairs surrounded the tables, replacing padded swivel rockers. The judge's bench had been moved from its former location of behind the jury box to where the judge now sat directly across from the jurors. The witness box was on the far wall halfway between the judge's bench and the jury box so that the unfortunate person who took the stand was totally isolated and bore the scrutiny of both judge and juror alike. Even if a witness had a lawyer, it would give him little solace. The counsel tables were back against the wall facing the witness. It was as if the room's unimaginative designer was a student of the "four corners" school of bland design, thought Pres.

A gavel sounded and Harry muttered, "The empress has arrived."

"Holy shit, she's wearing a robe," Pres thought. When he had left Montgomery County, Judge Cole had been on the bench. He was a natty, anal little man who wore white on white shirts with bow ties and a black suit coat which he had cleaned every weekend. Robes were eschewed. They were still not worn in southern Indiana. Country people viewed them as being pretentious and phony, costumes donned by fops and dandies.

"Mr. Prosecutor, it is my understanding that you have a criminal affidavit to present to the court," Judge Adamson said.

"That's correct, your honor," said a young man seated at the prosecutor's table.

"His name is Craig Terry," whispered Harry. "He doesn't know jack-shit. You'll eat him alive." The prosecutor stood and walked to the bench. He handed a sheet of paper to the court reporter, who in turn handed it to the judge, who began reading it aloud.

"I, Mark Rodgers, being first duly sworn hereby represents to the court, the following: That on the eighth day of July, of this year, a woman known to me as Marie Hart did commit a crime against the person of James Hawkins to-wit: murder in the first degree in that she, with premeditation and malice, discharged a firearm into the back of the head of said James Hawkins, causing his death, all of which is against the peace and dignity of the State of Indiana."

"First degree murder?" Pres exploded. "Her cousin was trying to rape her."

"Who are you?" the judge asked.

"I'm her husband," said Pres, "and I guess I'll probably be her lawyer, if she is going to have to face a ridiculous charge like that."

"All I do is read the charge," said the judge. "As I'm sure you know, counselor, if you disagree with it, you need to talk to the prosecutor. Don't direct your anger towards me. Now, how does your client plead?"

"Not guilty," said Harry.

"Mr. Hawkins," said the judge, "I'd like to only have to deal with one family member and one lawyer at a time. Mr. Hart is it? How does your client plead?"

"Not guilty to this loathsome charge, your honor. May my client be released on her own recognizance?" Pres inquired.

"Mr. Prosecutor, what is your position on that?" the judge asked.

"Your honor," the prosecutor complained, "the charge is first degree murder. She should be held in jail throughout these proceedings. Bail should not be permitted."

"Your response counselor?" the judge said, directing her inquiry at Pres.

"Do you need sworn testimony, your honor, or will my representations suffice?" asked Harry rising to address the court. The old man spoke in a dulcet yet authoritative tone that for years had disguised his meager knowledge of the law. Pres pulled at Harry's pants leg to silence him, but the judge clearly wanted to hear more.

"Miss reporter," the judge said to her court reporter, "have you duly noticed the request from the defendant that she be released without bail and that the State wants the defendant to remain imprisoned with no prospect of bail?"

"I have your honor," the court reporter replied.

"As we all know," the judge said, "the right to bail is constitutional. To deny bail or to make bail oppressive is to presume guilt instead of innocence. Jail should be reserved for those proven guilty or for people who are a threat to flee beyond the jurisdiction of this court. You were saying Mr. Hawkins?"

"Your honor," Harry repeated, "my daughter is a Montgomery County resident and she has lived here most all of her life. She's not going anywhere. The man who died early this morning was my cousin. I'm his closest relative. If I have no complaints about Marie being permitted to stay at home with me, where she lives, who else is there to demand her imprisonment? I will personally guarantee her appearance at any and all proceedings."

"Thank you, Mr. Hawkins," the judge said. "Mr. Prosecutor, am I correct in assuming that the defendant is accused of killing a man who showed up in her bedroom in the middle of the night? Do you have any evidence that Ms. Hart invited the deceased into her boudoir?"

"We're working on that, your honor," the prosecutor replied.

"Do you have any reason to believe that Ms. Hart is a flight risk?" asked the judge, once again addressing the prosecutor.

"No, your honor," the prosecutor replied. "But judge, we have charged the defendant with a capital offense. In most murder cases, bail is routinely denied."

"Mr. Prosecutor, that applies when the defendant appears to be a menace to himself or others. I fail to see how Ms. Hart is a threat to anyone except a man who may well have appeared uninvited in her bedroom in the middle of the night," replied the judge. "The defendant is released on her own recognizance. Court stands adjourned."

"Was I impressive or what?" Harry asked Pres and Marie. "I got my baby released without having to spend a dime or pledging the farm."

"You did good Harry," Pres agreed. "As a matter of fact, I don't think you need me at all."

"Daddy, you were wonderful," Marie said, "but I think we need Pres and right now my husband/lawyer and I need to talk. You go sleep and Pres and I will visit in your office while you nap. Can you drive yourself home all right?"

"I'll be fine." replied Harry as his body seemed to shrink. The elation caused by his legal success was short-lived as he realized that his cousin was dead and his daughter was charged with his murder. He decided he needed a drink.

"I don't know if I want to hear about what you've been doing since we separated," Pres said, "but I need to know what the fuck is going on and I don't think you are telling me everything. As a matter of fact, I'm sure you've been lying through your teeth."

"They are good looking teeth, though aren't they honey?" Marie asked, smiling widely. "My breasts weren't the only part of me that were shined and polished. You're looking at twelve thousand dollar incisors, bicuspids and molars, darling. After you left me, I was devastated. In case you never noticed, I loved you more than life. As a matter of fact, I tried to kill myself with pills when I realized you weren't coming back. Daddy saved me, just as he has always done. You couldn't accept the fact that as long as he lives, I will be here for my father just as he has been here for me. All you had to do was come back to me and none of this would ever have happened."

"Thanks for the big dose of guilt," said Pres. "If I'm not mistaken, it didn't take you long to find consolation in the arms of your recently deceased cousin."

Marie lit a cigarette. Pres noted that she still favored menthols. She took a long drag and let the smoke drift slowly out of her nose before she spoke. "You have always thought I was complicated. I am not. I am a one-man woman who has only loved two men. I thought I was free of Sonny when I met you. I would never have seen him again if you would have stayed with me. You chose to leave and I had nowhere else to go. I had to take care of my daddy and I had to have someone to love me. I went to Portland and got Sonny to return and take your place."

Pres hated the taste of menthols. He compared them to smoking Vicks. Nonetheless, he reached for Marie's purse and shook out a Capri. The match taste combined with the rotted fir tree aroma caused the dormant mucus in Pres's throat to stir and begin its slow, congestive journey down into the sensitive folds of bronchiole and lung. "These still taste like shit dipped in Pine Sol," Pres said. "Let's take a step back from us and concentrate on the mess you're in. For starters, why don't you seem to give a shit that your honey is dead?"

Marie inhaled again. This time the smoke lingered about her eyes. She blinked and a tear descended down her left cheek. It was clear that Marie was not crying, yet in a way, it was also clear that she thought she should generate some grief.

"I'm not inhuman, Pres, I'm sorry he's dead, but we were no longer lovers. I removed my pubic hair to please him, but my boob job really pissed him off. He started to see another woman. What am I saying? He was seeing an anorexic high school senior."

"You were no longer his prepubescent darling," Pres said; "you must have known your tits would turn him off. Now tell me what happened," Pres said, "and I don't want to hear any more of this amnesia bull shit."

"I woke up to find a man on top of me, and I shot him," Marie said. "I already told you. That's all I remember."

Pres took a hit from his cigarette and let the smoke flow from his nose. He then sucked it back into his mouth. It was an ostentatious technique he had perfected in high school. He used to stand in front of a mirror practicing the procedure over and over. When he was younger, Pres did the double smoke suck for effect. At age sixteen, he imagined it made him appear dangerous, someone you didn't fuck with. The illusion was frequently destroyed by fits of coughing, but Pres thought even the hacking made him appear to be more adult. Marie always looked at Pres with awe when he did his trick. Pres was so deep in thought that he missed his own performance.

"I'm going back to Paris Crossing," he said. "If anything occurs to you about how you shot your ex-lover, you might want to let me know."

Pres stood to leave. "When are you coming home?" Marie said. "I'm ready to be your wife again if you're ready to be my husband. Can't we see if we're still sexually compatible before you leave?"

"Marie, I don't think this is a good time for that. I would have a difficult time performing with the thought that you might blow my ass away if I failed to make you cum," Pres said "maybe next time if you promise to disarm."

"Is that what you think happened?" Marie said with a look of wonderment on her face. She reached for Pres's cigarette and lit a new Capri from the end of Pres's. There is a certain intimacy known only to smokers that occurs when the lit end of a cigarette passes from a man to a woman or a woman to a man. Marie returned Pres's cigarette. Then she smiled and said, "You are in no danger. You always made me cum."

CHAPTER THIRTY-FIVE:
CLARICE GETS HORNY

Many years ago, the word was "randy". It was defined as lascivious, lustful, libidinous or bawdy. The word was usually a feminine adjective. "Horny" was initially a male term derived from horns or similar projections. It is not difficult to see how the male penis could be compared with the ever-erect and hard phallic protuberance of the bull. Then women started to use it to describe their state of heightened sexual arousal. With sexual equality came definitional equality. Words such as "hot", which were formerly used by women to define their readiness to engage in lovemaking, became transformed into unisexual descriptions of attractiveness. Men and women alike use the term as in "she looks so hot," or, "isn't he a hottie?" Clarice did not take time to dwell on the various words that had been used to describe her condition. She knew only that she was eager to embark on a sexual adventure for the first time in years. Pres was many years her senior, but he was gentle and understanding. Clarice was frightened and insecure about her feelings and if she fell, she needed a soft place to land. Pres offered a safe harbor.

When she was seventeen, Clarice was pressured into having sex by a boy she thought she loved. He had been tender until that fateful night. His kisses had been sweet and his touch soothed and aroused. She was reluctant to remove her panties. Every other article of clothing had been removed in increments over seven Saturday nights in the back seat of his father's old Lincoln. Clarice gladly shed her sweater and her bra. As her young lover shed his jeans, Clarice eagerly removed hers. Their embrace was passionate and wet with sweat and saliva. He was on top of her for several minutes. First his leg and then his hand found its way between her legs. Clarice resented the invasion but wanted the attention and the love, and rolled so that she was on top. She was kissing her young lover when her panties were pushed to one side and his penis entered her. Mentally, she felt indignation and betrayal. Physically, she was wounded. A sword or a burning iron could not have hurt her as much as the unwanted entry. Enraged, she bit the lip she had been passionately sucking with so much indignant anger that her teeth clicked together and her mouth filled with blood. Her lover screamed and withdrew. Her relief was immediate. He began to sob. Clarice watched dispassionately as he tried to stem the flow of blood that streamed from his mouth and down his chest. She grinned as the first drops hit his now flaccid penis. She dressed as he continued to whimper. She listened politely until he paused long enough to call her a "cock teasing little cunt."

"Take me home, please," was her reply. Five weeks later she realized she was pregnant.

Dolly was distressed to learn of Clarice's pregnancy, but relieved to learn that Clarice wanted an abortion. Female sexuality is too complicated to ever be remedied by a pill. Too often it is shaped by the past and embedded in the psyche. The smell of a man's cologne or the taste of a peach can send hormones over the edge. Memories of a male kindness, the shape of a man's ass, the taste of Juicy Fruit gum on a tongue, might combine to melt one woman's heart, yet leave another female unmoved or even repulsed.

The abortion took but a short time and within an hour, Dolly and Clarice were walking out of the hospital in Louisville.

Their entry was unimpeded, but a crowd was gathered when they exited from the front entrance. Dolly had chosen the hospital because no one in Paris Crossing would ever know of an abortion that took place sixty miles south of their little town. Dolly also had learned from her more cosmopolitan sister that this hospital was well known for its aggressive "pro-choice" stance.

"Which of you is the murderess?" a masculine voice thundered from a loudspeaker. Dolly was stunned and then indignant. Embracing Clarice, the much smaller Dolly marched with her head up towards her car. As Clarice trembled, Dolly replied, "My daughter was raped. You owe her an apology, you sanctimonious asshole," Dolly shouted toward the little man holding the white microphone. "How can you or any man judge an injured woman? How can you possibly relate to what she has endured?"

"She killed an innocent babe," was the reply, and the little man reached Dolly's car at about the same time as Dolly opened the passenger's door and helped her sobbing daughter into her seat. The microphone was thrust into Dolly's face and the little man was about to blast his hatred into Dolly's ears when she pushed the wide circle of the microphone with all her might. The narrow end went into the little man's mouth as far as it could, striking the back of his throat with its metallic circle. In the lawsuit which he filed two days later, he alleged that Dolly had acted with malice, "striking him with great force and violence causing him to be severely and permanently injured." In fact, the microphone had temporarily widened the little man's mouth and did some minimal damage to his vocal cords.

The lawsuit was successfully defended by a team of lawyers who were hired by Dolly's homeowner's insurance company. Pres found a clause that obliged State Farm to provide a lawyer to protect Dolly from claims "arising out of acts of self defense." After the trial was over, Clarice rode silently back to Paris Crossing until she and Dolly were only a few miles from home. "No more sex for me," Clarice said. "Look at all the harm it's done." Dolly thought briefly about protesting but remained silent. The mother in her was relieved but skeptical.

Clarice kept her word. Throughout college at Franklin, she had been friendly but unapproachable. When Jimmy Fountain left Dolly in the lurch, Clarice volunteered to take an absence from school in order to resurrect the Parley Vous. The opportunity to return home was both a burden and a relief to Clarice. She needed only a few more credits to graduate with a major in history. She was educated but uncertain. College can do that to those who choose a liberal arts education. History majors are about as employable as blacksmiths or telegraphers. Clarice could use the time to decide what to do with her degree; besides, it would not be difficult to be celibate in Paris Crossing.

Dennis the dentist was different. His car had been brushed and overturned by a semi on the interstate, and Red had invited the shaken but unhurt dentist to have coffee at the restaurant until Triple A arrived. Dennis seemed smitten with Clarice. He rose from his seat when she appeared at the table to take their order and he complimented her on both her hair style and the shade of her lipstick. Clarice beamed. Red fumed. Dennis insisted on paying for the coffee and he produced two business cards, which he handed to Clarice. "My number is on both. Please write your number on the back of one and return it to me. I want to see you again." He left a five dollar tip.

"That guy seemed a little strange to me," said Red after the dentist had left.

"He was very much a gentleman," replied Clarice.

"You might be wise to stay away from him," Red said and repeated, "he seemed a little strange to me." He had been trying to stop smoking, but he reached for his pack of Kools as he envisioned his virginal Clarice in the arms of another man.

The next day was Thursday. Dennis called a little after seven p.m. He asked Clarice if he could see her on Saturday. Clarice was both excited and frightened. She agreed to the date, but thought that she was being rushed. Was she ready, she wondered? It had only been four years. Then it struck her, four miserable, lonely years.

The dentist arrived in a bright yellow Mustang convertible. "It's a loaner," he explained to Clarice. "I'll be driving this until they fix my Jag. How about going to the riverboat?"

The Caesar's Palace people had recently opened a new gambling establishment on the Ohio River near Jeffersonville. Clarice had never been to a riverboat. "I'm not dressed for anyplace fancy, and I don't have any money to gamble," she protested.

"You are so charming," Dennis replied. "People do not put on their finery to go gamble; at least not around here, and you don't need any money. I'll stake you. Incidentally, you are ravishing."

Clarice blushed. Not once in her life had she ever dreamed she would be told she was ravishing. Dennis opened the passenger side door for her and as they started south, Clarice turned and faced her date. He was not bad looking, she thought. He obviously worked out. His arms were slim and muscular and his waist was small. He was wearing a yellow Lacoste golf shirt which pleasantly contrasted with the green alligator. His pants were tan and tight. He wore boots and Clarice suspected that without them, she would be taller than her date. Even with boots, Dennis was a snappy dresser, Clarice concluded. She was certain that Dennis had spent more money on his shirt than she had spent on her entire outfit.

Nothing prepares you for the noise. One minute you are in the relative quiet of the casino entrance, then the door opens and caucophony reigns. Bells, laughter, shouts and sirens combine to assault the tympanic membrane. In the distance a gathering of fools are shouting "WHEEL OF FORTUNE." Clarice thought she might be crashing a convention for the mentally ill.
"Let's go play the slots for a while and then we'll get something to eat," Dennis said. It seems as if every casino in the world has the same three features, lots of slot machines, a buffet, and a steakhouse. Caesar's was no exception. The steak house was named Portico and Dennis told Clarice that they had reservations for seven p.m. "There will be six or seven other couples. I hope you don't mind, I want to show you off."
Clarice did mind. She silently appraised her blouse and skirt outfit and found it wanting. At the same time, she was impressed by her date and excited by her surroundings. In the middle class there is a sense of sin and lawlessness about public gambling that is intoxicating. Dennis led her to a bank of machines that featured fruit and seated Clarice in front of a slot machine that required her to pull a long handle to play. Dennis put three one hundred dollar bills in the bill sucker slot and said, "Here's the deal. We split your winnings. I'll be back in an hour. If you decide to quit, or if this merciless devise treats you badly, I'll be over there," he said pointing to a crap

table just a few rows over from the blackjack table area.

"Bet at least five dollars on every pull," Dennis said, kissing Clarice on the forehead. "You are so special," he said as he walked away.

Clarice tried to examine her feelings. She decided she liked being with a rich man. She thought she could relax around him. She didn't think he would hurt her. She pulled the handle on the machine. The fruit spun. She had forgotten to make more than the minimum bet and the two cherries increased her stake by only five dollars. Clarice thought briefly of cashing out and impressing her date by returning his investment together with change. That moment soon passed and Clarice hit the maximum bet button and pulled the handle.

Clarice was only dimly aware of a hand touching her back. She had filled two popcorn-sized cups with five dollar coins and was oblivious to everything but the spinning fruit. The machine's tally showed that she had in excess of four hundred dollars more within its metal reservoir. "You have been kicking ass, pretty girl," Dennis said. "Can you tear yourself away for supper?"

"Must I?" Clarice beamed. "God, this is fun." She hit the cash-out button and filled two more popcorn cups. The cashier peeled off eleven one hundred dollar bills, a fifty, a ten and four ones.

"Let's see," Dennis said, "after you pay back my three hundred, you will owe me four hundred thirty two dollars, and after the death I died at the table, you should pay for supper."

"I will if we can have supper by ourselves."

Dennis paused before answering, "Clarice, I was only fooling you. I want to buy you the first in a long series of meals. Come meet my friends."

In the weeks to come, Dennis took Clarice to a hockey game, a boxing match, a horse race and two professional basketball games. At each event, they always ran into or accompanied three or four of Dennis's friends and their wives. Clarice came to like the women. She tolerated the men, who seemed to go out of their way to ogle her. One made it a point to lick his cigar whenever Clarice glanced his way. Dennis was a perfect gentleman. He opened restaurant doors, stood when she approached, and nuzzled her cheek when they parted. Six weeks had passed and Clarice had not even been kissed. "It's all right though," Clarice said to Debbie. "I really don't need a man for anything more right now. I'm happy just to be treated like a lady."

"Honey, you're dating a queer," Debbie replied. "Trust me. I once worked in a gay bar and I know homos. Look at you. You're a good looking girl. If I were a man, I'd be all over you on the second date and have your pants down by date number four. That's how men are, and that's how we want them to be. Does your dentist specialize in any specific area?"

"Pediatric orthodontia," Clarice said.

"There you go," Debbie replied. "How many parents would want their babies to have the fingers of a sodomist in the mouths of their precious sons or daughters? Have you run into his friends on every date?"

"Yes," Clarice replied after some thought and then she became a little indignant. "Why do you equate everything with sex? Just because you and Red do it all the time doesn't mean that everyone should act the same way. You're starting to piss me off."

"I'm sorry," Debbie replied, "but you've described a man in need of a beard.

I've seen a lot of them. Gay men who can't afford to come out of the closet need a disguise, so they put a lovely girl on their arms and make sure they're seen by everyone they know. Some men even marry their beards. If I remember correctly, Elton John was married for a time and so was Michael Jackson."

"I think you're wrong," Clarice replied. "I have found a rich, cultured gentleman, and you're just jealous."

"I hope you're right," said Debbie. "And maybe he's just what you need right now, but sooner or later you are going to want to get laid and the tooth fairy ain't gonna want to go to bed with someone who doesn't have a dick."

A month and several dates later, Clarice was beginning to think that Debbie was right. Dennis was displaying more affection, but his kisses, hugs and caresses seemed to take place only when his friends were present. Dennis never suggested that Clarice should stay overnight with him at his home on the south side of Louisville. Instead, he always drove Clarice back to Paris Crossing. His conversation during the trip was witty and entertaining, and Clarice enjoyed being with her romantic, good looking gentleman. That was enough for now, she thought.

Another month passed and two more quickly followed. It was late August. The hot and sultry air lent itself to lust. Spring is for romance, but summer is for passion. They had been to a Louisville River Bats baseball game. Her supper had consisted of hot dogs and wine. Dennis had limited himself to one beer, but Clarice wasn't driving and she had three plastic glasses of an insidious Beaujolais. On the drive back to Paris Crossing, Clarice began caressing Dennis's arm. His response was to give her a "kiss kiss" gesture with his lips. Clarice dropped her hand to Dennis's leg when they were about ten miles from her apartment above the Parley Vous, and she began to feather touch the inside of his leg five miles or so away from her home. As the dentist's car pulled into the restaurant parking lot, Clarice moved her hand so that it lightly brushed Dennis' crotch. "How about coming inside for a cup of coffee before you leave?" Clarice said, gently squeezing what felt like a nicely equipped package.

Dennis turned and gazed into Clarice's eyes. At the same time, he gently removed her hand from his groin. "I'd love to," he said, "but I've got to be in the office bright and early tomorrow morning to see the mayor's son about some braces. You know it's quite a coup for me to be the dentist of the famous. Give me a kiss goodbye."

Clarice turned her head away from Dennis's proffered lips and without saying a word, left his car and entered her apartment. She was embarrassed, hurt and pissed at Debbie for being so goddamn right. At the same time, all tied up in the same emotion, was sexual frustration, which Clarice reluctantly realized might be healthy. For the first time in years, Clarice wanted a man.

As was his habit, Dennis called Clarice on Thursday to ask her for a Saturday date. "Not interested," she said and hung up the phone. Not more than ten seconds passed before the telephone rang again. Clarice finally picked it up on the twenty-seventh ring. She said nothing. After a brief pause, Dennis began talking. "I really want to see you. Twelve of us, including wives and girlfriends, are going to see Miss Saigon and have a late dinner at the Majestic. Didn't you tell me that the chef there was from Paris Crossing? I was in charge of the restaurant selection and I thought you'd be pleased if we ate food cooked by one of your own. Clarice, please speak to me. Please come with me. It's very important to me."

Clarice seethed. She had told Dennis how Jimmy Fountain had run out on Dolly and left Clarice with a responsibility she accepted but did not especially welcome. Clarice had suspected that Dennis heard only what he said and selected minimal parts of her conversation to absorb in order to appear as if he gave a shit. The fact that he was inviting her to a show she was dying to see was tempting. Dolly had made sure that Clarice had been exposed to Puccini and the heartbreak of "Madame Butterfly," and Clarice yearned to see the twentieth-century version. She waited for Dennis to say, "Clarice" four times before she finally said, "Pick me up at the usual time." Even before she hung up the phone, Clarice was thinking of how she could embarrass Dennis in front of his friends by shitting in Jimmy Fountain's hot dog gravy.

There comes a time in Miss Saigon when everyone wants to scream "Dump the American girl!" The ending comes soon afterward and the death of the faithful lover causes convulsive sobbing even among the most jaded. Some stories are too sad and too beautiful to tell. Dennis and Clarice were both gasping for air as involuntary moans escaped them. Dennis may have initiated the contact, or maybe it was Clarice who turned and began the hug. Both clung to one another for several minutes as the theater began to empty. Clarice knew before the embrace ended that she could do nothing to harm or embarrass the man who had been so kind to her. Dennis gradually pulled away but kept his hands on Clarice's shoulders, and as they sat facing one another, he asked, "Will you marry me?"

CHAPTER THIRTY-SIX:
MARIE AND PRES

They sat in the conference room of
Harry's office in Crawfordsville. Books
lined the walls. Scattered portraits of
Harry, Jimmy, Lincoln, and an autographed
picture of JFK were interspersed between the
*Indiana Reports, Martindale Hubble, Proof of
Facts* and various other unread tomes designed
more to impress than to educate.

"There used to be a picture of me in
here," Pres said.

"Harry took it down when you left,"
Marie said. "I salvaged it. It's in my
bedroom. Would you like to see it?"

Pres stared at Marie. She had changed
so dramatically from the shy, needy girl he
had loved so desperately at DePauw. She
oozed sensuality. He tried to keep his eyes
off her breasts, but she was wearing a low-
cut peasant's blouse that revealed powdered
tops just above what he knew were
extraordinary nipples. Marie had aged much
like Sofia Loren. "We've got to talk about
your trial," Pres said.

"I know what you're thinking," Marie
said. "How can I ask you to love me again
after my two year absence? How can you ever
forgive my occasional unfaithfulness? I have
answers. I can explain. In my way, I was
true to you. I didn't divorce you. Don't
forget that you left me."

"We've got to talk about your trial,"
Pres repeated. "Does anyone know that you
and Sonny were lovers?"

Marie glowered at Pres. "Stick to the
point. I have only been loved by two men.
When you left me, my world collapsed. I need
to be held. I need the intimacy that only
sex can bring. I did not want to be untrue
to you, so I didn't seek anyone new. I went
to Portland to talk him into returning to

Crawfordsville but I didn't live with him. I used him. He was only pinch-hitting for you. He was just a safe dick to me. "

"Jesus, Marie," Pres began.

"His ex-wife knew about us," Marie said. "She caught us, and that's why she divorced him and moved back to Costa Rica. "

"Wait a minute I never heard this story. What was Jimmy doing with a Latin wife? "

"He met her when she came to Indiana as an exchange student," Marie said. "She was having some problems with immigration and she needed a lawyer."

"I don't understand why I was never told about a foreign wife. I knew her name was Elana or something, but I didn't know she was not American."

"Elia," said Marie. "You were not told because you never asked. If you remember, darling, you did not want me to think about or talk about my dear uncle ever again after we were married. Little Elia had a passport that said she was seventeen when she married Jimmy, but Daddy later told me that she was barely fourteen. Jimmy was a pedophile to the end. He was sleeping with barely legal girls in Portland and he was rumored to have made overtures to a sixteen-year old daughter of one of Daddy's best clients. At first, after you devastated me, I tried to please him. I shaved my pubic hair, but when he barely noticed, I got my new breasts. After that, Jimmy seemed repulsed by me and would only give me a pity fuck every now and then. "

"Is that why you killed him? "

"Whoa, my lawyer hubby. Right now I would rather be held than cross-examined. " Marie reached across the table, but Pres refused to respond. Marie dropped her arms, clearly hurt by the rebuff.

"Did anyone else know about your sexual relationship? " Pres asked. "Your father's faithful Hannah seems to be wise to the two of you."

"Hannah never saw us doing it, if that's what you want to know," Marie said, flinging her words like knives toward Pres's eyes, his mouth, his heart. "I'm sure she suspected. Secretaries know everything, but they can usually be trusted. It's not for nothing that the first six letters in secretary spell secret."

"It's important that a jury think of Jimmy as an invader, a potential rapist, instead of a lover. We don't want them to believe that he had an open invitation to your bedroom," Pres said to a glowering Marie.

"Where do we stand? That's what I want to know," Marie said. "Are you going to act like my husband again? I want you, goddamn it. Do I have to beg you to make love to me?"

Pres stared at Marie for a full minute. He was trying to separate the lawyer from the husband. The lawyer wanted to focus on the trial; the husband wanted to fuck his wife's brains out. They both voted. The husband won.

Marie wanted Pres to spend the night and Pres was reluctant to leave. "It isn't clear to me yet what I should do," Pres said as he left the room in which Jimmy spent his last minutes on earth. "I know Harry needs me. I know you need me. I just don't know if I want to abandon a comfortable living in a no-stress environment for one where both of you will want so much of me. I do love you, Marie. I have always loved you. I'll be back in three days, on Saturday morning. Hopefully, we can spend as much time working on your defense as we spend in bed."

Marie grinned and blew Pres a kiss. "They will be waiting for you, lover," she said, brandishing her remarkable breasts.

CHAPTER THIRTY-SEVEN:
THE ROUND TABLE

Barnacle Bill the Sailor, Melanie Griffith, Marjorie Main, Wimpy, Panera Bread, chili in a bread bowl, Boston Blackie, Eliot Ness, racquetball, My Cousin Vinnie, rufous-sided towhees, blackjack, Dick Clark, and the non-existent ozone layer were discussed in November, 2000 along with the Elvis Syndrome.

Harold Meeker, with a hook where his left hand used to be, sat at the table. Harold was an old school farmer who preferred to farm his own ground with his own machinery instead of relying on a sharecropper or a cash renter. He was a retired Purdue professor who had taught both agronomy and classical English literature. Twelve years ago, Harold had purchased two hundred acres of hardscrabble land and several pieces of ancient machinery. Harold was well liked and the men at the round table looked forward to his occasional morning visits to the Parley Vous. Harold's profane language skills were admired by all. "He is the only man I know who can call me the offspring of an Aids ravished cocksucker and a syphilitic anal whore and make me smile while he's saying it," said Bill Walsh. At age fifty-five, Harold had married a twenty-nine year old named Lindsey. In her presence, he reverted to being a respected, dignified, pipe smoking pedagogue. Around men, he became a cigarette smoking, glib, obscene old farmer with a flair for creative profanity.

Last year at harvest, Harold's corn-picker had apparently wanted to add some meat to its diet and seized Harold's hand when he attempted to dislodge a clog. Harold was lucky. Corn-pickers use augers to deliver the grain to the wagon and the circular motion of the giant screw grabs, pulls, crushes and grinds bones and sinew. Whole arms and even bodies have been eaten by this mechanical T-Rex. "I wouldn't let the cold-hearted fucker pull me in," said Harold, lighting a Lucky he had fished out of his breast pocket with the hook. "When it grabbed me, I put both feet against the machine and let it chew, but it apparently didn't like the taste of this Southern Indiana dirt gouger, because it let me go after only taking my hand and my Timex. Blood spurted every time my heart beat, but thank God for bungee cords. They have to be a farmer's best friend. I used my right hand and my teeth and was able to wrap a cord just below my elbow to get the bleeding down to a trickle."

"Jesus, Harold," Doc said. "The pain must have been excruciating."

"It hurt, Doc," replied Harold. "But you know it hurt worse after I was in the hospital before the drugs kicked in, and then it really hurt when they put on this pirate's hand. You don't know what it's like to forget you have one of these sharp mother-fuckers and your eye itches. By the way, I need a parrot. Does anybody have a big-assed green and yellow bird who'll scream, 'Your mother cuts socks in hell'?"

"Was that the worst of it?" asked Bill Walsh.

"Hell no," said Harold. "Elvis died trying to shit, and that almost happened to me. I had been regular all my life. Fifteen minutes after that first cup of coffee found me on the stool ready for my first dump of the day. On occasion it would be a double flusher. Oftentimes, I would have an afternoon encore performance, and if I ate restaurant food for supper, I would hit a triple. I would drift off to sleep knowing that I had just had a perfect day."

"I had a professor in med school who proclaimed there was nothing better than a good bowel movement," Doc said. "At the time I thought either I didn't know how to shit or he didn't know to fuck. Now I'm beginning to realize that evacuation may even be better than ejaculation."

"It was the fucking pain killers," Harold continued. "It was like someone put a cork in my ass. I felt as if I had to shit, but those constipating mother-fuckers turned my stool to stone. Enemas helped a bit, but they always give that job to the ugliest, meanest nurses. Those bitches were all former members of Hitler youth organizations with names like Helga or Hilda. They would ram the tip of that un-lubricated nozzle into my ass, which with all the straining was ringed with roids, the size of hog livers and they would squeeze that bulb until I felt like I'd been anally impregnated by Santa Claus. Then they would say, "You will defecate now." Maybe three-fourths of a tiny concrete turd would escape, but that would still leave enough shit to fill an eight-gallon wash tub."

"Not too many nurses volunteer for that job," Doc said. "You generally get the puke scrubbers and the bed pan sloppers to do the asshole-related tasks. No wonder they're mean."

"When they did the autopsy on Elvis they found about seventy-eight pounds of shit," Harold said. "All those fucking narcotics had turned his crap into steel. Can you imagine trying to shit rivets? Anyway, I finally had the mother of all shits. It took me the better part of two days. Lindsey set up a table in the bathroom so I could shit and eat cornflakes at the same time, but can you believe it? That disloyal, uncaring wench would not stay in there with me. She wouldn't even give me a blow job while I was evacuating my bowels. What a cold hearted bitch. "

"Why did you opt for the hook?" asked Bill. "Aren't they making artificial hands? "

"Because my insurance wouldn't pay for it and it would cost me about thirty-five thousand dollars, " replied Harold. "Besides, Lindsey likes the touch of steel. I put on an eye patch and tie a sash around my belly and it makes her hot. I've put a flagpole up in our bedroom and whenever I hoist the skull and crossbones, she's all over me. "

"Debbie likes me to wear a gun to bed, " Red confided. "She says it makes her feel dangerous. I always unload it, " he added, pissed at himself for revealing a confidence.

"The older I get, the more thankful I am for the comfort and excitement a good woman can bring to an old man, " said Harold. "Look at us Red. You and me, and for that matter, all of us. Why would some great looking woman want to put up with a belching, farting machine with a big belly and a tiny dick that only hardens when the proper chemicals are ingested? Were it not for Lindsey, in a year or two, my sorry wrinkled ass would be sitting on the edge of a nursing home bed wondering why no one has come to change my Depends. "

CHAPTER THIRTY-EIGHT:
CLARICE MAKES A DECISION

All her life Clarice had wanted a proposal of marriage. She had dreamed about a man loving her so much that he would ask her to be with him forever. It seemed that her dreams had been with her long before puberty, early in grade school. Dolly had made marriage seem like paradise, and almost before memories began, Clarice had heard of her father and of her mother's perfect union with him. Then what Dolly referred to as "the rape" occurred, followed by the "abortion," Clarice's dream of a wedding disappeared along with her longing for a husband. She found herself despising men; then along came Dennis. He was kind, affectionate, generous and gentle. He treated her better than she dreamed any man would; best of all, he made no effort to make love to her.

If he had proposed to her a month ago, she might have accepted. But a month ago, she still would not have welcomed a sexual advance. A month ago, she would still be thinking of him as shy and considerate of her feelings. Things had changed. She realized that she wanted to be wanted again. Ironically, it was Dennis who had rebuilt the trust necessary for mature passion. At seventeen, we find ourselves in hot, burning lust. When that inferno subsides, it leaves burned fingers, thighs and hearts behind. Once we are wounded, the wise ones among us are frightened of the fire and it can only be rekindled by someone we know will not hurt us again. Clarice knew Dennis would never hurt her, but she also knew that he would never want her.

There was very little room for Dennis to kneel, but Clarice had not responded to his entreaty and he reacted by getting on his knees and producing a velvety box. Several people on their way out of the theater paused to look at the couple. Women elbowed their men, speaking without talking of how they would have wanted to be wooed. Men grabbed the arms of their women and steered them toward the exit, silently cursing the ostentatious asshole who was bathing them in guilt.

Dennis opened the box. The theater was awash in light allowing for a comfortable exit, and the orchestra was winding down. The strings were all that remained, and they replayed the last heartbreaking scenes. The diamond glistened. It seemed to want to leap from its cushioned shackles onto the fourth finger of Clarice's left hand. "I would love so much to announce our engagement tonight at supper. Please marry me. We would be perfect for one another," Dennis entreated. His voice quivered as his fear of rejection reflex shifted into high gear.

"Can we talk about the fact that you're homosexual?" asked Clarice.

"I guess you figured that out," replied Dennis. "Until last weekend, I didn't think that would be a problem. You told me going in that you had been burned pretty bad, and I guess I assumed that you would not miss having a heterosexual man around. Maybe I assumed wrong, but listen, I'm rich. I'll have my lawyer draw up papers guaranteeing you one hundred thousand dollars on our wedding day and another ten thousand a year for each year you stay married to me."

The crowd had nearly emptied the theater. Those that remained cast only a passing glance at the kneeling man and the pretty woman who seemed oblivious to all but each other. "I'm so confused," said Clarice. "I want to be happy. I want to be

in a normal relationship. I want to be rich.
I don't know what you do with men. I don't
want to know, but I don't want to see it. If
I agree to this, how will I know that you
won't bring someone who's murderous into our
home or if not him in person, his disease?
Why me? Why anyone? Can't you just come out
of the closet and leave me alone? I hate
men. Either you're vicious, or you're queer.
Goddamn you all. Get up. I'm hungry. "

Louisville hates its longitude. It wants so much to be as far as south as Macon or Montgomery, Savannah or Baton Rouge. Just as the younger sister of Miss America longs to be as beautiful as her sibling, Louisville tries hard to be as southern as its more geographically advantaged rivals. The Kentucky Derby helps the city forget that it is closer to Chicago than Memphis and closer to Cleveland than Atlanta. These days most of the horses come to Churchill Downs from New York, Florida, Ireland, California or the Middle East. A thoroughbred or two always shows up from one or more of the fine stables located near Lexington, but the days of Kentucky three-year old dominance are gone. Nevertheless, on the first Saturday in May, the women always wear hats, savor mint juleps, and drawl as thickly as the smoke produced from cigarettes made from only the finest Kentucky tobacco.

The Derby never really leaves. Like the cicada, it merely lies dormant. During its hibernation reminders of the great race are everywhere and nowhere is the run for the roses more in evidence than at the Majestic. The restaurant was named the Citation Room. It comprised half of the enormous Citation Conference Center. When the Majestic was not hosting a convention, workers pulled brass handles and rolled recessed panels from hiding to create a more intimate thirty table setting. On the walls were scenes of the track from different vistas and enlarged finish-line photos of Gallant Fox, War Admiral and Exterminator. The first race was run in 1875 and every horse that ever won the great race had its photo somewhere in the hotel. The servers were gaily festooned with silks worn by the winning jockeys. The tables were named after Derby winners and Dennis and Clarice joined Dennis's large contingent at Ponder, Count Fleet, Go For Gin and Riva Ridge. At Dennis's urging, the tables were pulled together. He had hoped to announce an engagement, but failing that, Dennis had yet another opportunity to show the world that he was a devout heterosexual. He kissed the back of Clarice's neck after he had pulled out her chair. Nearly no one noticed the flash of revulsion on Clarice's face after the intimate moment passed.

"Hello, I'm Margaret," the tiny black waitress said. "Does everyone want one of our complementary Mint Juleps? They are part of your Derby experience."

Everyone nodded in approval and one of the women held up her hand. "What is in it?" she asked.

"We serve the official mint julep of the Kentucky derby," the diminutive waitress replied. "We try here at the Majestic to be as authentic as possible. As I'm sure you have noticed, all of us are dressed in the silks of the jockey we represent. I am honored to be wearing the colors of Oliver Lewis, a black jockey who sat astride our first winner, the noble Aristides. Mr. Lewis weighed only one hundred pounds."

"Oh, my," the questioner replied. "Was he the smallest jockey to ever win the Derby?"

"No, ma'am," the waitress replied. "That honor belonged to a little man who weighed even less than me. He was named Swim and he weighed ninety-seven pounds when he sat atop Vagrant in 1876. Our mint julep is made with Early Times Kentucky whiskey, fresh mint, sugar and water. When I return with yours I'll bring you the recipe. All of us are proud of our restaurant and its Derby theme and I'll be glad to try to answer any more questions you may have concerning our prestigious race after I put in your food orders."

Clarice opened the slender menu. She expected to be offered expensive choices. She looked for filet mignon, swordfish and crepes. She found meatloaf, spaghetti and meatballs, catfish, pork chops and hamburger steaks. "Jesus Christ," she thought, "it's the same shit he offered when he was at the Parley Vous."

"Dennis," she said, "why are we here and not at Dennys? Do you realize you can get a chicken pot pie there for a third of the cost?"

"Clarice, I realize you and Jimmy Fountain are not exactly the best of friends," Dennis replied, "but give him a break. This is the place to be in Louisville. You can't get this type of atmosphere any place else in town. Besides, my dear, I'm buying." Dennis reached for Clarice with his right arm to pull her into an embrace, but she shrugged away and began a conversation with the woman seated to her right.

"Is there a special tonight?" questioned the chatty woman who had earlier inquired about the mint julep.

The waitress smiled, "You're in luck. Chef Fountain fixed an extra large batch of hot dog gravy and he is offering that over mashed potatoes with peas for only thirteen ninety-five. It comes with soup or salad and Louisville's special dessert, Derby Pie."

Clarice audibly choked. She knew that the meal cost less than two dollars per person to prepare. The rest of those assembled at Dennis's gathering were excited by Chef Fountain's generous offering and all but a few took him up on his special of the day. Most ordered additional drinks. A tall man and his equally tall wife ordered from the wine list. Clarice ordered a salad, a cheeseburger and a gin and tonic, eschewing the mint julep and the special. In truth, Clarice liked Jimmy's hot dog gravy, but she refused to enrich the man who had dragged her back into the Parley Vous.

Margaret returned with Clarice's salad and the drink orders. "Your meals will be out in about fifteen minutes. Do any of you have any questions about the Majestic or the Derby?"

"What's in the Derby Pie?" asked the tall woman.

"Only the Kern family knows," replied Margaret. "Derby Pie was created in Prospect, Kentucky about fifty years ago by Leaudra and Walter Kern. We know that it is a blend of real chocolate and California walnuts, but the name and the recipe are registered with the U.S. Patent office and the Commonwealth of Kentucky. Does anyone else have any more questions?"

"I do," said Dennis. "How did you get to be so smart?"

"Mr. Frey is a perfectionist," the tiny waitress replied. "Before anyone can work with the public in the Majestic, they have to attend Derby school, a week long series of classes conceived by Mr. Frey, and pass a difficult test. Only twenty-three percent are good enough to work at the Majestic," Margaret proudly concluded.

"I didn't know there were any Negro jockeys," the cigar licker declared.

"Many people are ignorant about that," smiled Margaret defiantly. "Thirteen of the fifteen riders in the first Derby were African-American. Eleven African-American jockeys rode a total of fifteen Derby winners. That hitching post statue you might have in your yard originally depicted a black jockey. It does not denigrate us. It honors the memory of men like George Garret Lewis who rode Fonso to victory and later died when he was tossed from his horse at a race track in Saint Louis shortly after his eighteenth birthday. May I bring anyone another drink?"

Willard Frey's menu was plain and unimpressive. Jimmy Fountain knew how to prepare gargantuan portions of simple fare, but if that was all they had going for them, they would have barely eked out a living. They had much more. Jimmy was willing to work eighty hours a week and Willard was Kentucky's finest host.

Willard's first memories were of the great stallions and the little giants who stood astride the thunder. Ocala made Willard believe that he was born to own a Derby winner. His first thoroughbred was a big, sweet-natured gelding for which he spent fifty thousand dollars. Most race horses are so high-spirited they need stall companions such as cats, dogs or even chickens to calm them. Willard's gelding needed only the company of humans. It would raise its ears and lope to the stall door whenever anyone appeared. The big horse almost purred when its head was stroked. Willard's father was incredulous when he learned of Willard's purchase.

"Son, that horse has no balls," the elder Mr. Frey said. "What is he going to do when a stallion with nuts of steel comes up on his right shoulder as he enters the home stretch? A horse with no balls has no heart. You just pissed away fifty thousand."

Willard almost proved his father wrong. The gelding with the pretentious name of "World Beater" was an over-achiever. He won his first race by six lengths, his second by four-and-a-half. He broke his leg in a fall in a calamitous third race when the horse on the pole broke sideways out of the gate, felling its jockey in front of the gelding. It was as if World Beater had attempted to save the life of the stricken little man on the track by jumping over him. The attempt would have succeeded had not the desperate jockey on the ground risen in a panic as the big, brown animal was on top of him. The gelding's right front hoof gave the jockey a glancing blow, but it was enough to fracture the spindly fetlock of the thoroughbred. Willard insisted on firing the rifle that ended the life of his sweet, game horse with no balls. Willard's dream of owning a derby winner died when his big gelding's eyes closed for the last time. Willard turned his hotel into a tribute for his big horse. World Beater's portrait hung over the marquee of the Majestic. The gelding was the only non-derby winner to be memorialized in the hotel. His gentle visage was displayed on the napkins, matchbooks and business cards of "Willard Frey d/b/a World Beater Enterprises."

Clarice nibbled at her salad and finished her gin and tonic. Another was ordered and just as quickly consumed. She fell asleep with her head on the table before the others finished their meals. Clarice was vaguely aware of being carried to the car. Dennis had fallen in love with the convertible and had purchased the Mustang to complement the Jag. Tonight he lowered the top and as the fresh, sweet-smelling air swept over Clarice; she began reluctantly to awaken from a dream about birds, clouds and snow on a mountain top in Utah. There was a man with her and while she didn't know who he was, she knew she loved him and he loved her. She tried to re-enter the sleepy fantasy, but Dennis was rubbing her leg.

"It seems that almost everyone these days is emerging from the closet. I can't. I don't want to. I play poker with the men we were with tonight. I play golf and I hunt and fish with them," Dennis said. "I laugh at their jokes about queers. I even wrote a song ridiculing homosexuals. I am a dentist who specializes in straightening children's teeth. If I'm found out, my relationship with my friends would collapse and my practice in staunch, conservative Louisville would wither and die. Can't you see that we would be perfect for one another? Should any doubt ever arise as to my sexual preference all anyone would have to do would be to look at the hotty I married and you would erase any and all doubt. You will benefit because I'll make you rich. You'll never see any of the men I sleep with, nor will I ever let you be harmed in any way by my homosexuality, and if you need to be laid from time to time, I'll understand so long as you're discreet about it. Come on Clarice, say you'll marry me."

"You wrote a song?" Clarice questioned.

"What does that have to do with anything?" Dennis stammered.

"Sing it to me."

"God-damn-it Clarice," Dennis said. "Didn't you hear anything I said?"

"I heard you say you wrote a song," Clarice replied. "Sing it to me."

"If you're not going to get serious about this, just forget about it."

"Okay," Clarice replied, and for the next ten minutes or so, neither of them spoke. Then Dennis began to sing:

"He's just a little bit queer.
He likes advances to the rear.
His mince and lisp are so sincere, my dear,
He's just a little bit queer.

He's just a little bit gay,
He'd like to blow his life away.
No need to say pretty please
To get him on his knees,

He's just a little bit gay.

You'd never know it to look at him
He plays his cards close to his vest.
But he'd rather lick
Some other guy's dick
Than to nibble on some hot honey's
breast.

He's just a silly little queer
Who'd like a pat upon his rear?
So buy your balladeer a beer, my dear
   And I'll make him disappear. "

   "You perform that when you sing it,
don't you? " Clarice said. "I can see you
swishing and singing. You wrote your
autobiography and you put it to music. That
was a very brave thing to do. You hide who
you are by revealing who you are. You don't
need me. You are far too clever for any of
your friends to ever find out that you are
really Clark Kent, and speaking of Clark,
wasn't he in drag when he put on his Superman
suit? Blue leotards, a cape and red
slippers; it's a bird; it's a plane, its Mrs.
Doubtfire. "
They spent the rest of the ride back to Paris
Crossing silently regretting that they could
not be the person either of them wanted.
Dennis knew he would never be more
comfortable with a woman, and Clarice thought
she would not again find a man she would
trust not to hurt her.
   "Will you at least think about my offer
to make you rich? " Dennis said as he pulled
into the drive next to Clarice's apartment.
Clarice turned to Dennis and grasped his
shoulders. She pulled on his left one and
pushed on his right. They were face to face.
Clarice could smell onions mixed with fear
emanating from Dennis's breath and his sweat.
"I really love being with you, " Dennis

said. "You're smart, you're funny, all of my friends adore you."

"I have loved being with you, Dennis. I only wish you liked girls, because for weeks I have wanted you to make love to me. I never thought I would feel that way again after I was betrayed in the back seat of a Buick. I am grateful to you for making me feel that way again. You have shown me that there are kind, gentle men out there. Men I can trust. I am grateful to you for making me horny again." She removed her hands from Dennis's shoulders and placed one on each cheek with her thumbs under his chin. She kissed him deeply then and for an instant, Clarice thought she detected a hint of reciprocal movement from an inert tongue. She held on to the kiss, encouraging, wanting, and needing a tactile reply. The response she received was akin to kissing a corpse.

"Goodbye, Dennis. Take care of yourself."

Clarice opened the door to the Mustang and before she had a chance to leave, Dennis squeezed the back of her shoulders. "You make me wish I was straight," he said.

"That makes two of us," Clarice replied.

CHAPTER FORTY:
DISCOVERY

For one hundred fifty years in Indiana trials, neither party had the right to know the identity of the witnesses that would be called by the other side. No exhibits were required to be revealed or exchanged. The process was called "trial by ambush" as lawyers would hide witnesses in order to spring a trap that would damage or destroy an opponent's case. New discovery rules had been passed to eliminate the inequities of hidden evidence, but in criminal cases the State often waited until the last possible moment to reveal exhibits and names. As Marie's trial date grew near, Pres waited apprehensively for the State to let him know who would take the stand to prove Marie's guilt. Pres was staying in Paris Crossing, tending to his practice, Monday through Thursday. Friday through Sunday, he tended to Marie.

The State's list of witnesses was given to Pres twenty-two days before Marie's trial was to begin. It was surprisingly short. Technical people needed to describe entrance and exit wounds were on the list. The coroner and the sheriff were going to testify about the time of death and the description of the crime scene. Harry was on the list, Pres was a bit puzzled by his inclusion. The final witness listed was the last person Pres wanted to see at the trial: Jimmy's ex-wife, Elia Hawkins.

Pres requested a hearing immediately after he received the State's list. In his petition Pres asked the State to produce Elia Hawkins so that Pres could take her deposition. "In order to discover what she plans to testify concerning the guilt of my client."

The judge's response was immediate. She ordered both parties to be present the

following day.   The State's position was
predictable.

"Judge, we plan on having Ms. Hawkins
here the day before the trial begins," the
prosecutor said.   "We will make her
available for Mr. Hart to question then.
Otherwise, he can always go to Costa Rica
like we had to do.   Besides, Mr. Hart knows
that Ms. Hawkins will tell the jury that his
client was screwing Ms. Hawkins's husband."

"Mister Terry," the judge said loudly.
"You will talk properly in my court.   Mr.
Hart's request is not unreasonable.   You will
have Ms. Hawkins here ten days before the
trial is to begin so that Mr. Hart may take
her deposition; any questions?"

Clark Terry was constantly smiling.   He
used his friendly countenance to disguise
contempt, anger and hostility.   His grin was
not nearly enough to mollify the judge.
"Judge, since you ruled that Ms. Hawkins has
to come here early, could she stay with
you?"

"Mr. Terry, that will cost you either
one hundred dollars or twenty-four hours in
jail," the judge said quietly.   "Madam
bailiff, since our barred accommodations are
rather crowded at the moment, please call the
Sheriff of Parke County to see if he has a
cell for our prosecutor.   Ask him if the one
formerly occupied by Mister Terry's old
friends the Benson boys is available."

The Benson Boys

The Bensons were named Edward and Edwin
but they were called big Ed and little Ed.
Little Ed was six four and weighed nearly
three hundred pounds.   Big Ed was bigger than
Little Ed.   They had not caused many problems
until two years ago when they were saved by a
visiting Maranatha preacher.   Their mother

was Methodist and their father was a farmer. The boys attended church only when Mother Benson insisted. One Sunday her pleas became demands. The Methodist minister, the Reverend Smoot, had chosen that day to yield his pulpit to the darkly handsome, "King of the Soul Savers for Christ," the one, the only, Burt Masterson.

The very Reverend Masterson, or "Baptizing Burt" as he preferred to be called, had a simple message. He believed that total immersion in natural creeks, lakes or ponds would wash away the devil and give sinners a second chance to "sit at the feet of Jesus" in paradise. The Methodists were only sprinklers, barely wetting hair with spray bottles during their baptismal ceremony and Reverend Smoot knew that he was going to be in trouble with the Methodist hierarchy when the Indianapolis bishop he feared, got word of Smoot's heresy.

Smoot had invited "Baptizing Burt" to preach on Smoot's watch because he felt that his diminishing flock needed a jump-start. Masterson was a local television celebrity who had an eight a.m. Sunday program on Louisville's WHAS. The Methodist minister knew that Masterson would attract a crowd. Smoot hoped that some of those who came this Sunday would return to see what their innovative Methodist minister had in store for them next. Smoot also believed that his faithful would be amused by the antics of "Baptizing Burt." No self-respecting Methodist would view Masterson as anything but a religious diversion, not to be taken seriously. Unfortunately, the Benson boys were not at all self-respecting, and they were convinced that Masterson's message of total immersion had been delivered to "Baptizing Burt" by John the Baptist himself.

At the end of Masterson's impassioned sermon, he invited sinners to leave their pews and come to him in order to find salvation in the healing waters of Sugar Creek. "I have a van outside capable of taking twenty to God's throne. There are at least a hundred souls here and all of you need each and every part of your body immersed and purified, so it may become a holy vessel worthy of the love of God that will pour into you when you are cleansed. I want to make five baptismal trips to the blessed waters, so that all of us are guaranteed salvation. Let us pray. Blessed Jesus, I sense hesitance in this congregation. Your servant, Reverend Smoot, gave me the opportunity to send your message to Methodists and while Methodists know you and love you, they are hesitant to publicly acknowledge their commitment to Christ. Lessen their inhibitions, Lord. Let them not be ashamed to stand and begin that walk up the aisle, toward me, toward the cleansing water that leads to eternal life. Tell them to come to me, God. Make their legs move and their spirits soar. "

Masterson's head remained bowed. At first, no one stirred, and then a middle-aged woman stood and began singing "Amazing Grace. " Later, most agreed that she was in league with "Baptizing Burt' " but at the time, the effect was electric. Several people began to sob, and soon many entered the aisle, marching toward Masterson, who was now standing, his arms raised in a Christ-like pose, beseeching and preaching. The Benson boys had been seated in pews opposite one another, but they rose as one to join the other supplicants on the road to paradise.

Exactly nineteen souls crowded into the van that bore the name "Holy Water. " Burt drove and the woman who led the singing in church sang hymns all the way to Sugar Creek. The songs of saved souls are loud and predictable. They always include the sin cleansing trio of "We Shall Gather at the

River," "In the Garden," and "The Old Rugged Cross." The Bensons did not join in. The mammoth brothers sat silently with their eyes forward and their shoulders erect. If you looked closely, you could see tears flowing from four large eyes, down four large cheeks.

Sugar Creek is a large stream when the spring rainfall totals are normal. It is as wide as a small river when the spring rains become "duck drowneders." The creek was well above flood stage when the baptizing van pulled into the public access driveway near Darlington. The upstream villages of Thorntown and Kirkin had been turned into small islands. Carp floated in basements and snakes took refuge in trees. Down river, the canoe rental businesses were closed. Two canoes escaped detection and were gaily bobbing and spinning their way toward the Wabash River. They were joined along the way by uprooted saplings, the debris from bank side campfires, and one white plastic lawn chair of the type purchased by the millions in the nineties. The creek water gained momentum as it passed Rockville and thundered toward the Wabash; then, almost imperceptibly, it began to slow and broaden. Swollen creeks do not overwhelm flooded rivers. Wild streams become docile. Wolves become collies. Deprived of the ability to empty into rivers, creek banks vanish and the water becomes a silent, persistent destroyer of property, as it drowns crops and muddies indoor-outdoor carpeting. Floods bring with them a smell of rot, as if turkey vultures have vomited partially digested catfish or buffalo.

Masterson surveyed the scene with a mixture of horror and revulsion. In order to accomplish his sworn goal of total immersion, he and his penitents would have to wade through about thirty feet of ankle deep water certain to mud-suck the shoes off men and women alike. The part of the creek where the water was deep enough to accomplish the baptizer's goal was torpid and stagnant. A turtle's head rose and seemed to sniff the air. Finding the smell revolting, the turtle dove for cleaner water. "Takes a lot to offend a fucking turtle," thought Masterson. "What am I going to do with these people?"

"Does anybody know someone who owns a pool?" Masterson implored. "It looks like Jesus would want us to look for clean water to cleanse our sins. Jesus is everywhere. He can even find us in chlorine."

"If we are going to find Jesus, we had better be looking for him here," Edwin Benson said. "He ministered to lepers. He washed the feet of the unclean. He would want us to wash away our sins in his water. He will cleanse this creek with our souls. Isn't that what you just finished telling us, Preacher? You get in the creek and me and my brother will bring the sinners to you."

The singing lady began again. This time it was "Michael, Row the Boat Ashore," as the Bensons carried souls to "Baptizing Burt" who had uneasily deposited himself in hip-deep water. Edward worked from the van carrying soon-to-be-saved souls to Edwin, who was located midway between the "Holy Water" and the preacher. Edwin completed the symbolic journey across the river Styx and gently immersed each sinner as directed by the baptizer. Edwin would then return the redolent, but cleansed soul to Edward, who would exchange his sweet-smelling, sinful burden for Edwin's saved and pungent one.

The singing lady provided pilfered motel towels and reams of "Wet Ones" to the sodden but saved souls and all looked toward the stream as the Bensons were reborn. Each of the mammoth men was immersed in turn by his brother as Masterson intoned the ancient, mystical phrases of salvation. Jesus became real again for the occupants of the "Holy Water" as they returned to Crawfordsville.

The singing lady chose the militant "Onward Christian Soldiers" as her final number as if to remind the saved of their duty to save others. The Bensons got the message.

Sugar Creek has wide beaches in Turkey Run State Park. This bucolic setting south and west of Crawfordsville features trails, cliffs, scenery and canoeing. It attracts thousands during the warm months and it was an ideal setting for a pair of serial baptizers.

The Benson brothers would loiter in the water near the swimmers in the most congested swimming areas. Pretending to frolic, one of the big Jesus lovers would submerge an unsuspecting floater while the other intoned holy words. "In the name of the Father, Son and the Holy Ghost" was the phrase most often utilized, although other magical sentences containing Savior, Redeemer, Prince of Peace and the like were sometimes intoned. The immersions were brief, and most people tolerated them, especially when they learned of the big men's motives. You are inclined to trust big, jovial, gentle men who talk of Jesus.

As a matter of fact, only one complaint had been registered before Clark Terry went swimming with his wife in Sugar Creek. The complainant was a rather corpulent woman in a two-piece suit, the top of which covered nipples and aureoles and nothing else of her blue-veined, oversized mammaries. Her dunking freed her breasts from their fragile restraints and the blue and white flowers which adorned her yellow top were swept away by a canoe paddle and hoisted atop a makeshift mast. Edwin ran to shore to borrow a towel while Edward stared wondering why one breast floated while the other broke surface tension and submerged. The woman noticed too, and shifted her body to try to drown the floater, but it remained buoyant and cheerfully defiant while the sullen tit stayed under water.

.The woman's ire had all but vanished when she made her report to the Park Ranger. "I know they were just having fun," she said, "but they are so big they might hurt someone." The incident was duly noted and the Bensons were perfunctorily questioned. Their response -- "We were doing God's work" - was quoted in the record that was made for that day, but no explanation was sought. As the ranger later testified, "They seemed to be nice, young men, and they are so goddamn big."

Clark Terry did not like water. As a matter of fact, he was afraid of it. Showers were fine and a tub was fun. He would not set foot in an ocean because as he explained, "there are denizens in there that will eat you." Sugar Creek was doable, but frightening. Terry would wade into water that was knee high, but if it touched his testicles, he would run for dry land.

Terry had noticed the two big men speaking earnestly to a group of teenagers near the middle of the creek. The young people were nearly neck deep in water while the Bensons navels were showing. "Look at those big bastards," Terry said to his wife as he turned to head for shore. Suddenly the water seemed to explode as the big men turned toward Terry and his wife and attempted to submerge and save the two sinners. Terry turned to see what was going on, but his wife, sensing trouble, started for dry land. Terry followed, but he was not quick enough. His heart pounded in his chest, ears and anus as he was held under water. He resurfaced flailing wildly as the bigger Benson assured Terry that he had been washed in the blood of the lamb.

"You stupid sons-of-bitches almost drowned me," Terry screamed hysterically and added the line favored by lawyers the world over, "I'll see you in court."

Following their arrest on charges of criminal assault, the Bensons listened solemnly as the Parke County judge read the affidavit containing the charges. "So if I understand this correctly, you two attempted to baptize the Montgomery County Prosecutor," said the obviously amused judge. "And Mister Terry took offense at your attempt to make him see the light? Is that correct?"

"We are guilty, your honor," said Edwin, "Guilty of cleansing the soul of another sinner."

"I have no doubt that Mister Terry's soul needed cleansing," said the judge smiling at his court reporter and bailiff. "But you boys had no right to attempt a forcible conversion," the judge continued. "I'm going to sentence you to thirty days in jail, but I'll suspend that sentence, if you two apologize to Mister Terry and promise me that you will stop this baptizing foolishness. The authorities at Sugar Creek tell me that this is not the first time you two have attempted to harvest souls on their property and it's just got to stop. Do you understand?"

This time Edward spoke, "Your honor, I reckon we'll do the thirty days. We can't stop saving souls. That's our calling."

Two weeks passed. The Bensons had been given the run of the jail. They were the only inmates in the ancient, spacious ruin and they spent their days roaming from cell to cell. They carried a boombox with them which the First Methodist Church had provided. A local radio station offered twenty-four hour God rock and new age Christian standards such as "Jump for Jesus," "Rock Around the Cross, and "Our Savior Rocks". They were played constantly. The volume control on the radio was turned to its maximum level and the Bensons sang along with the music. The resultant din disturbed even the pigeons. The jail had for years been one of their most favored places to sleep and shit, but the great flock took wing during the second chorus of the "Samson and Delilah Twist."

Sheriff Butler was beside himself. The sheriff and his wife lived in a comfortable home across the alley from the jail. One of the very substantial perks of his job was that the house, its furnishings and all of the utilities and expenses were provided by the county. In addition, he was given a generous allowance to provide food for his prisoners. Instead of buying meals from restaurants, the sheriff's wife Marcie went once a week to the Kroger in Terre Haute and purchased the meats and vegetables which she cooked in large quantities for the inmates. The county council looked the other way, willing to let the sheriff pocket the profit so long as his prisoners were well fed. Unfortunately, the Bensons were prodigious eaters. The ladies from the church visited them daily bringing chocolate cookies and eclairs, cakes of various flavors and blueberry muffins. These were all quickly consumed, as was the food Marcie supplied. The once a week trip to Kroger became a twice and then three times a week thing. When she wasn't shopping, Marcie was cooking, stirring the large pots, and slow cooking the cheap cuts of beef to make them edible. All the while the cacophony created by the loud Christian music and the singing and chewing of the Bensons was turning Sheriff Butler into a whining, pitiful creature.

"Judge, you've got to let them go," pleaded the sheriff. He had adopted a supplicant's posture in the judge's chambers and was pulling at the judge's sleeve.

"Sheriff, I've been meaning to talk to you," said the Parke County Judge, prying the Sheriff's hands from his Gant shirt. "The ladies from the Methodist Church are concerned that you aren't feeding your prisoners well enough. They tell me that the Bensons always seem to be hungry."

The sheriff started to cry. Soon he was sobbing uncontrollably.

"Marcie's talking about moving in with her mother and I'm having to feed those big bastards out of my own pocket," Sheriff Butler said between convulsive sobs. "For the love of God man, have some mercy."

"Mister Edwin Benson, Mister Edward Benson, you are free to go," said the judge to the brothers who were standing before him in the otherwise empty courtroom. "By the way, in case you are asked, please say that you apologized before I cut you loose."

The brothers looked at one another and Edward spoke. "We are sorry Judge," he said. "From here on in we're going to try to only baptize people who have souls."

"Yes," Edwin added "No more lawyers for us."

Elia Hawkins

Harry wanted to question Elia. "I will absolutely devastate her," Harry bombastically proclaimed to a horrified Pres. Trial lawyers know that it is a difficult task to destroy the credibility of a witness. Weepy confessions are the stuff of weekday television. "Besides," Pres protested, "this is only a deposition. Its purpose is to find out what she plans on saying at the trial. For all we know, she might not hurt us at all."

"Fat chance of that happening," Harry replied. "Terry may be dumb as a box of rocks, but he sure as hell didn't bring that bitch all the way from Costa Rica to say nice things about your wife."

Pres was pissed. Harry had learned the art of cross examination by imitating his father, who had learned it from his father, ad infinitum. The method employed was to ask the deponent a critical question. When the answer was harmful to his client's case, Harry and the pettifoggers who preceded him would argue with the witness. "Now Mrs. Hawkins," Harry would say, "everybody in this room knows that you did not truthfully answer that last question. Perhaps you didn't understand it." Where-upon Harry would ask the question again. When the same answer was given, Harry would turn stern and righteous. "Mrs. Hawkins, do you know the penalty for perjury in the state of Indiana?" Harry would intone and then he would pick up the large black book lying on the table in front of him and read aloud from it perjury's definition and punishment. Harry would then ask the court reporter to repeat the question. If the same answer was given, Harry would leave the topic only to return later with the same question accompanied by the same theatrics, only louder.

Pres realized that people were no longer frightened of lawyers. Harry's tactics were sometimes successful in the days prior to I Love Lucy, but then Perry Mason was overwhelmed by LA Law. Lawyers began to be portrayed as flawed men and women and the general public took notice. The respect for officers of the court faded and when the mighty fall, everyone wants to put a bullet into the body. Attorneys were viewed as vanquished bullies. If the trend continues, Pres thought, trial spectators will soon be provided with eggs and spoiled vegetables to toss at the once mighty masters of the court room. Pres knew that any chance of them getting any favorable answers from Elia at trial would vanish if Harry laid his heavy hands on her during the deposition.

"Harry," Pres said, "you asked me to defend Marie and I agreed. Now, let me do my goddamn job. I will depose the former wife of Sonny Hawkins."

Four days later, Elia Hawkins swore to tell the truth to Pres while a glowering Harry looked on from a seat two rows removed from the action. The introductory questions were asked and answered. Elia testified that she was indeed married at one time to the deceased and that she lived in Costa Rica not far from the place of her birth, and that she knew the defendant, Marie Hawkins. Elia spoke in a pleasant, soft manner with just a trace of a Latin accent. Pres found himself liking her. She was not beautiful but she was definitely cute, verging on pretty. Pres knew that a jury would want to believe every word she said.

"Mrs. Hawkins," Pres asked "are you acquainted with my client, Marie Hart?" Pres nodded his head in the direction of Marie who sat next to him.

"Yes I know her," said Elia. "Except for the fact that she's older and her breasts are bigger, she still looks the same as she did when I caught her fucking my husband."

Elia spoke softly without rancor or emotion. The "fucking my husband" line is seldom delivered in a monotone. It is usually punctuated with tears, screams, and sarcasm, sometimes combined with false bravado. Elia, Pres noted with a hint of admiration, had none of the above. She just no longer gave a shit.

The rest of the deposition went quickly. Elia was going to testify at trial that Marie and Sonny had been lovers. A jury would know that Sonny was no stranger to Marie's bed. Pres was not without emotion. He kept his composure outwardly, but he was inwardly raging over the fact that the prosecutor was going to publicly reveal the fact that Marie had been sexually molested as a child. Worse, he was going to get by with it because it established motive. Pres was beginning to get desperate. His client was no help. Trial was approaching and he had no clue how he was going to keep Marie out of prison.

CHAPTER FORTY-ONE:
THE ROUND TABLE

Chocolate, French dressing, escargot, walleye, bleu cheese, butterscotch, the lickable crease where the inside of a woman's leg blends into her pelvis, fortune cookies, sushi, walnuts, quail gravy, steaks broiled Pittsburgh style, shrimp cooked on the grill, nipples coated with apple butter, food, pussy and death were the major topics of discussion at the round table in December, 2000.

Red toyed with his eggs. He liked them over-easy, almost snotty. Clarice had killed his eggs and undercooked his bacon. Red morosely wondered about trichinosis as he chewed the barely-cooked strips. Clarice had not been herself since Pres had been gone. Red reluctantly accepted the fact that Clarice did not want Pres to return to his wife.

"I have a new guest," Bill Walsh said; none of his guests stayed very long. "How many of you remember Hazel Nutter?"

"Jesus, Bill," Doc said. "I thought she was dead years ago. How old was she?"

"Ninety-eight," Bill replied. "She lived by herself with no outside help except for the "meals on wheels" people who brought her food five days a week. Every Saturday, she would drive to the IGA in North Vernon in her enormous Cadillac to get her paper goods, cigarettes, bread and beer. According to the folks at the grocery store, she almost always purchased a case of Miller High Life and two cartons of Marlboros. They got a kick out of the fact that she loaded up on the free catsup, mustard, napkins and salt and pepper packets, and talked the cashiers into giving her matchbooks. She lived like a beggar, but I'll bet she died a millionaire. Her stockbroker is making the arrangements."

"What a cruel name to give a girl," Red mused. "Hazel Nutter. Her mom must have hated her."

"I think it might have been her father," Bill said. "According to the obituary her son dropped off this morning, her father was named Chester "Chess" Nutter and she had a sister named Pea."

"You've got to be shitting me," Red said. "Did she keep up the tradition? Were her kids named Mixed, Cashew and Wall?"

"She never married and she had only one child, a son named Mack," Bill said.

"Thank God," Red exclaimed.

"Probably short for Macadamia," Doc snorted.

"Holy Christ," said Bill. "He said his name was Mack, but I'll bet you're right. Maybe that's the reason he wrote such a shitty obituary. Do kids with cruel names become cruel adults? Do children with stupid names become stupid adults? I don't know whether to give it to the papers or shit-can it. Anyway, here's what he wrote; I suppose I could abridge it, but he's the paying customer. I don't know what to do. I'll read it to you and I'll welcome any suggestions.

"Hazel Nutter," Bill began, "born July 7, 1902 and died December 3, 2000." "I'll skip the ancestry appetizer I just gave you and get to the main course." "Lincoln was called the great emancipator. Hazel was the great emasculator. Her conquests included the father of her child, her only son, and the over 400 employees of the auto repair business she inherited known as Lug Nuts. Hazel hated men and barely tolerated women. She was born angry and she died pissed-off. The family is taking applications for pallbearers, since no volunteers can be found. The first six to apply will be paid one hundred dollars each."

"Still upset with his mom because she named him after a hard-shelled, solid-textured, one-celled fruit, huh?" Doc inquired. "Sounds like Hazel wasn't the only cuckoo in the family tree."

"Actually," Red said, "I thought they were both pretty nice people, but they got crosswise over Velma Richardson."

"Velma Richardson," Doc said. "Now there's a name I haven't heard in years. What connected Velma to the Nutters?"

"If you remember correctly," Red said. "Velma was a looker, but there was a weirdness about her. She wore a long fur boa year round. It dangled from her neck in the summer and she wrapped it around her breasts when fall arrived. In the winter, it went around her ass a time or two and she pinned it to her skirt with a pin that looked like a monarch butterfly. She was always bare-legged and wore black high heels regardless of the weather or the season. Those heels were always shiny and she put a racing stripe of lipstick on each toe to match what she was wearing on her lips."

"Jesus Christ, Red," Doc said. "What kind of panties did she wear on her buttery little ass? Did she rouge her nipples?"

"Doc, you're disgusting. I barely noticed Velma, but Debbie was fascinated by her. Velma was only here for a few months, but she came into the restaurant two or three times when Debbie was helping out and for days later Debbie would talk about what Velma had on, how she held her cigarettes, the shade of her lipstick."

"I don't remember her at all," said Bill. "I must be getting really old. How long ago was this?"

"About ten years, wasn't it Red?" Doc asked.

"Yup," Red answered. "Nineteen ninety-one to be precise. I re-read the file right after I heard that Hazel died."

"File?" Doc asked. "What kind of file?"

"A criminal file," Red replied. "Mack Nutter had been through a nasty divorce in Memphis and he'd come home to mama to re-group. Hazel had been feeling poorly the month before Mack arrived and she'd checked into the hospital in Madison. Velma was a night shift nurse and Hazel was an insomniac. The two took a liking to one another and when Hazel was discharged, she took Velma home with her. Velma's job was to cook, make sure Hazel took her medicine, and keep Hazel company. Hazel told me that Velma was well paid."

"Did you mention her tits?" asked Bill. "I remember a nurse with really big ones who used to come in here."

"Actually, Velma had next to no breasts," Red replied. "She had a great ass and thick, sensuous lips. She carried herself regally, like she was queen fucking Elizabeth."

"I am so sick of aging," Bill gloomily proclaimed. "I wonder if this faux Alzheimer's might be worse than the real thing. At least with 'Old Timers' disease, as some of our rural elders call it, you don't realize that your brain is turning into viscous horseshit. How could I not remember a young woman with a great ass and Julia Roberts' lips?"

"She was not really all that young, was she Red?" Doc asked.

"She took care of herself," Red replied. "And she looked younger than she was. When I ran her records before filing theft charges against her, I was surprised when I learned that she was forty-five when she fled the county."

"That explains it," Bill gleefully exclaimed. "I wouldn't have paid any attention to a woman that fucking old."

"You are so full of shit," Doc said. "I have seen you drool over any number of geriatric widows who have hired you to put their poor dead spouses underground. Let's admit it. A fifty-year old woman doesn't look too good to a twenty-year old man, but she's a hot looking piece of ass when you're sixty. Can we get back to the Nutter saga? What happened to them, Red?"

"I really shouldn't tell you any more," Red said. "Hazel swore me to secrecy. I wish Pres were here to let me know if Hazel's death released me from my promise to keep quiet."

"Of course it did," said Doc. "Besides, you'd really be a prick if you didn't finish what you started. What would Debbie do if you got her all hot and bothered and then turned on NYPD Blue, or whatever you law enforcement shit-heads watch?"

"I guess it will be all right," Red said. "To make a long story short, Velma started servicing both Mack and Hazel."

"At the same time?" Doc asked. "Jesus, that's really sick."

"Sexual depravity in Paris Crossing, and I can't even remember the main character," Bill said mournfully. "I might as well go lay down in one of my eternal bed-e-byes. 'Guaranteed to last forever' the sales literature says and the poor bereaved bastards believe it. Like who's going to unearth Grandpa two hundred years from now to see if his mattress is moldy."

"According to Hazel," Red replied to Doc's question, "neither she nor Mack knew that Velma was screwing them both. This went on for sometime with Velma hopping from one bed to the other, sometimes doing both Nutters in the same night."

"What was in it for Velma?" Doc asked.

"Hazel's stash," Red replied. "Hazel had several lockboxes in the North Vernon State bank loaded with cash, jewels and various coin collections and she gave Velma access to them. Hazel liked to wear her baubles around her house and she didn't like to wear the same jewelry more than a day or two at a time. She also liked to count her money. So Hazel would have Velma run to the bank to exchange the jewelry and return the cash. Problem was that lots of rings and things never got back into Hazel's lockbox."

"So why was she doing Mack?" asked Bill. "Didn't you say that his ex-wife cleaned him out?"

"Mack co-signed for Velma to buy a new car" Red said "a yellow Mustang convertible with a black top. Mack didn't have any money but his credit was good and Velma traded in her eighty-eight Olds with over a hundred thousand miles on it to seal the deal. I think the payments on that fully equipped mustard colored beauty were around three-twelve a month."

"Anyway," Red continued, "Velma slept in Hazel's room in a twin bed next to Hazel's four-poster canopy king and one night Mack decided to pay his mom and his lover an unannounced visit. According to Hazel, her bedroom door was always locked, but Velma had left the room earlier to go pee-pee and had apparently forgotten to snap the dead bolt back in place when she returned. When Mack opened the door, his mom was spread-eagled and Velma's face was down where it could do Hazel the most good."

"Jesus," said Doc, "how revolting. To see your mother naked must have been bad enough, but to see her being licked by your lover? That's some really bad shit. What happened next?"

"Velma ran out of the room and Mack beat the shit out of Hazel," Red said. "If Velma had not made the 911 call, Mack might have committed matricide. The old lady was damned near dead when I arrived."

"His mom?" Bill asked. "He tried to kill his mom?"

"According to Hazel, Mack kept yelling about Hazel being responsible for taking away everyone Mack ever loved," Red said. "Hazel thought that had to do with her leaving Mack's father who Mack seldom got to see after his parents split."

"What happened to Velma?" Bill asked. "God, I wish I could remember her. Were these people ever on Springer?"

"Nothing much happened at first," said Red. "Jerry didn't come calling, Hazel didn't check her lockbox right away and Mack quietly went on a state-by-state quest searching for his lost love. He told me he would forgive her if only she would let him prove to her that he was all she would ever need in the bedroom. Then Hazel discovered that Velma had been taking valuables out of Hazel's lockbox and Mack started getting calls from The North Vernon State Bank wanting its money for Velma's car loan. Hazel swore out a complaint on a Monday and Mack came in two days later to swear out one of his own."

"Did you bring them to justice?" Bill asked in his most dramatic timbre. Bill thought he sounded a bit like John Wayne. Red was reminded more of a bronchial Daffy Duck.

"Very few people understand this part of my job," Red said. "I don't just throw somebody in jail because somebody else alleges that their neighbor poisoned their cat, peeked through their window, or stole panties off their clothesline. My job is to take the complaint to the prosecutor. His job is to shit-can it, take it to a grand jury, which is the same as shit-canning it, or take it to the Judge."

"So the prosecutor doesn't have to prosecute?" asked Bill. "Seems to me that makes him one powerful son of a bitch."

"Bingo," said Red. "The prosecutor wouldn't prosecute and so there wasn't a damned thing I could do."

"What kinda shit is that?" asked Doc. "So he just let that cheating, eating, thieving, bitch get away?"

"I was pissed about it at first," explained Red, "but after I talked to Pres, it all made sense. Hazel couldn't prove that she had anything in her lockbox. Only she and Velma knew what was in there and Velma sure as hell wasn't talking. Think about it. Bill, you and Inez know what's in your safety deposit box but even if you've told me that you have a shit pot of E Bonds in there, that don't prove squat. That's why you can't insure a lockbox against the theft of its contents."

"But what about the car?" Bill asked. "She stole the fucking Mustang, didn't she?"

"Did she?" Red asked. "In order to show his love and trust, Mack put the car in Velma's name and you can't steal your own property."

Clarice was usually quiet about making her entrance. Dolly had taught Clarice to be unobtrusive so as not to disturb the men as she warmed coffee with her ubiquitous pot. This time was different. Rushing from the kitchen, Clarice appeared with both her pot and a telephone. "Pres's father-in-law just died," she loudly exclaimed, handing the phone to Bill, "and Pres wants to talk to you."

CHAPTER FORTY-TWO:
THE TRIAL

Harry Hawkins's life had been notable for sound. As a boy, he had spoken loudly to gain attention and to distract bullies. As an adult, he had added bass to the volume to seduce and persuade. Cigarettes and Jim Beam had turned his lower register into a growl. Death came quietly, sneaking first into his kidneys and then into his lungs as he lay sleeping. Harry awakened just long enough to realize what was happening. He tried to yell, but had no breath to form words. In the split second before sliding down into the abyss, Harry realized that he had nothing more to say. "Goodbye," his mind screamed in terror. "Goodbye," echoed and resounded throughout Harry's dreams and nightmares. Patiently waiting wolves finally got to tear. Fetid sewers rushed into petrified lungs. Harry's body fell and on this truly last occasion, it slammed into the earth.

Marie was quiet while Pres made Harry's funeral arrangements. She spoke only once, grabbing the telephone from Pres to tell Bill not to notify her mother or to include her mother's name in the obituary. "That bitch has not even telephoned to see how I'm doing," Marie exclaimed to Pres after he had finished talking to Bill. "Her only daughter is on trial for murder and she doesn't care any more about me than she did about poor Daddy. I have no mother and now I have no Dad."

Pres braced for the emotion. Marie had initially looked in on Harry at 7:30 a.m. Seeing nothing amiss, she had softly called for him and returned to his kitchen to pour his coffee. Still suspecting nothing, Marie gently touched Harry's arm and found it wet with his spittle. Harry's open mouth had produced copious amounts of drool. Death had frozen his eyes in place. Marie screamed and still Harry's unblinking eyes stared at nothing. It was then Marie realized that her Daddy had abandoned her.

Tears for the dead are really tears for the living, and Marie had none to shed for herself. Still, her sense of loss was enormous. Her neck felt as if it would not support her head. The air that she breathed tasted heavy and viscous. She swallowed every few moments, trying to rid herself of the marble-sized lump that had formed on the rear of her tongue. She knew that grief was expected of her. She wanted to cry, to lose herself in the delirium of hysteria yet she feared ostentatious grieving would somehow diminish Harry. She did not want to create a distraction that would take attention away from her memory of the great Harry Hawkins. She would keep her sorrow to herself. Pres, on the other hand, suddenly saw Harry's death as a way to preserve Marie's freedom.

For weeks, Pres had wrestled with the Fifth Amendment. Unless you were O.J., your ass would go to jail if you failed to explain yourself. Jurors interpreted silence as an admission of guilt. Many a marginal case turned in favor of a conviction because of a juror's unspoken belief that silence meant you had something to hide. Judges could lecture and instruct to the contrary, but it still would not remove the image of televised scum invoking their constitutional right to remain silent.

Marie could take the stand. Pres supposed, but what would she say? "I found my lover on top of me, so I grabbed my gun, reached around, and shot him in the back of the head?"

"What a crock of shit," Pres thought. It was sure to brand her as a liar. The prosecutor would point out to the jury that Marie would be physically endangering herself by putting her head in the path of the bullet, not to mention the contortions she would have to put herself through in order to reach around Sonny's head and pull the trigger. From the physical evidence alone, the jury could infer that Marie arose from her bed and shot Sonny as he lay sleeping; cold blooded murder. Marie would not take the witness stand, Pres concluded, but if his plan worked, Marie would still get to "testify."

Pres' mind continued to race. He knew, as did all of the best criminal lawyers, that truth was irrelevant. His job was to vindicate his client whether she was guilty or not. Marie had admitted to firing the fatal shot. She also claimed to be acting in self defense while resisting rape. These two statements had to lead to only one conclusion. Marie was lying; but about what? There was only one way to attack the State's case; blame it on someone else. Pres would blame Harry Hawkins.

Trial began as scheduled. It took one day, working until 7:00 p.m., to select the six men and six women who would determine Marie's future. Unlike most trials, no one wanted to ask the Judge to excuse them from what promised to be several days of sex and blood. Pres kept exercising his preemptory challenges on women and the prosecutor countered by trying to get rid of the men. Both lawyers believed that Marie would charm the men but the women would want to hang her. Finally, the Judge tired of the process and suggested that the jury be equally divided. "Otherwise," she said, referring to the lawyers, "you gentlemen are going to be wasting the Court's time while you embarrass the whole county with your sexist behavior."

The State had the burden of proving Marie's guilt and so on day two of the trial, Craig Terry rose and buttoned his coat, as he had seen every lawyer on every television

court drama do, and proceeded to tell the
jury what the State's evidence would be.
"We will prove," Terry began, "that the
defendant Marie Hart killed her long time
lover by shooting him in cold blood as he lay
sleeping. We will also prove that the bullet
fired by Marie Hart entered the brain of the
deceased and caused massive trauma, thereby
ending his life. We will prove that the
fatal wound was to the back of the deceased's
head, thereby ruling out any argument of
self-defense."

"Objection," Pres exclaimed, nearly
leaping from his chair. "The 'ruling out
self defense' remark is argument and should
be stricken. We ask for a mistrial."

"Your mistrial motion is overruled,"
the Judge said. "However, the self-defense
remark is argument and will be stricken and
the jury is instructed to disregard it."

"Members of the jury," the Judge said
turning toward the six men and six women
eagerly waiting for the lurid tale of sex and
murder to begin. "When I say that you
should disregard something, you must treat
the event as if it never happened."

"And you Mister Terry," the Judge
said, turning her attention to the
prosecutor, "will have ample time to argue
this case at the conclusion of the evidence.
Get back to your opening remarks and confine
yourself to what you intend to prove."

"Yes, your honor," Terry said, a
little rattled by Pres's interruption. As
minor as it might seem to an outsider, the
first objection set a pattern. If the ruling
was in your favor, the jury would be inclined
to believe that the defendant's lawyer was a
lightweight, only speaking to hear his own
voice. Lose the first ruling and lose the
invaluable presumption of first impression.
Momentum had shifted and the trial had barely
begun. Terry had hoped to slide slowly into
the sordid details, building anticipation

with suggestion until it became foreplay. Pres had spoiled the moment much as the strident ringing of a telephone can ruin a first advance. Terry knew that he now had to regain favor with the jury and in order to do this he had to dispense with the wooing and get right down to the fornicating. Let the side-show begin.

"You will meet a woman named Elia who flew all the way here from Costa Rica just so she could testify in this case. Elia's last name is Hawkins and she used to be married to the deceased. She and Sonny had just celebrated their fifth wedding anniversary the week before Elia caught Sonny in bed with his young cousin, the defendant, Marie Hart."

An attractive middle-aged juror who had identified herself as "Mrs. James Tingle," audibly inhaled a vast amount of air through her mouth. All of the jurors turned their eyes toward Marie with the exception of a male juror named Abernathy who had inexplicably shown up that morning wearing a bandana on his head, pirate-style. The juror, who had been dubbed Captain Kidd by the bailiff's staff, was already staring at Marie and had been since he had entered court. His look was that of a ravenous beggar eyeing a piece of fried chicken.

Terry continued with his opening statement. "We will prove through various witnesses that the defendant moved to Oregon following her separation from her husband Mr. Hart, who is also, strangely enough, her lawyer."

Pres was waiting for just such a remark and he pounced: "Objection," he shouted. "Once again the prosecutor has forgotten that he may only tell the jury in opening statement what his evidence will be. Any snide comments concerning my relationship with my wife are insulting and improper. There is nothing strange about my loyalty to her and I would ask the court to instruct the prosecutor to remain silent about a matter that is none of his business."

"Your honor," whined Terry, "counsel is testifying."

"I agree," said the Judge, "but you invited his comments when you characterized Mr. Hart's relationship with his wife as weird. If you stick to what you should be doing Mr. Terry, you would not give Mr. Hart an opportunity to sock it to you. Now let's move on."

Terry continued by telling the jury, in an abbreviated and hurried manner who his witnesses were and what they would say. Then he abruptly sat down, his confidence clearly shaken. His last words to the jury had been the prosecutor's tired cliché. "After hearing all the evidence, we are certain you will return a verdict of guilty as charged." These words were delivered with verve and bravado. They always were. The jury expected them. For the first time Terry wondered if a conviction was as inevitable as it had seemed when Marie had first reported her lover's death. "I killed him," she had said. "It was self-defense," she had said even as Sonny Hawkins lay face down in her bed with a bullet in the back of his head. Still, Pres had proven to be a formidable foe. Who would have thought her cuckold of a spouse would have anything to do with that murdering bitch. Let's see what he has to say.

"Mister Hart," the Judge said, "are you ready to make your opening statement?"

Pres rose and immediately violated the lawyer's code of dress by leaving his suit coat unbuttoned. He knew that the spirits of hundreds of rigid, unyielding pettifoggers silently moaned at this unforgivable breach of conduct. He intended to give them more reason to convulse in their graves before he was done. "With the Court's permission your honor, we would move to defer opening statement until the conclusion of the State's evidence. "

Terry shot to his feet, forgetting to button his coat. "He can't do this your honor."

"Mr. Terry," the Judge replied, "you have every right to make an objection, but let's do it like we were taught in school, shall we? Now did you mean to make an objection, or were you just favoring us with your opinion?"

"Now Judge," Terry said, trying to regain some of the high ground, "you know how excited I get when I'm representing the good people of our county. I was just trying to object to Mr. Hart's highly unorthodox request."

"Mr. Terry," the Judge said, "I know your term is up in a matter of months, but now is not the time to run for re-election. If you have an objection, tell me why the law is not in favor of a deferral of opening statement."

"Your honor, it is simply not the way things are done around here," Terry said. "In every case I have tried or witnessed, the State makes an opening statement and then the defendant says his piece and the State presents its case."

"That's it?" said the Judge. "You are objecting because it's not the way things are done around here?"

The prosecutor sat and began to shuffle papers. "Well while you were chattering, I did what lawyers are supposed to do," said the Judge. "I looked up the law. My Indiana Case Law disc talked to my Dell and my Dell talked to me. It does appear that Mr. Hart's request is unusual, but it also appears that it can be granted at my discretion. Since I see no harm in it, and since the prosecutor has not given me a legal reason to decline it, the motion to defer opening statement is granted. Proceed with your case in chief, Mister Terry.

"Perfect," thought Pres. "now Marie can see some of her trial."

CHAPTER FORTY-THREE
THE FIFTH AMENDMENT

O .J. tried to speak at his trial. His lawyers asked the Judge to let him say a few words without taking the witness stand. Presumably, the intention was to dispel the presumption of guilt that surrounds a defendant who won't talk. The Judge properly denied the request. The rule is that the State gets to cross-examine you if you open your mouth. But if you keep silent, you don't have to explain anything. O. J. was able to avoid all those embarrassing spousal abuse questions.

Marie would not have to give an explanation for her ludicrous claim of self-defense. Somehow in order to save Marie, Pres had to come up with a plan that would let her "testify" without ever taking the witness stand. An idea had been forming in Pres's mind. It all depended on Marie's reaction to what he was going to do. Pres thought he knew his client pretty well. Marie's life might depend on it.

Pres knew that one of the definitions of "testify" was "to give evidence in any manner." Throughout history, witnesses have made non-verbal declarations by pointing, scowling, laughing, nodding (affirmatively and negatively), cheering, clapping, and by making gestures of disgust, loathing and joy. Many of these silent statements are made while testifying, but many are not. "If it don't fit, you must acquit," was one of the best closing arguments in recent memory. It was not based on sworn testimony from the witness stand, but rather on O. J.'s struggle with the glove while seated mutely in the defendant's chair.

The Montgomery County Sheriff was the State's initial witness. By calling a lawman first, Terry was following the same script that had been written long before Darrow was in diapers. It was yet another time for the utilization of the presumption of first impression. Find an articulate police officer, dress him in uniform, and coach him to say "Yes sir" and "No sir" before answering a question. It never failed to swing precious momentum back to the side of the State.

Sheriff Matthew Hasp was an impressive looking man. A retired major with a Vietnam resume, he had a presence about him that dared you to disagree with anything he said. Pres did not intend to argue with the State's first witness.

Sheriff Hasp testified that although he had not taken the call, he had been on duty when Marie telephoned his office.

"Do you have a recorder that tapes all incoming calls?" Terry asked.

"Yes sir, we do," the Sheriff replied.

"Does your recorder contain a message?" Terry asked.

"Yes sir, it does," the Sheriff answered.

"Did it contain a message when the defendant, Marie Hart called your office?" Terry continued.

"Yes sir, it did," the Sheriff replied.

"Would you play that message for us Sheriff?" asked Terry.

"Yes sir," said the Sheriff. "May I leave the stand to get my equipment, your honor?"

"Yes you may," said the Judge. "Mister Hart, do you have any objection to playing this recording?"

"No, your honor," said Pres having heard the message several times before. It was delivered in a monotone indicating that the speaker was reading from a form which had probably been prepared by the prosecutor.

The message advised the caller that his words were being recorded. A "Miranda" warning followed warning the caller that anything said could be used by the State to prosecute the caller.

"Did the defendant hear this message before she began speaking with the officer about the death of Mr. Hawkins?" Terry asked when the tape finished playing.

Pres rose, "Objection, your Honor," he said. "The defendant is the only person who can answer that question."

"Objection sustained," the Judge said. "Rephrase your question, counsel."

Terry paused before continuing, "Was this message played to Mrs. Hawkins?" he finally asked.

"Pretty much the same objection, your Honor," Pres said. "How could this witness know the answer to that question?"

"Pretty much the same ruling," the Judge said. "Objection sustained."

There was a lengthy silence. Finally Pres spoke, "Look Terry" he said in a dismissive manner, "if you are trying to get Marie's statement in evidence, just say so. We have no objection."

Pres knew he was giving up nothing. Sooner or later Terry was going to get to play Marie's confession to the jury. The Judge would eventually rule in the prosecutor's favor. She was not about to do anything that would allow Marie to "get off on a technicality." Her constituents would not permit it. In addition, Pres wanted the jury to believe that the confession was unimportant. He had established himself as the alpha lawyer. If he regarded Marie's admission nonchalantly, the jury was likely to do the same. He hoped.

The courtroom was soon filled with Marie's frightened voice. Pres had to admire the sound system. Indiana was filled with law and order proponents and they spent freely on their jails, courts, and police. Marie sounded younger, almost adolescent, when she was scared and the speakers picked up every nuance of her tear-stained voice. "This is Marie Hart and I would like to report a shooting."

"Yes ma'am, who got shot?" inquired the voice of the deputy who had answered the telephone.

"Sonny Hawkins," Marie's voice replied, "and I shot him."

"Why did you go and do that for?" asked the shocked voice of the deputy.

"Because he was trying to hurt me," Marie replied. "I shot him in self-defense. I think I killed him."

There was only a little left of the recording. The deputy told Marie to stay put and that an ambulance would soon be arriving. A belch was overheard during the pause in the deputy's cautionary instructions, bringing with it the usual tension-breaking guffaws and twitters. Then the recording was over and the prosecutor resumed questioning Hasp.

"Were you the first law officer to arrive on the scene?" Terry asked. The Sheriff said that he was and went on to describe what he saw.

"I was greeted at the door by the defendant, who was carrying a gun. I asked her to give me the weapon; instead, she took me upstairs and I saw a man in a bedroom who I later determined to be the victim. The man was lying on his stomach on the bed with what appeared to be a bullet wound to the back of his head. He was obviously dead. I again asked the defendant to surrender the weapon. This time she handed it over to me."

"What did you do next, if anything?" asked the prosecutor.

"I placed the defendant under arrest and yellow-taped the bedroom. I then called the coroner and the State Police."

"Why the State Police?" asked Terry. "Wasn't this your baby?"

"Its protocol," the Sheriff answered. "Anytime there's a shooting resulting in death or serious bodily injury. They have the forensic equipment and the manpower to do a more complete investigation if one is warranted."

"Did they get involved in this case?" asked the prosecutor.

"There was no need," answered Hasp. "This was a mortal lock."

"Your witness," said Terry.

"Mr. Hart?" the Judge said.

"Thank you, your Honor," said Pres. "So officer, were there any tests performed to show that the defendant fired a gun before her arrest? I believe television calls them paraffin tests. Is that the correct term?"

"You have asked a multiple question, counsel," replied Hasp smugly. He smiled at the jury. "My answers are no and yes."

"Thank you and thank you," said Pres, unperturbed by the sarcasm. "So no tests were run to see if the defendant had recently fired a gun. Is that correct?"

"That is correct," replied Hasp.

"Were tests run to see whose fingerprints were on the gun?" Pres asked.

"Mister Hart," Hasp replied, "your client, a confessed murderess, had a dead man in her bed and a gun in her hand. Why should we have checked the gun for prints when hers were obviously all over it?"

"Your honor," Pres said, addressing the Judge, "would you instruct the witness to just answer my questions?"

"Yes," replied the Judge. "Officer Hasp, just answer Mr. Hart's questions. These extraneous remarks of yours are unwarranted and unnecessary. Do I make myself clear?"

"Yes, your honor," said Hasp. "No, we did not check the gun for fingerprints."

"Thank you Judge," said Pres. "Officer, did you do any testing to see if the gun had been recently fired?"

"No."

"Did you remove the bullet from the skull to see if it came from the gun taken from the defendant?"

"No."

"Did you do anything to find out who owned the gun?"

"The gun was registered to Harry Hawkins, the defendant's father," replied Hasp.

"Sheriff, did your office ever have the occasion to investigate alleged criminal conduct by the deceased?" asked Pres, shifting gears in his questioning.

The courtroom, which had previously been quiet, lowered its volume to tomb level. The Judge sat perched in her chair, anticipating an objection. The sheriff spoke:

"We had two separate complaints involving the deceased. The first was for child molesting, involving a sixteen-year-old girl. The second was also child molesting and since the juvenile girl in question was only fifteen, it was also for statutory rape."

"What time frame are we talking about?" Pres asked.

"I don't have the exact dates before me but the first incident took place about two years ago."

"What was the girl's name?" Pres asked.

"You know I cannot reveal the name of a minor," Hasp replied.

Pres shuffled through his file and picked out what appeared to be a cancelled check. Looking at it, Pres said, "You may not be able to reveal the girl's name, but I can. Was it Cathy Whitworth?"

"Objection," Terry said while leaping to his feet. "Don't answer that question, officer."

"Mister Terry," the Judge said, "in case you have forgotten, I'm the only one who can instruct the officer not to answer a question. In this case, the toothpaste is out of the tube and neither you nor I can put it back. This is a murder trial. Officer, please answer the question."

Hasp grimaced before he replied, "Yes."

"How about the statutory rape?" Pres asked. "When was it supposed to have occurred?"

"The statutory rape took place two weeks to the day before the decedent was murdered. We figure that's why your client killed him."

Pres jumped to his feet to object, but the Judge beat him to it. "Members of the jury, you will disregard that last remark. Madam court reporter, you will strike the last sentence of Sheriff Hasp's testimony, and Mister Prosecutor, while I know this was none of your doing, I am inclined to entertain a motion for mistrial if Mister Hart requests it. Mister Hart?"

"I do request a mistrial, your honor," Pres said.

"That motion will be taken under advisement for the time being," the Judge said. "Are you through with this witness?"

"Yes, your honor," Pres replied.

"Any re-direct?" the Judge asked of the prosecutor.

"Yes, your honor," Terry replied.

"Very well," said the Judge. "When the lawyers are finished with you, Sheriff Hasp, I hereby order you to go to the county jail, pick out your favorite cell, and lock yourself in it. Do I make myself clear?"

"Yes, your honor. I'm sorry, your honor," Hasp said.

"When I am convinced of your contrition, I may set you free. In the meantime, I want an essay from you. It must contain at least five hundred words. Its topic must be two-fold. It should tell why a witness should confine himself to answering questions and it should also give reasons why a Judge's orders should be obeyed," the Judge said. "Proceed with re-direct, Mister Prosecutor."

CHAPTER FORTY-FOUR:
THE ONLY BOOK

"I brought you gentlemen back into my office to coordinate our calendars," Judge Adamson said. "I believe I have no choice but to grant the motion for mistrial. Mister Terry, Mister Hart, can you be ready to start over again a week from Thursday?"

"But that's only nine days away," Pres said with a bit of a whine. His momentary elation at the granting of his motion had been replaced. In its stead came the sense of foreboding that accompanies Pyrrhic victor. He felt like a fool.

"The State can be ready, your honor," said Terry.

Pres hesitated. In large jurisdictions, a mistrial was as good as a "not guilty" verdict. Calendars were so clogged that often months and sometimes years passed before a miss-tried case found its way back to the front of the line. In the meantime, exhibits could vanish, and witnesses frequently died, moved, or became too addle-brained or intimidated to testify. Just his luck to be in a county where a loss of a place in the queue meant a nine-day delay. He should have known better.

"I'll withdraw my motion for mistrial," Pres said. "I don't want to have to start all over again. I like my chances with this jury, in spite of Hasp's attempted mind-poisoning."

"Very well," the Judge said. "Let's go to lunch and then Mr. Terry, you may proceed with your case in chief."

Hasp's re-direct had been perfunctory, even apologetic. The sheriff wanted desperately to stay out of his jail and so with Terry leading the way, Hasp explained that his outburst concerning motive was without fact or foundation. Two doctors followed the sheriff to the stand. The first testified that Sonny had died due to the gunshot wound to his head. The second physician had performed the autopsy and stated his opinion that Sonny would likely have lived out his life expectancy of twenty-seven more years had he not been shot. Pres had no questions for either witness. Elia Hawkins was the State's next and last witness.

Terry had done a good job of dressing his star. She was modesty personified. The hem of Elia's full skirt rested just above her knees as she sat in the witness chair. She wore a ruffled white blouse which featured glasses suspended by a gold chain around her neck. The only incongruity was her lipstick which surpassed blood, cherries, roses and fire engines in its redness. It had a sheen to it that reflected light. Topping off the ensemble was a wedding ring which Pres suspected had been given to Elia by the late Sonny. Terry couldn't get a real widow. Sonny and Elia had been divorced for several years. So the prosecutor tried to manufacture a grieving spouse. There was only one problem, Elia was not unhappy to see Sonny dead. No tears were shed as she recounted her early years with the handsome, American lawyer. She had begun having sex with Sonny when she was sixteen, married him when she was eighteen, and divorced him when she was twenty-six.

"And was there a single act that occasioned your divorce?" Terry asked.

"Yes," Elia replied. "I caught the bastard in bed with that little bitch."

Elia pointed at Marie. Marie pointed back. The two women stared and pointed at one another for a full minute. The jury stared at them both. Finally, Terry broke the deadlock.

"What happened to the defendant after you divorced Sonny Hawkins?" Terry asked.

Elia slowly lowered her arm. Marie lowered hers in unison. Elia replied, "She went off to school, married Mr. Hart, left him, and took up again with my ex. She followed him to Oregon and came back here to Crawfordsville when he returned."

Pres rose, "Objection, your honor. The witness must be relying on hearsay. How does she know what the defendant was up to? Mrs. Hawkins was in Costa Rica."

"Your client sent me letters," Elia said, reaching into her purse and withdrawing several. "Would you like to read them?"

"Yes, thank you," Pres said rising from the defense table. He took the letters and returned to his seat. "You wrote her?" Pres whispered to Marie.

"I thought she was my friend," Marie whispered. "I know it was stupid, but I hoped she would be happy for me once I married you. When you and I split, and I went to Portland, I wrote to make her understand; stupid, stupid, stupid."

"No further questions," Terry said. Pres rose. This time he buttoned his jacket. No questions came immediately to mind, but he knew he must question the State's star. "Weren't you and Marie once friends?" he asked.

"I suppose," Elia replied.

"Didn't Marie refer to you as Aunt Elia?" Pres asked.

"Yes," Elia replied. "She and Sonny were only second cousins, but she called him uncle and me aunt."

"The two of you were pretty close in age, weren't you?" Pres continued.

"I guess," Elia replied. "I am six years older than Marie. Our birthdays were both in November."

Pres made a quick leap to a dangerous area. "In addition to the rage you must have felt, didn't you feel a little sorry for Marie when you found her in bed with your husband?" he asked.

Elia did not reply. Pres persisted. "The man seduced you when you were very young. Didn't you feel a little sympathy or empathy for Marie?"

"You don't know much about women, do you Mister Hart? Look at you, married to a murderess who followed a man to the Pacific Ocean so she could continue to sleep with him."

Foolishly, desperately, Pres struck back. "I don't care what you think of me, but you just called Marie a murderess, and yet you don't know that she murdered anyone do you? Isn't that just your hatred showing?"

"In all fairness, Mr. Hart, I misspoke when I called your client a murderess." Elia paused for effect. "But only because I don't consider the killing of a cockroach to be a murder."

Pres suddenly decided that he had no further questions. The State rested its case and it was time for the defense to make its opening statement. Pres again rose and buttoned his coat. "You've heard from the State," he said. "Now it's our turn. We will cause you to have reasonable doubt and acquit the defendant and it will only take us two witnesses to do it. We will first call the defendant to the stand. She will testify as to what actually happened to cause Sonny Hawkins death. Our second and last witness will give you reason to believe that the deceased was shot to death by the defendant's father, Harry Hawkins."

Pres heard the book before he saw it. It sailed just past his left ear, before opening and fluttering harmlessly into the eager hands of Captain Kidd. Later, the juror would tell Montel and then Geraldo that

Pres tried to recover the book and offered to pay dearly for it.

This was not true. Computers with access to every case ever published had replaced books and law libraries in every law office in America. Books were now just for show. The one thrown by Marie had been salvaged from a dump-bound pick-up. Pres had liked its black cover. He carried it into court with him to impress clients and juries. It was the last law book he owned. It was a well worn, hopelessly outdated 1948 list of Indiana's criminal statutes. Captain Kidd could have it.

The sound of human keening is both pathetic and embarrassing. At first the sounds coming from Marie's prostrate figure were indecipherable. The muffled sounds preceded what seemed to be "Daddy." The same phrase was repeated again and again. Each time "Daddy" was followed by a wail that sounded like a small animal being slowly strangled to death. A juror finally served as interpreter.

"She's saying please don't hurt my daddy," he said. He was right.

Pres slowly returned to stand beside his wife. He felt guilty. Her reaction was what he expected. His plan to acquit her had worked. He could now explain away Marie's failure to testify; and yet he had wounded her deeply. He had exposed her heart to strangers. He had used her vulnerability. He had treated her like shit.

Marie became aware of Pres's presence. She slowly quieted. Then raising her arms like a child wanting to be lifted, she repeated her plea looking directly into Pres's eyes. "Please don't hurt my daddy." Pres lifted her into his arms and carried her out of the court room. After waiting for a few minutes, the Judge broke the silence that

had enveloped the courtroom. "I think we'll
adjourn for the day."

CHAPTER FORTY-FIVE:
FARTS

When court convened the following day, Pres stood alone at the defendant's table. "Where is your client, Mister Hart?" the Judge asked.

"She has instructed me to tell you that she will not attend, testify, or participate any further in this trial, your honor," said Pres.

"Of course you realize that I have to hear that from her," the Judge said. "Failure to attend your own trial can have serious consequences, and I must advise her of the peril she may be putting herself into."

"I told my client you would want to speak with her," said Pres. "She's sitting out in the hall."

"Members of the jury," the Judge began after speaking with Marie, "the defendant has chosen not to attend the rest of her trial. That means she will no longer be present in the courtroom and she will not testify in her own behalf. She has a right not to testify and she does not have to be here if she does not want to be here. You are not to make any inference whatsoever concerning her absence from this courtroom or the witness stand. Mister Hart, call your next witness."

"Thank you, your honor. The defendant calls Hannah Burke."

Hannah's face had always been cherubic. At twenty, it had made her look forty. At sixty, it still made her look forty. Her angelic countenance sat atop a body she euphemistically described as portly. Hannah had gone through a period in her life when much of her salary as Harry's secretary had been spent adorning her body in clothing that was both tasteful and expensive. Lately, however, it seemed as if she had surrendered her sense of style. She was well on her way to becoming a frump when Harry died and it seemed as she approached the witness stand as if the transformation was now complete.

Clearly comfortable as she took her seat, Hannah waved. It was a fluttery little gesture directed toward no one, but it elicited smiles. Everyone knew Hannah, and she knew them.

"State your name, please, " Pres asked.

"Hannah Burke. "

"Would you mind giving the jury a bit of your personal background? " Pres asked.

"Well, after high school, I went to college and after college, I went to work for Mr. Hawkins, " Hannah began. "I have been a professional secretary all of my life. I've worked for you since poor Mister Hawkins died. I've never married. I've lived here in Crawfordsville at the same address for the last thirty-nine years. I guess that about covers it. "

"Are you personally acquainted with the defendant? " Pres asked.

"I held her on the day she was born. "

"I take it you also knew Sonny Hawkins? "

"Yes, " Hannah said, and nothing more.

Pres let the silence build for nearly a minute and then he asked, "How well did you know Harry Hawkins? "

"I knew him as well as anyone. He was a lonely man after his wife left him and when Marie went off to school, he just got worse. I couldn't stand seeing such a good man suffer, so I started to cook supper for him. We'd watch television or play cards after we ate until he fell asleep and then I went home and came back in the morning to make his coffee and get him to the office for his first appointment. "

"But Marie came home from time to time didn't she? " Pres asked.

"Yes and when she came home she took care of her daddy. You see, Mister Harry Hawkins had to have someone take care of him and when Marie couldn't, I did. It was a simple as that."

"Could you describe Harry and Marie's relationship with one another?" Pres asked.

Hannah was eager to answer. "It was more than father and daughter. The two of them were best friends. When Marie's mother left, it was as if it was the two of them against the world. They would do anything for each other."

Pres fumbled with his papers, letting Hannah's words dive deep through the cortex and into the gelatin of each juror's brain. "Did Harry ever fart in your presence?"

The courtroom exploded. Farts are uproarious in rural Indiana. "Yes I suppose he did," answered Hannah, clearly embarrassed.

"Did Harry belch in your presence?" Pres asked.
Again there was laughter, but it quickly subsided. Belches are not nearly as funny as farts.

"Where are you going with this, counsel?" asked the Judge. "May I assume your interest in noxious emissions has something to do with the subject at hand?"

"You may, your honor, Hannah, do you think you would be able to identify a Harry Hawkins' fart if you heard it in a crowded room?"

There was more laughter, but the character of it had changed. Jurors were poking one another and talking, each one trying to say something clever. Captain Kidd made a fart sound with pursed lips that drowned Hannah's answer.

"What did you say?" asked Pres.

"I said no. Of course not," replied Hannah indignantly.

"Miss Burke, have you heard the tape recording of Marie that was taken by the sheriff's office?" asked Pres, fully knowing the answer.

"Yes, you played it for me in your office yesterday," Hannah answered, relieved to be rid of farts.

"I'm going to ask you to listen to it again in the presence of the jury. Would that be all right?"

"Of course," Hannah replied, and Pres motioned the court reporter who pressed the play button releasing Marie's little-girl voice. Near the end of the tape the belch was again heard, but this time it elicited only smiles from the fart-jaded jury.

"Hannah," Pres said when the tape finished playing, "Did you hear anything on that tape that would cause you to believe there was someone with Marie when she was on the telephone with the sheriff's office?"

"Yes," Hannah replied. "Mister Hawkins was with Marie."

"Objection!" screamed Terry so loudly that the guide dog of the blind deputy clerk began to bark. The young girl had just entered the courtroom, lured by the laughter.

"Susan, see if you can calm Hairy Black," said the Judge to the deputy. "And Mister Terry, the question has already been answered. Proceed, Mister Hart."

"Would you explain to the jury, Hannah, how you know Harry Hawkins was present when his daughter was talking to the police?" Pres asked.

"I recognized his belch," said Hannah. "He always made the same sound, like an 'arp!"

"Like how most people refer to AARP?" asked Pres.

"Exactly," replied Hannah.

"Miss Burke," Pres said, "having worked for Harry Hawkins for such a long time, would you recognized his signature?"

"Yes, of course," replied Hannah.

Pres stood with what was clearly a check in his hand. "Hannah I am now handing you defendant's exhibit A. Can you tell the jury what it is?"

Hannah took the exhibit, looked at it a moment and replied, "This is a cancelled check for twenty-nine thousand dollars made payable to Cathy Whitworth."

"Has it been endorsed?" Pres asked.

Hannah turned over the check and looked at the signature on the back before replying, "Yes."

"Who endorsed it?" asked Pres.

"Floyd Whitworth for Cathy Whitworth," Hannah replied.

"Who signed the check?" Pres asked.

"Harry Hawkins."

"The defendant rests," Pres said.

CHAPTER FORTY-SIX:
HOW CAN YOU BELIEVE A MURDERER?

Pres timed the prosecutor's final argument. It took just a little over thirteen minutes. The final part of Terry's summation dealt, as expected, with the confession. "The vast majority of women who kill, murder their husbands or lovers," Terry argued. "These are usually crimes of passion; battered women who can't take it anymore. Their actions cannot be condoned, but they deserve our sympathy and understanding. The defendant deserves neither. She promised to explain to you how she shot her lover in the back of the head in self defense. She did not, because she could not. It was cold-blooded murder, ladies and gentlemen. She killed him. She told the police she killed him and she told you she killed him. This is an open and shut case and you need to now shut the door with the prison bars on it."

Terry sat down and Pres stood up. His argument was even shorter than Terry's. "I don't have to prove anything. I don't have to prove anything. I don't have to prove anything. I don't have to prove anything. I don't have to prove anything. The State has to prove guilt beyond a reasonable doubt. The State has to prove guilt beyond a reasonable doubt. The State has to prove guilt beyond a reasonable doubt. The State has to prove guilt beyond a reasonable doubt. The State has to prove guilt beyond a reasonable doubt. In case you're counting, I said, counting this time, I don't have to prove anything and the State has to prove guilt beyond a reasonable doubt six times each. I could say them a thousand times and it wouldn't be enough. They are the cornerstone of our American criminal justice system. Over here on the good side of the water, we are innocent until proven guilty. I don't have to prove anything. The State has to prove guilt beyond a reasonable doubt. There I said it again."

"The State's case is based entirely on the defendant's confession. They have nothing else. I know what you're thinking. Every juror has the same thought right now. Shut up and sit down, mister lawyer. Your client admitted she committed murder," Pres replied. "What if she's lying? Would you trust a murderer to tell the truth? How about a thief, an arsonist, a rapist, a perjurer, for crying out loud? These people are criminals and natural born liars. Isn't it just as probable that my client is not a murderer, but one hell of a good liar?"

"And here's the paradox," Pres continued. "The State wants you to believe one half of the defendant's story and disbelieve the other. They want you to believe that she was telling the truth when she said she killed Sonny, but they also want you to think she was lying about doing it in self defense. Isn't it just as probable that she was lying about killing Sonny and telling the truth about it being in self-defense?"

"My client wouldn't want me to say this, but I think her father killed Sonny," Pres said. "He had motive. Sonny couldn't stop fooling around with young girls, and he was bleeding Harry dry. Harry had opportunity. He was there belching in the middle of Marie's confession."

"Marie took the blame for two reasons," Pres continued. "First, she would do anything for her Daddy, and second, Harry never thought she would be convicted, let alone charged. The concocted self-defense story seemed perfect. A beautiful woman, a plea of self defense, no jury would ever convict her. Only one problem, the shot to the back of the head."

"Here's what I think happened," Pres said, "Marie may not have ever slept in that bed the night of the murder. She may have vacated that bedroom before Sonny arrived. Or another scenario, Marie and Sonny shared the bed and Marie got up to go to the bathroom or to sleep somewhere else. How about this? Harry shot Sonny in another room and put him in Marie's bed. In either event, Harry saw his chance to rid himself of an expensive problem. But Harry was not a professional killer. He probably never thought how hard it would be to prove self defense when he shot his nephew in the back of the head."

"Farfetched? THE EVIDENCE DOES NOT EXCLUDE THE POSSIBILITY!" Pres shouted. "If it could have happened the way I just described, then you must have doubt and you must acquit."

"I've decided to give Paris Crossing a try," Marie said. "There's nothing for me here now. You're the only man I have left."

Pres and Marie were sitting in Harry's old office. Pres had just opened his third beer and Marie was one swallow away from emptying a bottle of Merlot. The Judge had required Marie's presence during the reading of the verdict. She had barely spoken following the "Not guilty" pronouncement. Pres feared Marie would question him about his final argument, but she had not. Weather and crop observations were the only topics of conservation leading up to Marie's announcement.

I should have seen this coming, Pres thought, "Marie," he said, "a lot of water has gone under the bridge since we last lived together....."

"Is there someone else?" Marie interrupted.

"No," said Pres, "but there could be."

Marie was silent for a moment and then she spoke. "I know I haven't been much of a wife these past two years....."
It was Pres's turn to interrupt. "You haven't been any kind of a wife. You were with another man."

"You left me no choice. You knew I couldn't leave Daddy and I can't be without a man. Give me some credit, I didn't try and find someone new. I went back to the same loathsome bastard who molested me. In my head, I was still being faithful to you. I know that doesn't make sense."

"Marie, I've always loved you," Pres said, "and I'm willing to give it a try, but what if it doesn't work out? It's a mighty big load to carry around, being the only man you have left."

"I'll make it work," Marie said. "And I'll try not to be a burden to you. I'll only insist that you be faithful to me."

"What happens if I'm not?" Pres asked.

"I'll shoot you in your sleep," Marie replied.

I would like to thank Pam Lewis, John Shambach, my very talented graphics editor, Kathy Pieters, daughter Susan McDaniel who put up with her father's confusion about word perfect and Microsoft word and was the one who really put this book together, and the Wright brothers, John and Mark for being my editors. I could not have written it at all without Shirley, the love of my life.

I discovered "The Passing of the Backhouse" while sorting through my aunt's personal effects shortly after her death. No one claimed it at the time of its publication prior to 1923, so it was credited to that prolific author "Anomymous." Riley was thought to have written it, but he denied it and seemed embarrassed by its content which was considered to be risqué at the time. Charles T. Rankin later claimed to have written it and perhaps he did. The author thanks Jon Schladweiler who has spent a lifetime tracking down the roots of our sanitary sewers, for his assistance.

I am also grateful to Gordon Lightfoot and his publisher and rights holder, Academy of Management, for granting permission for me to use copyrighted content from
"The Wreck of the Edmund Fitzgerald".

Don grew up in Madison, graduated from DePauw and Indiana University where he got his law degree. After a brief stint working for the Supreme Court of Idaho, Don returned to Indiana where he practiced law in Covington with the Wallace law firm for over forty years. He and his wife, Shirley Campbell, PsyD., raised five daughters and now live in Naples, Florida.

www.ingramcontent.com/pod-product-compliance
Lightning Source LLC
Chambersburg PA
CBHW021044090426
42738CB00006B/171